gspocks

Mastering Pool

George Fels

cbi Contemporary Books, Inc.
Chicago

Library of Congress Cataloging in Publication Data

Fels, George.
Mastering pool.

Includes index.
1. Pool (Game) I. Title.
GV891.F43 1977 794.7'3 77-75726
ISBN 0-8092-7896-0
ISBN 0-8092-7895-2 pbk.

This book is dedicated to Dale Fels,
whose sufferance of my pool game is second only to mine.

The author is also proud and grateful for the cooperation of Bensinger's Billiards in Chicago in the photography for this book. The name has been active in billiards all the way through the 20th century, and it seemed fitting to shoot our pictures there.

Published by Contemporary Books, Inc.
180 North Michigan Avenue, Chicago, Illinois 60601
Manufactured in the United States of America
Library of Congress Catalog Card Number: 77-75726
International Standard Book Number: 0-8092-7896-0 (cloth)
0-8092-7895-2 (paper)

Published simultaneously in Canada by
Beaverbooks
953 Dillingham Road
Pickering, Ontario L1W 1Z7
Canada

Contents

Preface

" . . . that game with the fifteen numbered balls is the devil's tool. . . ."

—Meredith Willson, *The Music Man*

I know, I know: you can see the game played in some pretty scuzzy trappings, by characters whom you might call "exotic" if you were feeling charitable. And still, if you're interested enough to have opened the cover of this book, you have probably already recognized that the game itself is one of the most elegant on the earth.

Which is really the ideal start. How good you are ever to become at pocket billiards largely has to do with how much you respect the game. If that sounds startlingly cerebral for a table game, that's as it should be; you'll learn, as all expert pool players know, that the game is played in great measure in your head, far more than on a table.

Hopefully, you'll also be able to see that the game is imitative of life, and it pays to play it that way. Its best practitioners are never far removed from flawless fundamentals (which is why the best players always seem to make the game look easy). They are masterful when it comes to arranging sequences of individual tasks that are not hard to do, one by one. They'll gamble if they have to, but it will be a well-calculated risk rather than a leap-before-you-look flyer. And they'll be successful, under pressure, at recouping their own mistakes. (I'll admit that few of you have probably ever seen the game this way, but this is all straight stuff, and I'd generally prefer not to find it reprinted as a "Block That Metaphor" blurb in *The New Yorker* . . . oh, hell, we all enjoy free enterprise; their address is 25 West 43rd Street, New York 10036, and I think they used to pay $5 for that sort of thing.)

One sound reason for the unique nature of my views is the paucity of *any* written information on advanced pool playing. As I write this, every single legitimate billiards book on the market is generally repetitive of the next, all mostly primers that explain the game, with varying success, to readers who are completely uninitiated to the game. One of the game's all-time best-sellers espouses such wisdom as "Avoid scratching the cue ball"—this in the chapter on Advanced Play, which is much like telling Jimmy Connors to remember to bring his racket.

But I'm willing to assume that you've read at least one of those books, and/or have spent enough time fingering felt that you can pocket a ball now and then, maybe even five or six in a row. That is where I propose to pick you up and help you progress, perhaps even to breathe life into that delicious fantasy you have about running *all* the balls. (You *can* do it, you know. And if you can run one rack, you can probably run more than one.)

Let's play pool, Fast Eddie.

1 Advanced Straight Pool

I'm sorry, but I'll just bet you're hitting the balls too hard.

That's not as insulting as it sounds, because very few players ever do learn the knack of stroking softly, not even some super players. Sense of speed is invariably what cuts the trotters from the pacers when it comes to pool, clear on up to the game's highest level. And sense of speed really means sense of the *lack* of speed.

Here's one way to look at it: Big-league baseball players use bats that weigh between 36 and 40 ounces, to try and drive a 5-ounce ball into the next county. Your cue weighs about half what a bat does, the balls weigh just about what a baseball does, and you only have to *roll* them—on felt—a few feet, frequently a few inches. You begin to get my drift.

My reason for making this point first is that in virtually all pool games (excepting Rotation and its variants, in which the cue ball frequently *must* do some traveling), your sense of speed will contribute greatly to your accuracy. And putting the balls in the subway is what the game is all about.

Pool table manufacturers, over the past 15 years, have made the peculiar decision to render the world's most difficult game even tougher. As a result, most modern tables have tightly angled pockets that seem to enjoy rejecting balls that do not come straight down the middle. (Had this feature been introduced during any war of consequence, it would have been quite properly labeled an atrocity.)

But the same object ball that stands there wiggling, refusing to take the subway, and spitting in your eye, can be coaxed into falling after all. Just be nice to it and hit it softer, and you'll see how nice it can be to you. And here's why.

Those corner-pocket rejections occur when the object ball has touched the cushion on its way in. The cushion imparts *spin*—sideways motion—to the natural rolling motion. The harder the ball has been struck, the more spin it picks up this way. And the more spin it has, the less likely it is to absorb the rubber of the pocket jaws. It simply bounces straight across to the other jaw and back again, as though between pinball-machine bumpers, except that you don't get a ball in a hole.

But a softly stroked ball picks up less spin, and also bounces less far from the rail it has struck (and remember, we're talking about differences in millimeters. I told you it was a hard game). Thus it retains most of the motion of its natural roll and, upon contact with the pocket jaw, is much more likely to reflect backward—holeward—than straight across.

There's a second, equally important benefit to be derived from a soft stroke, too: It means you're much more likely to (a) keep your cue level, and (b) therefore hit the ball more smoothly. To use the baseball analogy once more, any player or coach worth his salt would certainly counsel you to go for line drives with a smooth, level swing, rather than to thrash out wildly for the fences. Next time you're in the billiard room where you play, take a look around and see how few players have the butts of their cues down where they should be. The vast majority (unless they've read this too) are sure to be shooting down instead of through the ball. If the room isn't busy, simply see how many little pinholes you can find in the felt. You seldom find one of these phenomena without the other.

Make that soft, smooth, level stroke your first objective if you want to play good pool. If you play with any frequency, you should see an improvement almost immediately; and just how softly most pool shots can be accomplished—even your break shots—will delight your eyes and consternate your friends.

(For a more practical concept than the mere word "soft," a good checkpoint is that the pocketed object ball should not touch the very back of the pocket, but rather tumble in off the lip.)

So relax your grip on that cue butt. Try to "think" the action of your stroke into your arm *from the elbow down.* Your wrist should be as limp as you can comfortably make it (no wisecracks, please). And just as tennis players are taught to concentrate on the racket head, you should focus on the tip of your cue, and the tender force it will apply to the cue ball.

I've seen top players like Bill Incardona and Billy Burge ("Cornbread Red") practically tear pockets off the rails, and it's all very intimidating and impressive, but those men have the gift of one-in-ten-thousand accuracy going for them. I'm assuming that you, too, find a little clay under your socks every so often.

How to Break

First, let's make a small mental adjustment: Being required to break the balls in straight pool usually means that your opponent will get the first clear shot of the game, right? Well, yes, but you've got the wrong attitude. Consider instead that your breaking the balls is simply going to leave the first *tough* shot of the game. In the first place, that's just what a good break will do (if it leaves any shot at all); secondly, your break will improve if you learn to think of it as an *opportunity,* rather than a hazard.

Next, I want you to picture the ideal break in your mind: the two corner balls wandering out of the stack timidly, like gophers with an eye out for hawks over-

Diagram 1: The rack isn't straight.

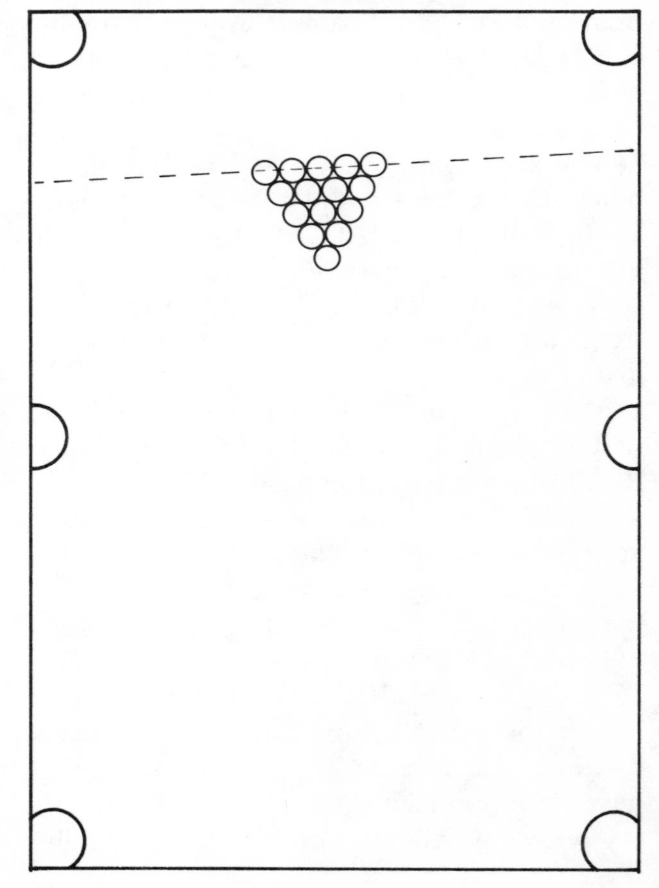

head, and returning back whence they came. This sort of mental rehearsal will benefit every single aspect of your pool game, and we'll be talking about it more. In his excellent book, *Sports Psyching,* Dr. Tutko goes a step further and recommends that whatever your sports event, you should mentally rehearse it *in slow motion* as well as in the speed with which it would normally take place. And if you've taken my advice and slowed down your stroking speed, you're already coming as close as you can, in sports, to simulating slow motion anyway.

Now take a good close look at the racked balls themselves. What we're looking for are assurances that (1) the rack is *straight,* that is, each row of balls facing you is exactly parallel to the bottom rail, and (2) the rack is *tight,* with each ball in contact with the ball(s) next to it. Balls that are crookedly racked, or that exhibit Terry-Thomas-type gaps within the rack, will just about obliterate your chances for breaking the balls safely. (See Diagrams 1 and 2.)

And the reason you should inspect the rack for these features is not that your opponent is a rascally scalawag with skulduggery in his heart; it's simply that in commercial billiard rooms, or any place where the tables come in for frequent play, it's increasingly difficult to rack the balls precisely. That's because the balls tend to "settle" into thin spots on the felt, where their last little wiggles will free them from contact with their neighbors. To ensure a tight rack, the player racking the balls should force them together by pressing his fingertips between the wooden or plastic triangle and the balls, by tapping the corner balls with the cue ball, or both.

Diagram 2: The balls aren't "frozen."

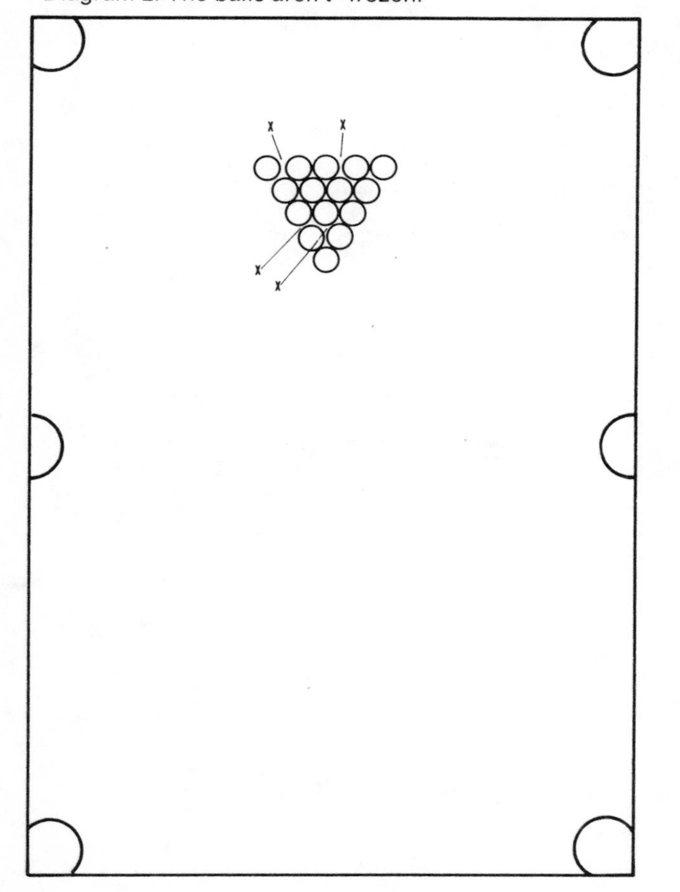

Diagram 3: Opening break position.

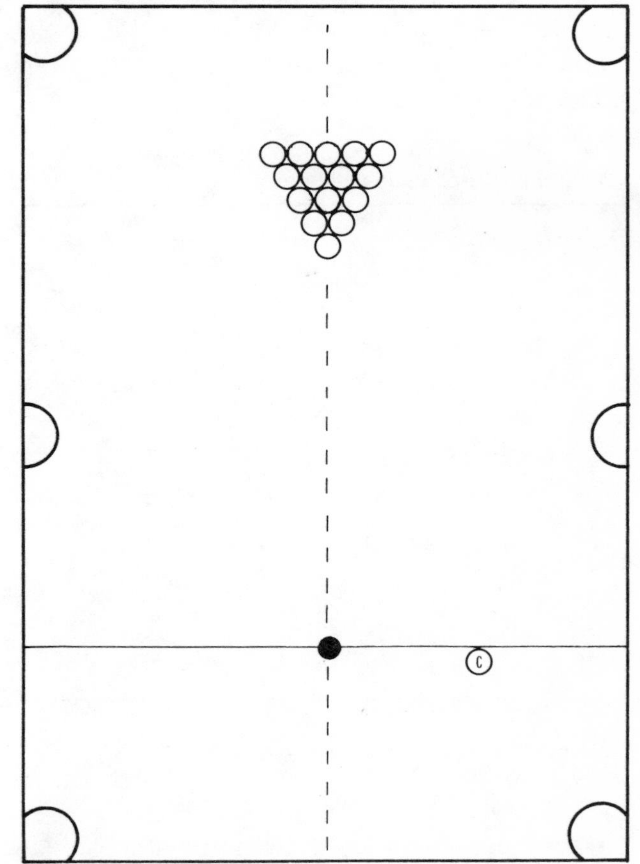

Now you've got the rack correct on the table, and the break straight in your head. Remember, you're not ready to break correctly without those two priorities.

Okay. The break shot is both the first shot of the game and the first shot to which we're going to apply our new theory of minimum force: The *softest* possible hit that will still accomplish the various objectives of any given pool shot is the *best* possible hit.

What we're going to do, accordingly, is take some speed off your stroke and replace it with some spin, or English. Experienced players will tell you to avoid excessive English, and rightly so; but there are two situations when English, judiciously used, can be a very valuable ally. One is when English can help create an angle you need; the other is to replace cue ball speed, therefore to move the ball someplace with greater control, and that's what we're going to do now.

Right-handed players will generally break off the right-hand side of the stack as it faces them, and lefties the opposite, although no rule says you have to. As you learn the fine points of cue ball control, it may well occur to you that you are somewhat more comfortable in your head with applying right-hand English than with left-hand, or vice versa. (All but the very best players feel that way too, deep down in their heart of hearts; and for some reason, most would rather draw a ball—bring it back toward them—than hit it with follow English.) But let's say that you've chosen to break off the right-hand side.

Set your cue ball along the head string, halfway between the middle of the string (which should be marked with a spot) and the long rail on your right. (See Diagram 3.) Select a point on your cue ball just north-

Diagram 4: Stroke cue ball here.

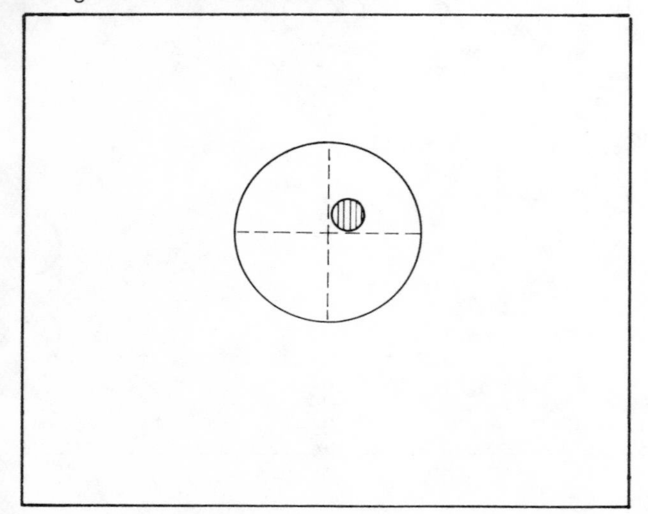

Diagram 5: Correct hit for opening break.

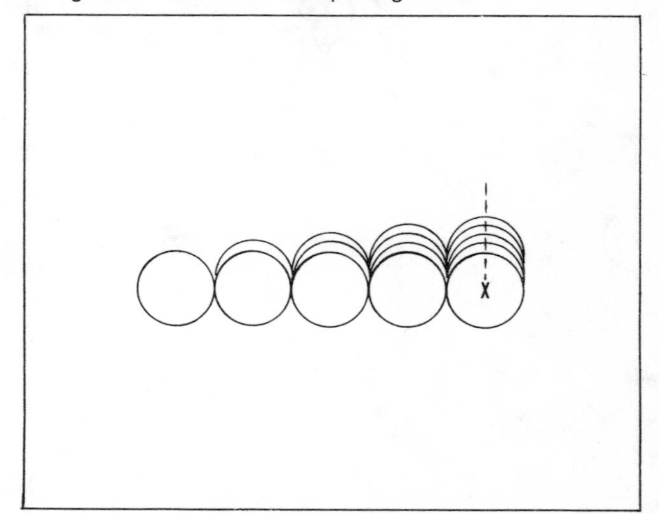

east of its exact middle, but no further from the middle than the width of your cue tip. (See Diagram 4.) Your point of aim on the corner ball in the rack should be that point at which it is exactly in line with the other four balls in its row (Diagram 5). Now relax, and try to *feel* the spin you impart to the cue ball. The correct speed, spin, and hit—and you do need all three—will produce the effect you see in Diagram 6, or very close to it. But on this shot, don't worry about the object balls; you should be focused on the cue ball. The very least you should accomplish is to get that albino fool back to the end rail, or very close to it. That way, if object balls are exposed and pocketable, you've forced your opponent to take the game's first *gamble,* a shot he cannot be sure of and the possibility of breaking more balls open for you. Winning pool is largely a matter of reducing *possibilities* to *certainties;* in competition between two evenly matched players, the winner over the long run will almost surely be the player who gambles the least.

It would be nice if you could break as in Diagram 6 every single time, but it's not the end of the world if you don't. Diagram 7 demonstrates some other typical leaves which, although playable, still offer positive aspects to you. (I have made *perfect* breaks, in which the two corner balls return to their original racked positions, several times over the years; and I can't remember a single occurrence in which I didn't lose the rack anyway. You can't always get what you want. As I said, the game imitates life.)

Examining the Stack

Now let's turn the picture around and consider that the balls have been broken by your opponent instead of you, and he has

Diagram 6: The ideal break.

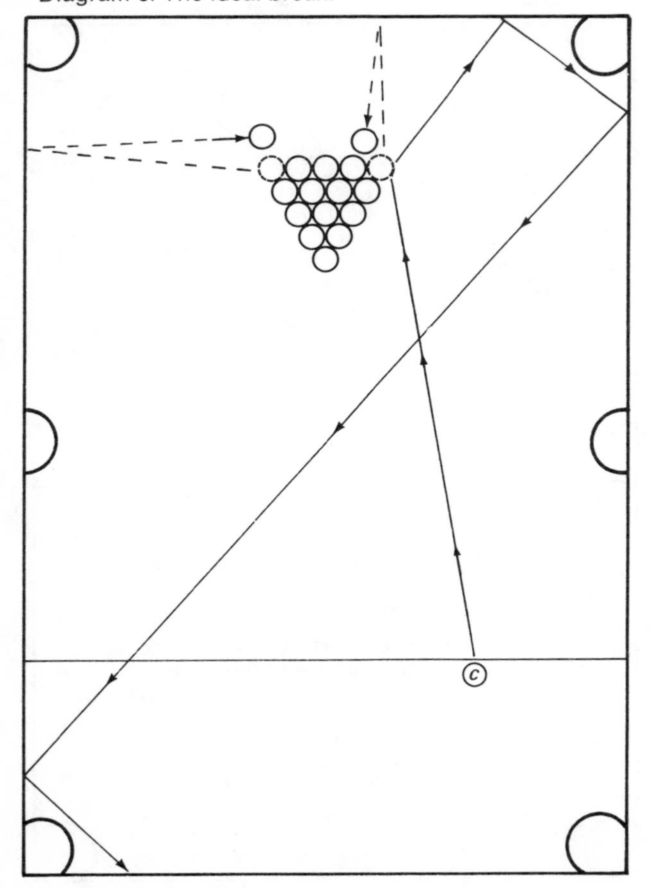
C

Diagram 7

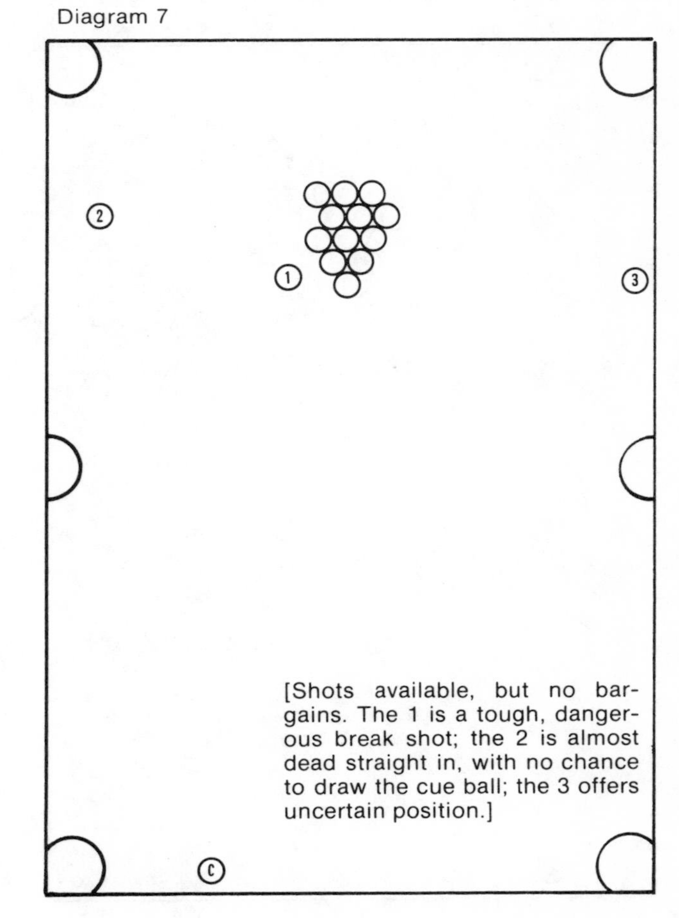
2
1
3
C
[Shots available, but no bargains. The 1 is a tough, dangerous break shot; the 2 is almost dead straight in, with no chance to draw the cue ball; the 3 offers uncertain position.]

been generous enough to leave you pocketable balls. Forget about them for a moment; they only represent possibilities, and we're going to look for certainties first.

You should examine the balls left clustered not only following the opening break, but *every single time that cluster is altered* in the slightest way. It's a very subtle game, remember, and it doesn't take much for a combination shot that can't possibly be made to become one that can't be missed.

Diagram 8 shows you a typical leave off the break that comes up often. Oddly enough, this shot generally occurs when the player breaking the balls has hit his break shot well. You'll note that the corner ball, which is now a mortal cinch for the corner pocket, has actually returned to a position very close to where it began, which would be perfect. See what I mean about subtle differences?

Anyway, his good break has now turned into an even better break for you, and here's how you ought to capitalize on it.

First, remember that in a cluster combination like this, the ball that determines whether your object ball can be pocketed or not is the ball twice removed from it. So no matter how many object balls stand between you and the one you're trying to make, *always read the third ball.* Diagrams 9 and 10 demonstrate a yes-yes and a no-no according to this principle.

Let's say that you've read "All Systems Go" for the out-of-the-stack shot you've been left. You cannot help but make that corner ball, and that's a clear mandate to rear back and pulverize that whole rack with one good wallop, right?

I can give you some pretty good reasons not to do that. Play the shot, sure. But play it under control. This is a certainty, re-

Diagram 8

[A perfect break—for the other guy. The 3 can't miss.]

Diagram 9

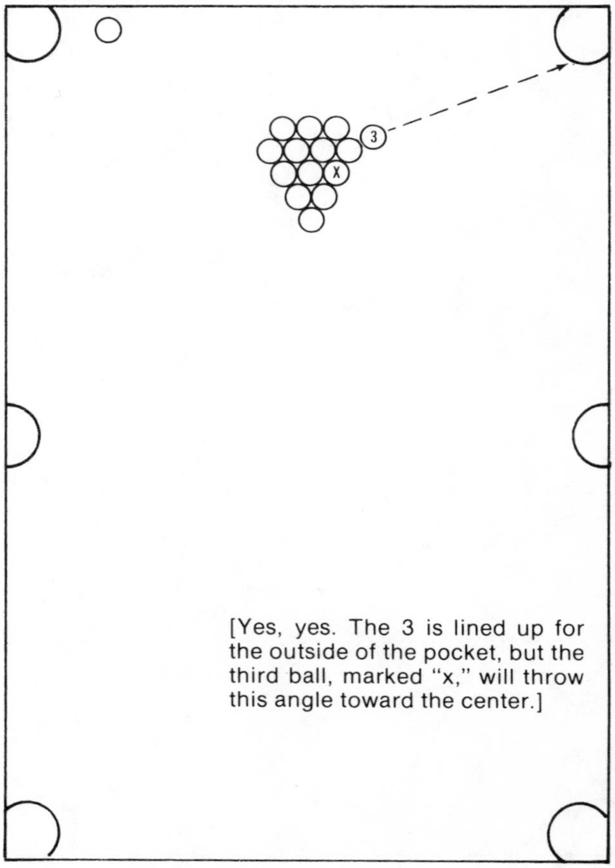

[Yes, yes. The 3 is lined up for the outside of the pocket, but the third ball, marked "x," will throw this angle toward the center.]

member, and certainties are just what we're looking for; let's not negate our sure thing by introducing the gamble of a howitzer stroke.

In the first place (and we'll talk more about this when we discuss the various single-ball break shots), you'll find that stacked balls react much better to being stroked smoothly than they do to being stroked hard. That's because a smoothly stroked cue ball transmits its force to more of the balls, whereas a cannonball passes its force along primarily to the first ball it touches and the last ball in the row. And as we've noted, it's much easier to achieve smoothness when stroking more softly.

And second, what you're considering is turning your cue ball loose, and that is truly one of pool's epic "Don'ts." The reason could hardly be simpler: When you turn it loose, you don't know where it will end up. So even if you do blast that stack into oblivion, object balls are going to be on all kinds of unpredictable journeys, and they can trap your cue ball, knock it someplace unplayable—or even into a pocket.

What we want to do at all times, in all pool games, is (1) pocket the ball, and (2) keep the cue ball free for the next shot. So even with a juicy cripple such as in Diagram 8, let's not be greedy. Increase your speed from soft to medium, but above all, hit it *smoothly*—and concentrate on drawing it back out of there, toward the center of the table. This will not only do a better job of opening the balls, but it will afford you the maximum options among the balls that are opened.

Let's consider another combination-shot leave off the break. This one looks like a real doozy, but actually it shows up quite a bit. You start looking for this one when

Diagram 10

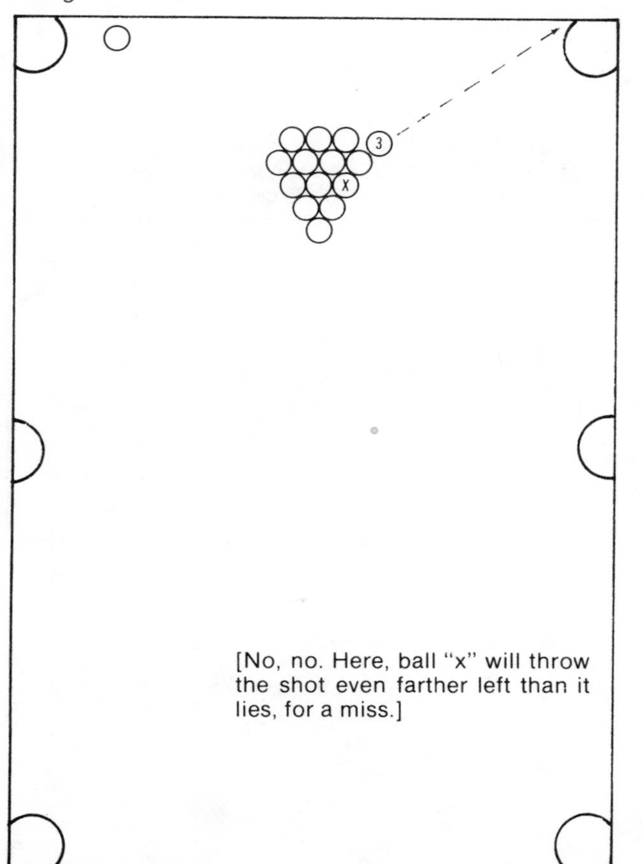

3
X
[No, no. Here, ball "x" will throw the shot even farther left than it lies, for a miss.]

Diagram 11: Check ball "x."

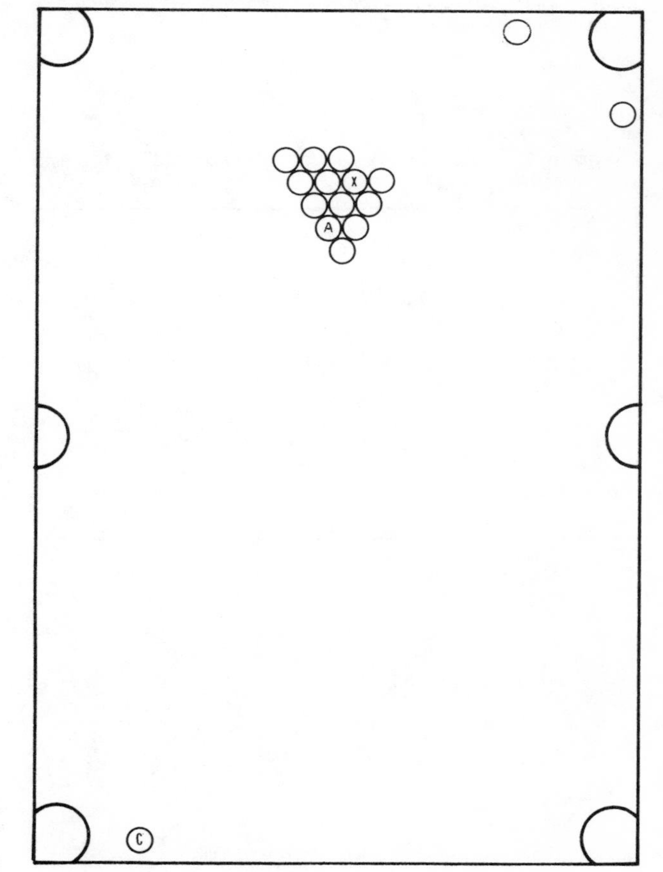

your opponent has taken both the corner ball and the ball immediately next to it out of the back row with his break. Now check Diagram 11. Believe it or not, that ball marked "X," seemingly buried in swampland, is really a pretty good candidate.

Diagram 12 shows you a closeup of the same situation. The reason Ball X is such a delicious stiff is that it's in immediate contact ("frozen") with the ball next to it, and will therefore be thrown into a can't-miss carom off that middle ball in the end row. Remember, it must be frozen on its neighbor, *and* clear of the ball in back of it, or else it's no stiff.

In fact, if the reverse of that situation existed, as in Diagram 13—where Ball X is *not* frozen on its neighbor, but *is* frozen on that last-row middle ball—Ball X wouldn't be within a foot of the pocket. But don't kiss off this situation completely, because with Ball X and the ball behind it frozen, the last-row ball becomes a pretty good candidate itself, as a carom off Ball X. (Incidentally, in carom shots of this nature, it becomes unnecessary to read the third ball removed, as we did in Diagram 8.)

To make Ball X in Diagram 11, you need only to strike Ball A head-on—but because of the position of Ball X, you're going to need some speed this time. Just focus on controlling your cue ball; hit it hard and just below the center. We've already determined that the object balls will take care of themselves. Get that white rock back in the center of the table.

The opportunities offered in Diagram 13 are a little trickier to come by. That middle ball can only be made by striking the remaining corner ball; again, you'll need speed, and the angle on that corner ball is such that you can't hit it full, at the risk of

Diagram 12: The carom will be off that ball in the end row, into the pocket.

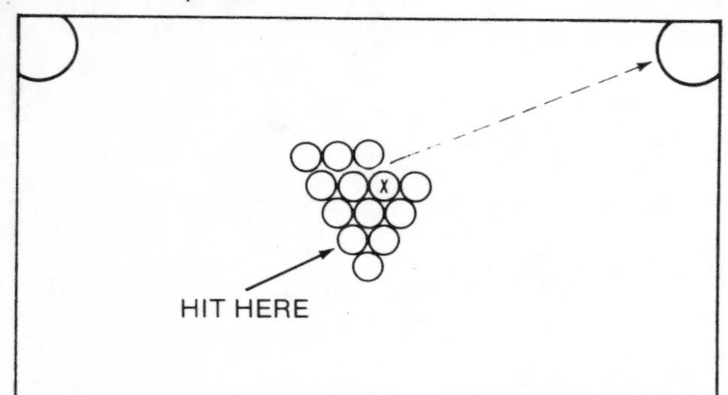

Diagram 13: Here, the last-row ball is frozen on ball "x," and will carom off it toward the corner.

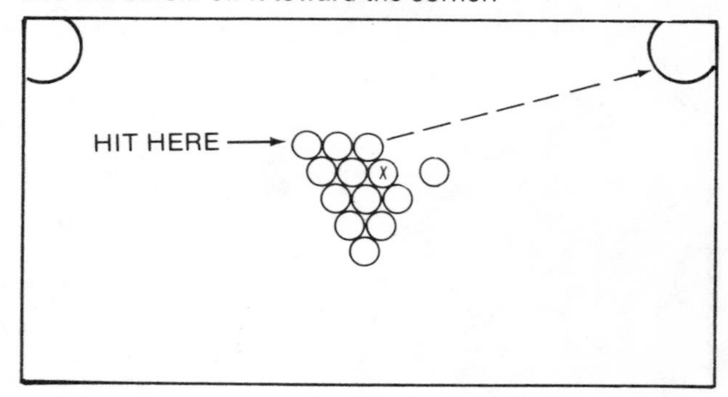

scratching off it in the corner. And that means you'll have to turn your cue ball loose, something we want to do as seldom as we can.

So hit the shot with a little reverse (in this case, right-hand) English. That will help negate your cue ball's speed coming off the bottom rail.

I'll limit the discussion of specific out-of-the-pack shots to these, because they do come up with some frequency, and because I obviously can't show them all. (Personally, I find new ones almost as often as I play, but I might never look at that same shot again.) Don't be intimidated by the profusion of words required to explain all this. These are all mental calculations that you'll quickly learn to do in seconds, once you're at the table with the balls, not diagrams, before you—and once you've learned what to look for. The important thing to remember is, always check the stack any time it's been changed at all. Check it from all sides; dead shots are often available to the side pockets and back pockets too.

Diagram 14

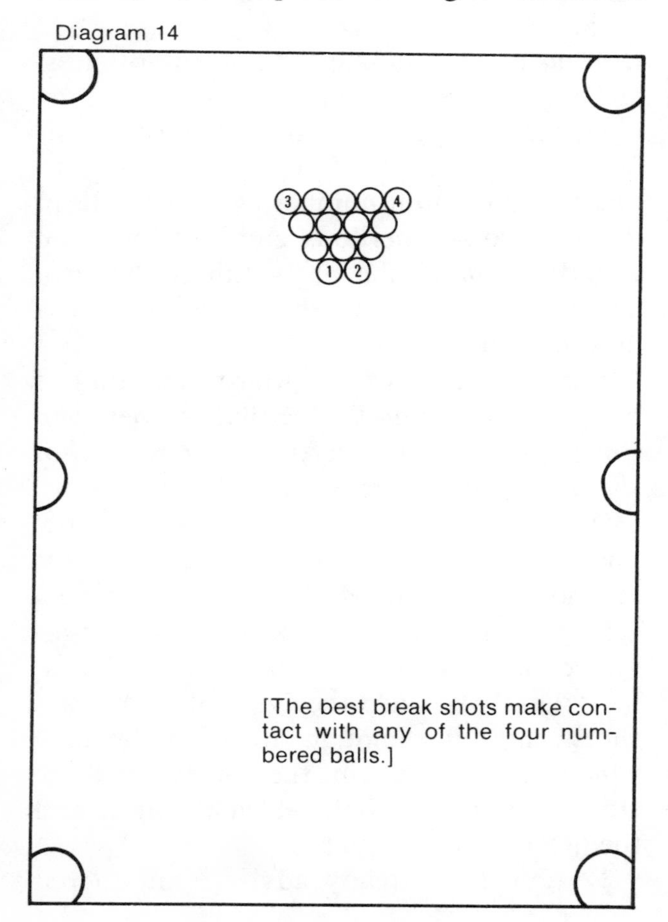

[The best break shots make contact with any of the four numbered balls.]

The legendary Mosconi has been quoted as saying, "There's *always* a playable ball." (But I wouldn't recommend that you test his theory for the sheer joy of experimentation in any games of consequence. If a shot looks merely comatose rather than truly dead, and you just can't work up your enthusiasm for it, pass it up and look for another option. We're coming to that.)

Break Shots

One way to define straight pool itself is to consider it as the only pool game requiring transitions from one rack to the next.

Accordingly, your ability at the game will always be equal to your ability to make those transitions: breaking the balls, and positioning yourself for future break shots. We'll take break shots first, and talk about sequence next, since in the first rack of the game, the incoming shooter following the break will very likely be confronted with a break shot early in his sequence.

Mentally, of course, break shots are among the game's most complex, because your concentration must be equally divided three ways:

1) Pocket the ball.

2) Break up at least some of the other balls.

3) Get the cue ball in the clear.

None of these three is worth a tinker's without the rest, obviously. The reason I make such a fundamental point in a book dedicated to advanced play is that a startling number of intermediate and even better players frequently forget about Number 3. They *want* cue ball liberation, naturally, but they forget to really concentrate on it. And that's just when it doesn't happen.

I agree, splitting up your concentration three ways is no cinch. *Two* ways would be much more comfortable. So why not do yourself a favor and stop dwelling on Number 2 instead?

Here's how I look at it: You already know that your cue ball is going into the clustered balls. It can't miss doing that. You've played position so that's just what *would* happen. There is just no way that you can hit the loose object ball anywhere near where you plan to and *not* hit the cluster. Okay?

Good. Then *close that cluster out of your head and focus on the object ball and cue ball only.* You'll find it just about automatic that if you pocket the ball, with enough speed and smoothness (remember, you *must* have both) to drive the cue ball free of the cluster after contact, object balls will be loose someplace. There is no point in following those balls in flight; you have plenty of time to look at them once they stop anyway. And *the danger in watching the stack is that you tend to jerk your head in midstroke, take your eye off the object ball, or both.* Either mistake is enough to yank you into a half-a-diamond miss.

You've got to "think" that cue ball free, both in your mental rehearsals and your actual stroke.

Once you master that technique, your break shotmaking will gain immeasurably in consistency, and therefore so should your whole game. You'll find it somewhat harder to do than it is to read about, but stay with it. It'll pay off.

The second major pitfall of break shots, and one that undoes even the very best players now and then, is excessive speed. We've talked about this already, and the principle still applies to break shots as well as open ones: *You can get the job done hitting the ball much more softly than you think.*

I'm not saying you should "baby" your break shots, nor shy away from them. You've got to hit them with authority. But you don't have to clobber them. Just as with those dead combination shots, the temptation is there to drive all the balls apart. But the fact is, you'll play better position, and eventually run lots more balls, if you'll learn that it's simply not necessary to move every ball in a remaining cluster. In fact, it's frequently harmful.

Overhitting a break shot is generally a sign of lack of confidence, rather than the opposite, as you'd expect. It takes real confidence to take speed *away* from the break shot, in my opinion, because of that nagging fear that the cue ball won't free itself. But it will.

Or at least you'll have given it the maximum opportunity to get clear. Again, when you make smoothness rather than power the objective of your stroke, your butt hand is more likely to stay relaxed, your stance will be firmer; and once the object ball is pocketed, you've got the maximum in cue ball action going for you. There are only a handful of players in the world who can hit a ball with both maximum speed and smoothness, and still maintain their accuracy; and even then, these players are simultaneously sacrificing cue ball control after impact and putting the maximum number of object balls in flight. That's a perilous combination. You wouldn't *believe* the nasty things that can happen to a cue ball when a break shot is hit too hard.

Which brings us to the third fine point of break shots; again, it's one that escapes even some pretty fair players. *A break shot should be just as precise as you can make it.* The very best break-shotmakers not only pocket the ball, free the cue ball, and get secondary object balls loose, but they have a very good idea of where those balls are going (or at least, the general area of the table). That's because they've looked at their shots carefully enough to know exactly which object ball in the cluster will be struck by the cue ball, at what angle, and the probable consequences.

I know I've already advised you to put

the stack out of your mind during the actual stroking of your break shots. But during your mental rehearsal of your break shot (you *are* remembering to do that, right?), which should take place before you even take your stance, I want you to plot the fate of those object balls as though you knew all their birth signs.

And that's not as hard as it sounds. After all, I've already advised you not to put too many of those balls in motion at once; on top of that, remember that you don't have to move a previously unpocketable ball very far to make it pocketable. Millimeters will frequently make all the difference.

Break shots, then, are largely a matter of *control.* Control your emotions about them (after all, they are the game's most important shots); and control your cue ball speed and action. Control of the broken object balls will invariably follow.

We can't revisit these three points often enough:

1) Focus on the cue ball and object ball *only* during your stroke.

2) Don't murder the shot. It is smoothness that gets the balls open. You'll find that the word "flow" might make a nifty little mantra to chant to yourself as you deliver the stroke; that's just what you want your stroke, and the cue ball, to do.

3) *Know* your break shots as well as you can. No cluster should be a total mystery to you; don't settle for potluck among broken balls, because you can't be sure of being accommodated. Just as in every other aspect of the game, we're trying to reduce variables to certainties.

Now let's look at some typical break shots themselves.

See the balls specified as 1, 2, 3, and 4 in Diagram 14? Whatever the break shot you're confronted with, those four balls represent the four friendliest neighborhoods for your cue ball to visit. You've probably seen good players place an empty rack on the table while they're clearing the balls off, to determine if certain object balls will be in or out of the rack area; the best players will determine not only if the ball will be playable, but what part of the rack will most likely be contacted—*before* the balls are racked.

The reason those four balls are so desirable is fairly obvious: Each is clear on one side, and that means it will be easier to keep your cue ball free after contact. I'm not saying you cannot break the balls efficiently *unless* you make direct contact with one of the Friendly Four; you can, but you'll generally require more speed, and sacrifice accordingly in control. The exception to this rule is any break shot in which the cue ball comes off a rail, rather than directly off the object ball, to break up the rack. If your cue

Diagram 15

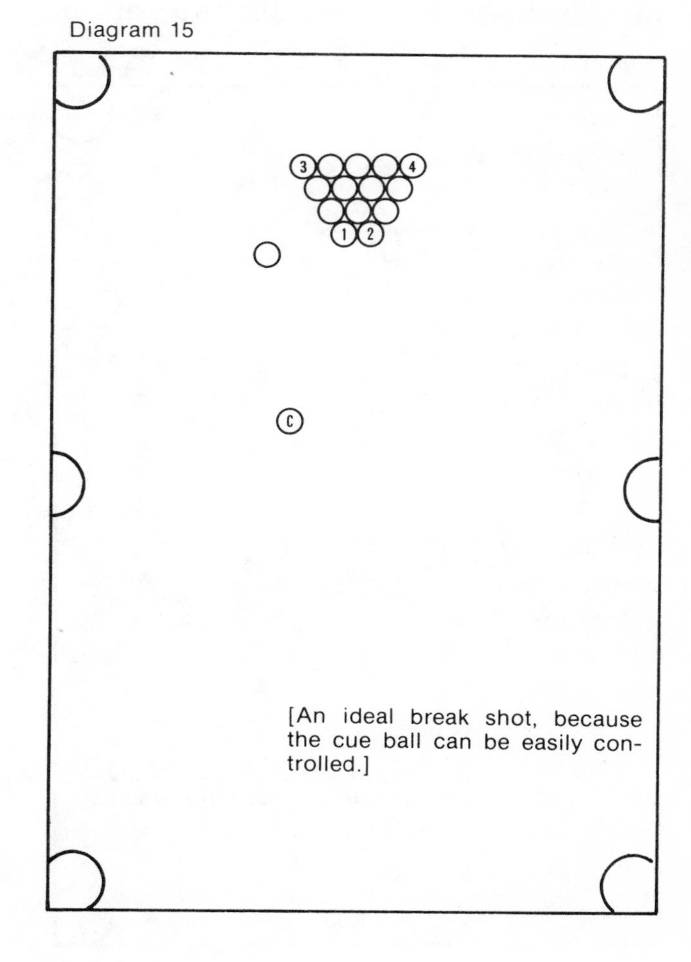

[An ideal break shot, because the cue ball can be easily controlled.]

ball comes off a rail and *doesn't* smack a corner ball, it's very likely to stick on the ball it does hit, and you'll have the dickens to pay. (Needless to say, all the break shots you'll see diagrammed here occur on the opposite side of the table too, and are to be played the exact same way. But generally, a right-handed player will prefer break shots on the left-hand side of the table, simply because they're easier to reach, and for the most part that's what we're showing here.)

If you could guarantee me the break shot in Diagram 15 every time I had a break shot to shoot, I'd ask very little else of life. Properly struck, this is the very easiest shot from which to get your cue ball to or reasonably near the ideal destination: dead center of the table. All it takes is smooth draw, and no more than medium speed. And it usually moves at least four balls free, in this case, the 2-ball, the 4-ball, and the two balls in between. The perfect speed for this shot will get the 2 in the vicinity of the side, the 4 down near the corner, and the other balls in some proximity to one another for another break shot proposition (Diagram 16). But again, concentrate during your stroke on cue ball and object ball only. No two breaks will ever be exactly the same; as long as your Kojak has some breathing room, you should have something to shoot at next.

Diagram 17 looks like the same shot—until you remember to look for the point of contact on the rack, like we just agreed to do. (But you knew that, didn't you? You're coming along fine.) Now you can see that this *is* a different shot than the last, and it's important that you not underestimate the difference.

In order to pocket the ball here, your cue ball is going to have to take on those interior balls between the 1 and 3. And in their

Diagram 16

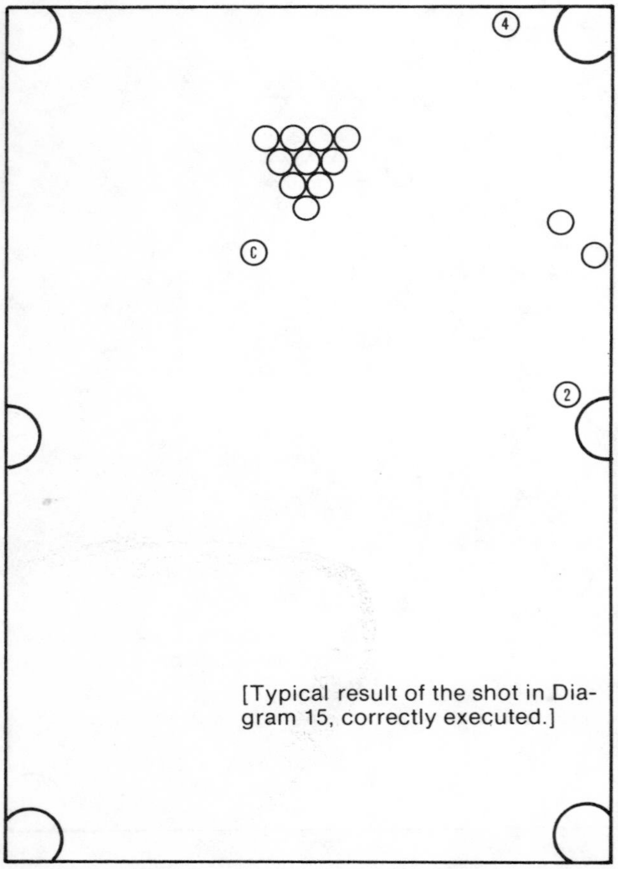

4
C
2

[Typical result of the shot in Diagram 15, correctly executed.]

Diagram 17

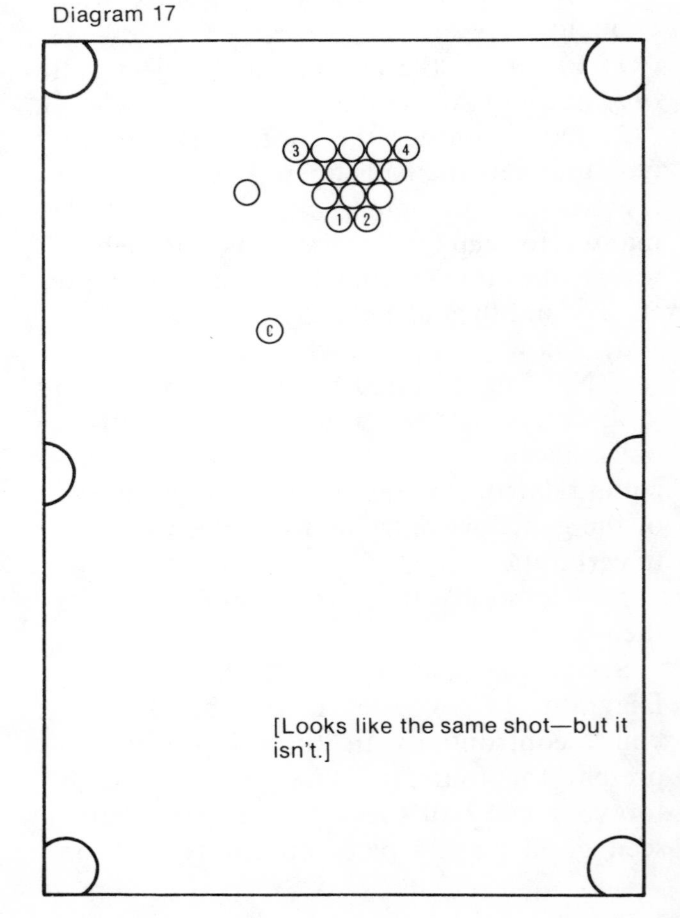

[Looks like the same shot—but it isn't.]

way, gram for gram, they can be as fearsome as the defensive Front Four of any Super Bowl team. They've got most of the mass of the rack behind them, and they can stand a pretty stiff jolt without coughing up any turf. So you'll need more speed, combined with the same smoothness, to get your cue ball out of there, and don't be surprised if it heads for the side rail, or at least in that direction. Hopefully, you'll have the 3-ball available next; most of the other broken balls will have been moved to the other side of the table, as in Diagram 18, which could be a problem if something isn't pocketable on your side.

But again, this break shot is nothing to fear; it's just that you ought to know its pitfalls. The shot is mostly a matter of confidence. If you hit your cue ball with anything less than a good firm stroke here, there's a big fat scratch waiting for you in the corner, so bear down and stroke through the ball. You can count on moving close to half the stack with the shot.

Diagram 19 shows you a break shot in which contact originates from the front rather than the side. What we want to do here is smack the 2-ball cleanly, rather than hit in the crotch between the 1 and 2, which would have a vastly different effect on the cue ball. (It might even spit Whitey back in the direction of the side pocket.)

Correctly hit, this shot will demolish the right side of the stack. But you can't draw your cue ball this time, because the force of your stroke plus the spin you pick up after contact would undoubtedly send you way the hell back up the table for a treacherous long shot next, probably off the rail too. None of that for us. We want to hit the cue ball absolutely dead center here. If you make solid contact with that head ball, and

Diagram 18

[A good leave off the shot in Diagram 17. It can be a lot nastier than this.]

Diagram 19

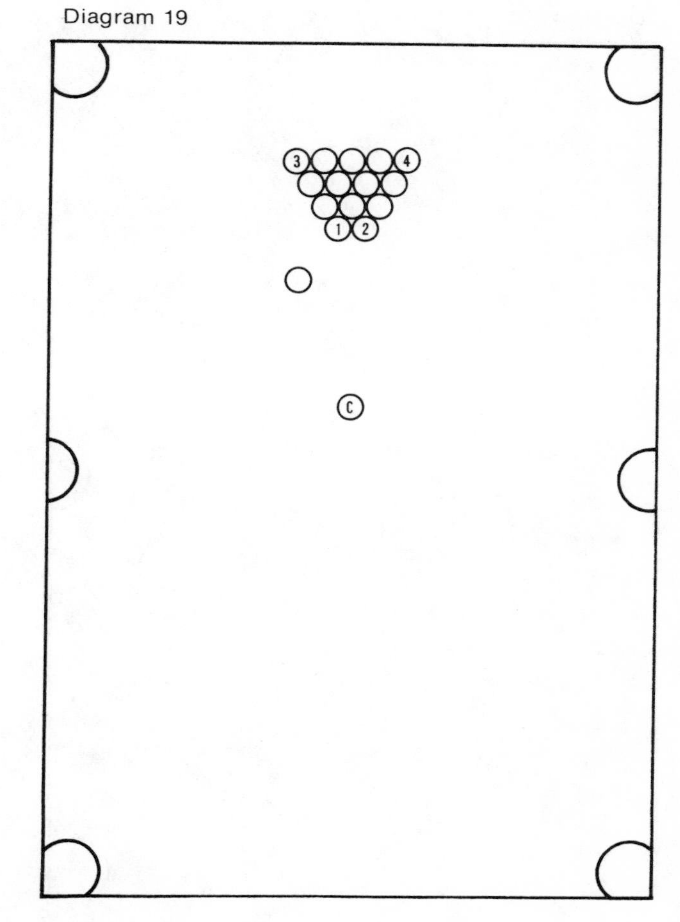

stroke smoothly, your cue ball should travel toward the right-hand side rail, *slowly*. If it shows faster sidespin than forward roll, congratulations; you hit it just right. Contact with the rail will cause it to spin back toward the center of the table. The only peril here, again, is overhitting the shot, in which case you run the risk of picking up some natural following English you didn't want, and Baldy will head for the corner rather than the side rail. Medium speed will do just fine.

Mosconi himself called the break shot in Diagram 20 the best of all. While nothing qualifies me to take Mosconi on intellectually or any other way when it comes to pool, it's worth noting that his opinion was formed in consideration of *clay* object balls, while the game has long since gone over to plastics. Plastic composition object balls came into prominence shortly before the advent of sharp-angle pockets, in the late '50s, and they're completely dominant today. As to what kind of difference that makes, ask any player who was around in the days of composition balls, and he'll likely tell you that he had to change important aspects of his game around to accommodate plastic balls. Nostalgia might soak his voice, too; pool with clay balls was really quite a different game than today's game, and lots of veteran players preferred the earlier game. You still hear some grumbling about that, even in the game's top echelons.

So much for technology. What a bang-on hit on the 1-ball, as diagrammed, will do is this: drive the 1 and 2 smartly out of the rack area; the cue ball will force-follow on through into the *next* row of balls and, hopefully, thence to freedom. (You can't draw this shot, either, for reasons already discussed, and even a center-ball hit on the

Diagram 20

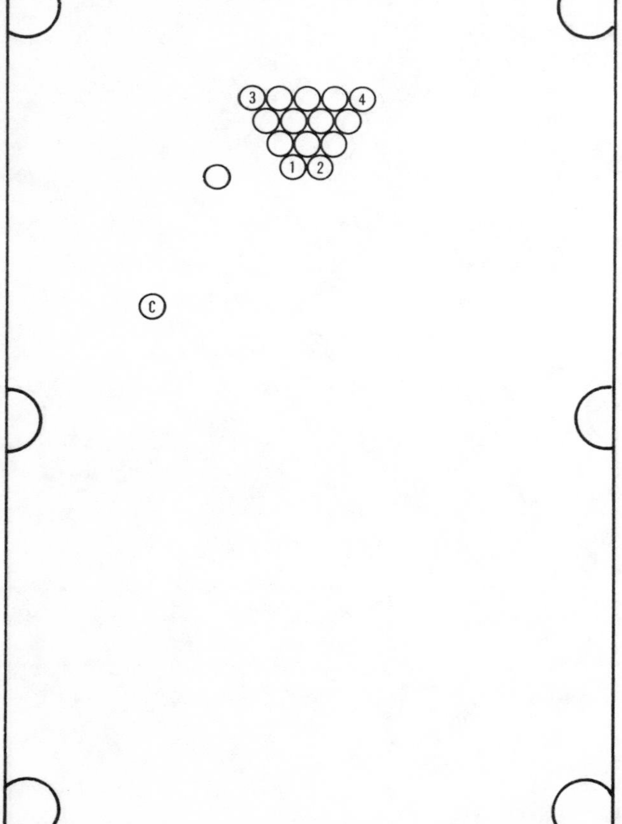

Diagram 21

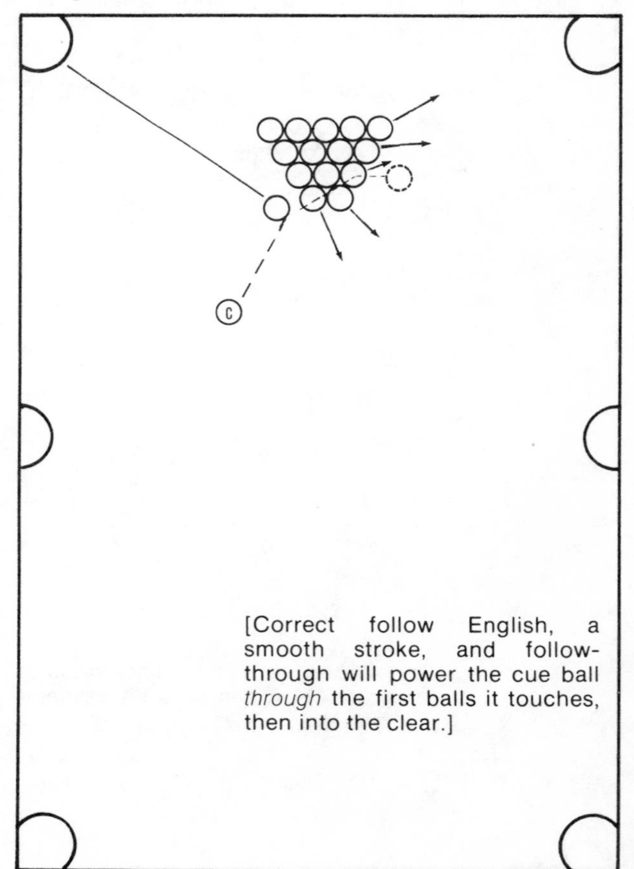

[Correct follow English, a smooth stroke, and follow-through will power the cue ball *through* the first balls it touches, then into the clear.]

cue ball will still produce the force-follow effect.) Naturally, you have to hit this shot pretty crisply; but even with smart speed and smoothness, don't be surprised if you get "buried" in there. It's a bit of hard luck, of course, especially since there will probably be object balls all over that you can't get to. But it's quite a common pitfall of the shot, and it happens to some of the best players in the world. Diagram 21 shows you a typical successful escape route for the cue ball; Diagram 22 shows you the disaster.

I'd rather have the break shot of Diagram 23 than that of Diagram 20, especially considering today's typical equipment. It's a thinner cut shot, as you can see, which means that the object ball absorbs a minimal share of the force you've applied to the cue. This shot, with correct speed and smoothness plus modest follow English—no more than the width of your cue tip above dead center on the cue ball—will move the maximum number of object balls, and may even open the whole stack. The only dues you pay for that are that the cue ball will probably go to the side rail and come back toward the center of the table where all those object balls are moving, and could possibly receive its fair share of abuse, such as winding up frozen on a lone ball. The other demon to watch out for, once more, is excessive speed, which can and often does lead to a scratch in the *opposite side pocket,* believe it or not. (See Diagram 24.) I know it will seem like hideous luck if it ever happens to you, but that scratch does exist, and has for quite some time now.

Players seem to settle for the break shot you see in Diagram 25 only as a last ditch; nobody wants to send a break ball into the side pocket. Yet you can turn up old-timers who will swear that the immortal Greenleaf,

Diagram 22

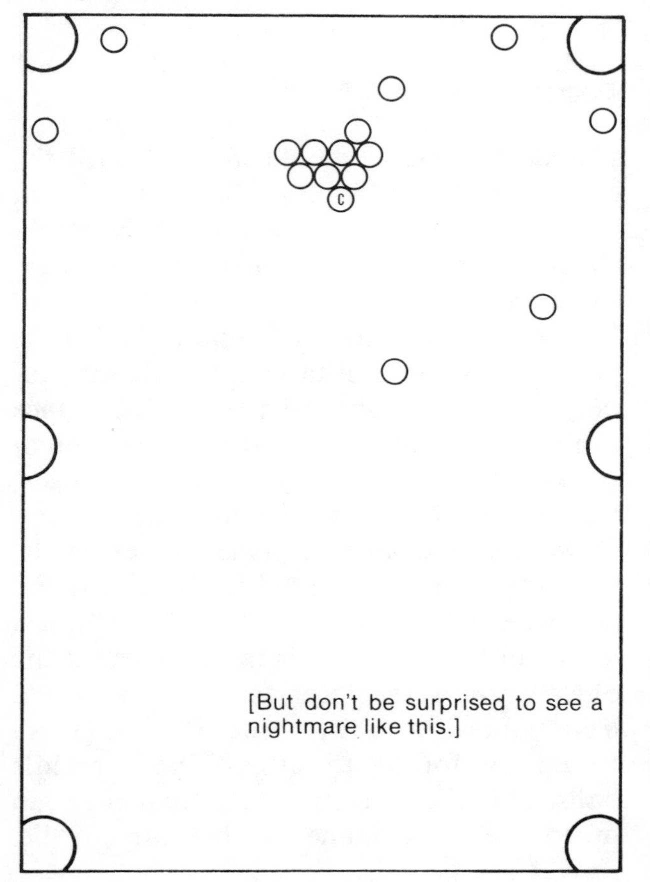

C
[But don't be surprised to see a nightmare like this.]

Diagram 23

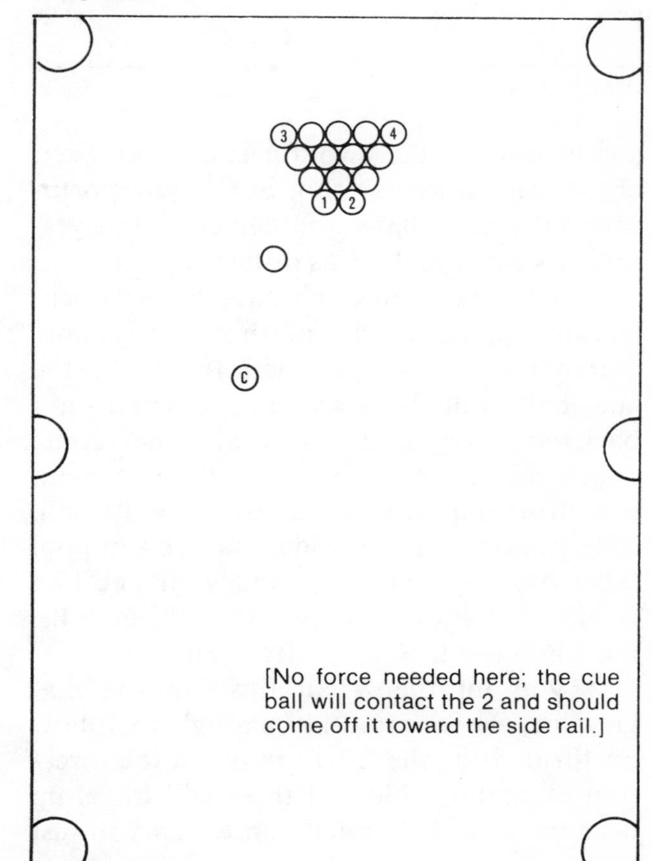

3
4
1
2
C
[No force needed here; the cue ball will contact the 2 and should come off it toward the side rail.]

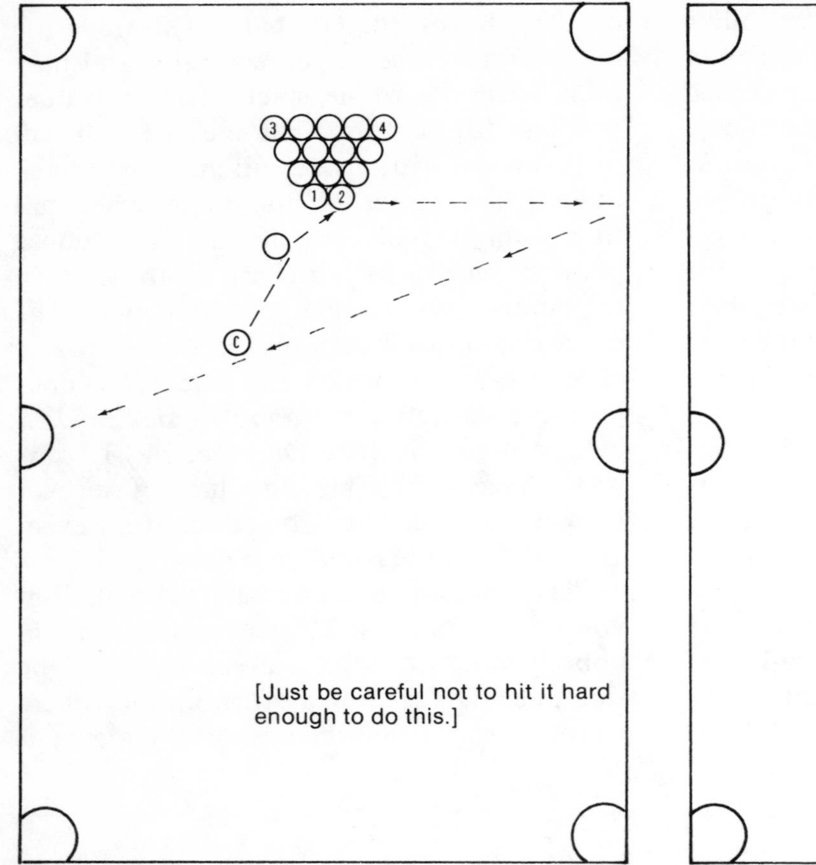

Diagram 24

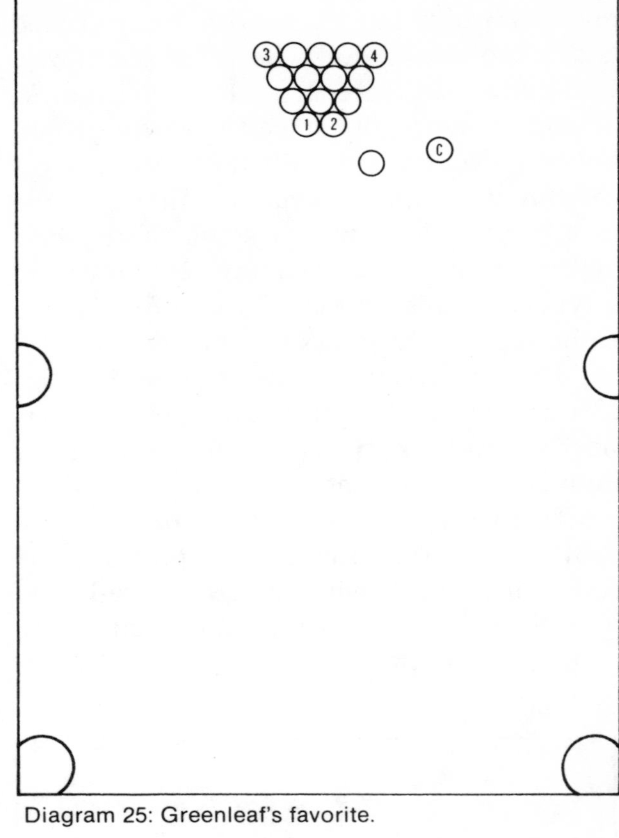

Diagram 25: Greenleaf's favorite.

surely one of the two finest players ever, chose this particular shot at every opportunity. (Perhaps that's another clue that yesterday's game really was different.)

And at that, you don't have to be Greenleaf to see the merits of this shot. Immediately following impact with the 2-ball, the cue ball will be traveling *forward*—not backward—in the direction of center table, which means you can stroke the shot with less effort than if you were drawing the ball. Side pockets are the widest target any pool table has to offer you. And your cue ball need only fight its way past two object balls, the 2 and the 1, to get to fresh air.

If you hit the 2-ball flush in the diagrammed shot, smoothly enough to follow on through it, the 2 will move in the direction of center table and the 1 will travel up near the same side pocket in which you just scored. The 3-ball should move toward the corner, and you will probably loosen at least one other ball at the rear of the stack. (Bear in mind that during any of these shots, you could contact the rack at the ball I suggest but a mere pinhead away from the point of contact I'm talking about, with totally different object-ball results. Once again, I'm simply suggesting what might *typically* happen, along with correct suggestions for getting your cue ball free.)

On this and all side-pocket break shots, you simply *must* avoid old Rock-Ribs there, in between the 2 and 4-balls. That is not a worry in the shot of Diagram 25; but if the object ball were closer to the rack, you'd have yourself a sticky wicket. Your cue ball would be forced to attack those middle balls, plus the balls massed behind them, in much the same plane as they already lie,

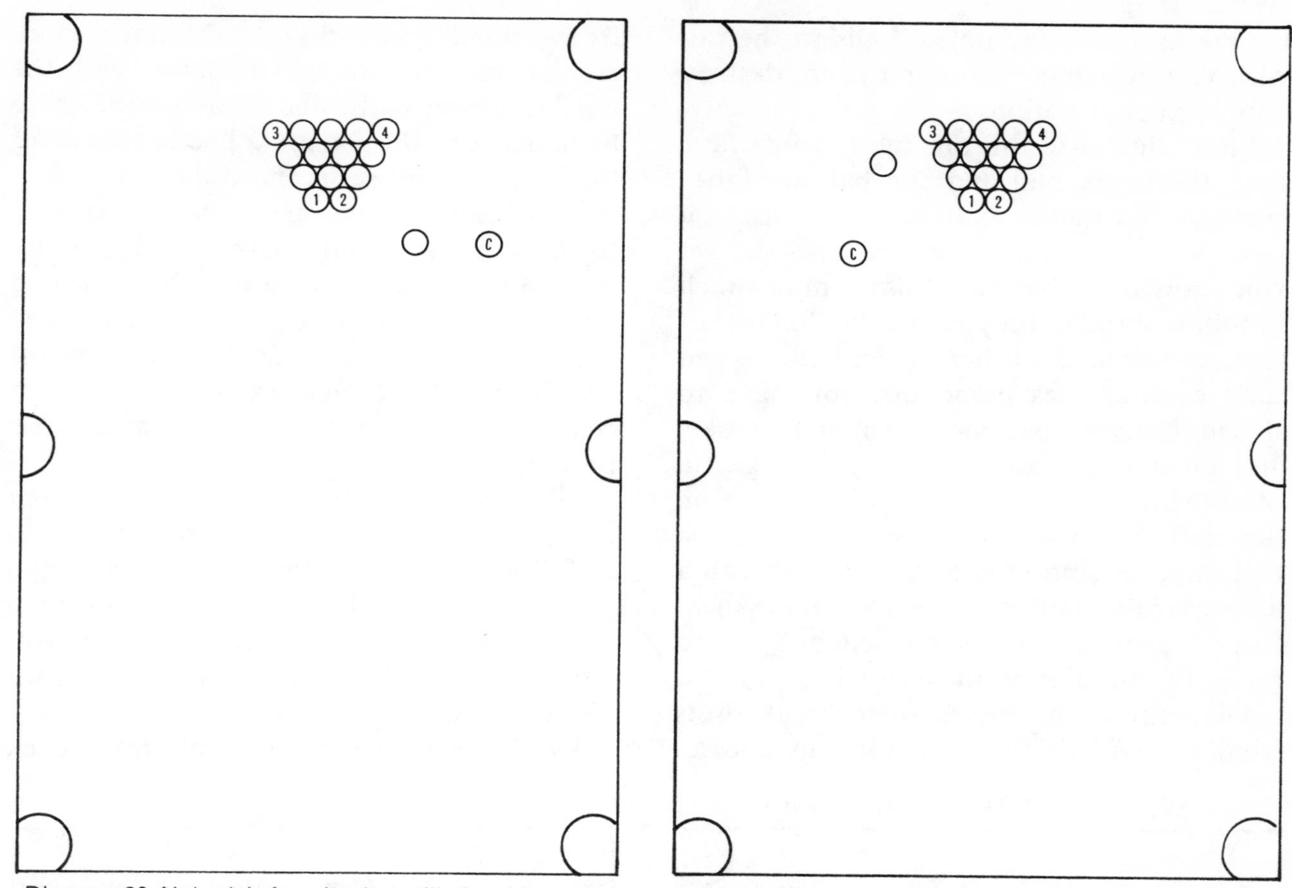

Diagram 26: Nobody's favorite, but still playable.

Diagram 27

and would have about as much future as Floyd Collins.* You can't hit the shot with draw, either, because you'd be almost certain to scratch in the near corner pocket.

Do your best to avoid side-pocket break shots that require you to cut the object ball thin. Note the difference between the shot in Diagram 26 and the one in Diagram 25. I'd try the Diagram 26 shot if it came up, but I wouldn't like it nearly as much. As a matter of personal preference, I like to be able to see the entire side pocket when I line up a shot like this, and that's not possible in Diagram 26; additionally, although I will engage the front of the rack as I should, I now have a mountain to move instead of just two balls, because of the angle involved. So I have to hit the shot harder, and take potluck with the subsequent position of the object balls. Also, I'd be wary of follow English on this shot, as I'm not particularly anxious to send the cue ball on an uncharted flight. Center cue ball would be better here.

Diagram 27 shows you another common break shot in which you must deal with the rack's troublesome balls. It's similar to the shot of Diagram 17, except you're going to follow, rather than draw, the cue ball this time, with enough force to drive through the corner of the racked balls. Your next shot will probably be one of the three balls between the 3 and 4; the dangers of the shot are (a) sticking at the point of contact, and

*Mining's most celebrated casualty. Poor Collins was trapped in a Kentucky cave-in in the late 1920s. A reporter somehow managed to shimmy down to him and interview him as he lay waiting for his rescuers. The reporter won the Pulitzer Prize; Floyd Collins died while still trapped. Always strive to show your cue ball a kinder fate than that, and the game will reward you in gratitude.

(b) taking too many object balls to the rail with you, which could inhibit if not destroy your next-shot options.

Shots similar to this one may occur where both the break ball and cue ball are fairly close to the racked balls. As a result, you have a shot requiring follow English, yet you really don't have a lot of room in which to follow through on your stroke, for fear of fouling one of the other object balls. When such a shot does come up, you have to shorten (a) your backswing, (b) your stroke, and most importantly, (c) your bridge (in other words, move your bridge hand up on the cue). You won't be able to hit the cue ball quite as smoothly as you would with a longer stroke, but the three shortening measures I propose should still enable you to get sufficient juice on the cue ball.

Diagram 28 introduces us to break shots from the rear of the rack. On this and all from-behind break shots, it becomes more crucial than ever to make contact with the outside object balls, and to avoid the three balls between the 3 and 4. The back row of the rack, of course, is the widest, therefore the toughest to open up. In the shot shown, for instance, you could get away with touching the ball next to the 4-ball, but it would alter the path of your cue ball, and you could very well find it moving back toward what's left of the rack, rather than toward center table. Which, to recall a familiar phrase, spells Trouble.

So hit your cue ball northeast of its center, and concentrate on contacting the 4-ball as full as you can. A smooth follow-through will drive the cue ball to the side rail, then toward the center of the table, and the principal object balls affected will be the four corner balls.

I've branded that middle ball in the back

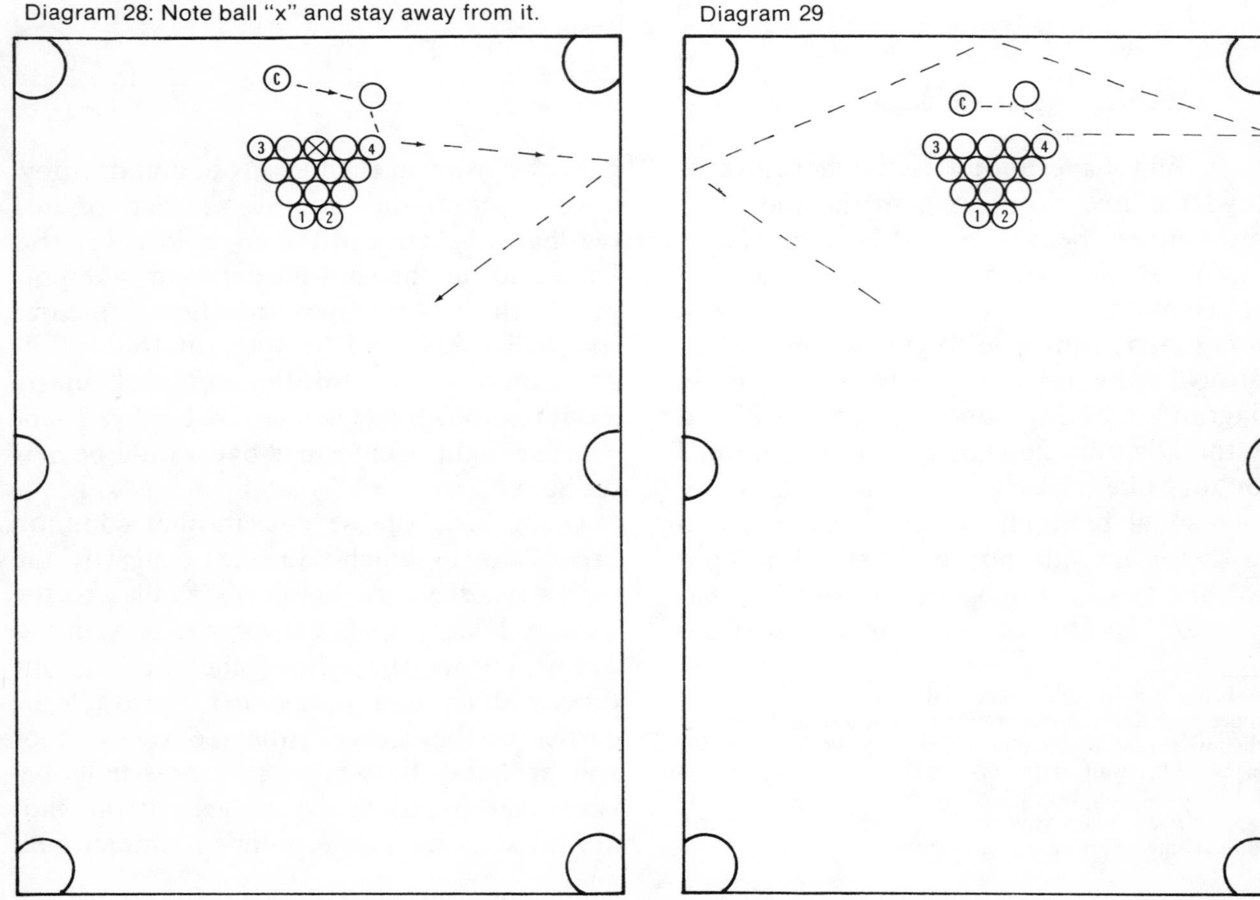

Diagram 28: Note ball "x" and stay away from it.

Diagram 29

row of the rack with an "X," even if it does seem melodramatic, for a good reason. You don't want anything to do with that ball, in any form of from-the-rear break shots. There is no tougher single point in the entire rack. If you hit the X-ball on the nose, your cue ball will stick there and will be well on its way to sucking deep swamp water. If you take on both the X-ball and the ball to either side of it in quick succession, you're an odds-on favorite for a double-kiss scratch in the corner. So if you're going to save a ball for a from-the-rear break shot, make sure that ball sits one side or the other of dead center of the rack.

With a less sharp from-the-rear angle, as in Diagram 29, it becomes more difficult to spin your cue ball off the side rail toward center table. So we'll take our cue ball the other way, with *left*-hand follow instead of right, and with enough speed to contact the

Diagram 30: Tougher than it looks.

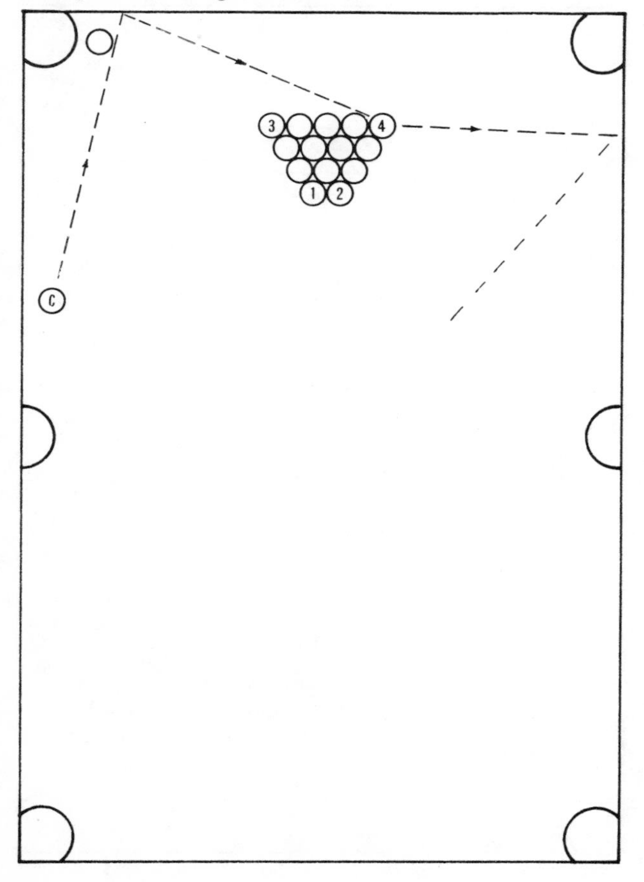

three rails you see diagrammed. Don't hit it too hard, or with too much English, or you'll send the cue ball back into the stack somewhere near where the 3-ball used to be, and enemies lurk there. Old-timers will tell you that this shot was a favorite of the fabled Ponzi. Just be careful with it, or it will make you look sillier than Fonzie.

The shot in Diagram 30 looks like something that Ray Charles could handle eight times out of ten, but then that first apple presented Adam with no visible dangers, either. Actually this shot represents a tough little billiard, from the object ball to the 4-ball, which you simply must hit. The farther up the table your cue ball is, at the outset of the shot, the tougher it becomes to take the rack on as you should; ditto as the cue ball is left farther off the side rail. You should hit your cue ball at about 5 o'clock for this shot. As usual, medium speed will do; and if you engage the corner ball, your cue ball will behave about as it did for the shot in Diagram 28. If you hit the ball next to the corner ball, you can count on either staying between the rack and the bottom rail, or getting stuck on the side of the rack. And if you hit the X-ball, be prepared to take a seat soon. In any case, don't be deceived by the simplicity of pocketing the object ball; this shot requires the tightest cue ball control you can muster.

The balls can be broken with the shot in Diagram 31, but it, too, is a shot that players usually choose only as a last resort; it's frequently the result of an improperly played sequence. At any rate, the shot increases in effectiveness with the sharpness of the angle between cue ball, object ball, and pocket. If the cue ball in Diagram 31 were closer to the rail, or the object ball farther from the rail, the shot would be treacherous; you'd have to both overhit it and force the cue ball into the rack, and those are two prime no-no's. As it is, you can pocket the ball with center cue ball hit or modest follow English; and again, be *sure* you contact the 1-ball on the way back. The inner balls will almost surely capture your cue ball and hold it hostage.

Actually, this is no bargain as break shots go. Even correctly executed, there are still the dangers of a scratch in the opposite side pocket, or a trip to the head of the table, sometimes even a scratch in the back corner. The only way to preclude all these horrors is to hit the ball softly; and if you overdo that, you won't do much of a job of opening the racked balls.

As you move the open object ball and cue ball of Diagram 31 farther down the table, toward the corner pocket you're aiming for, it becomes necessary to draw the cue ball, to be sure of smacking the 1-ball on the way back. And that amplifies the chances of sending your cue ball to the far country, up by the head rail.

Diagram 32 presents another deceiver. Pocketing the ball in the side is easy enough, but the shot is completely worthless unless you hit the rack at the 1-ball. If you hit off the side of the rack instead, only Dame Fortune can keep your cue ball out of the subway, and she can be very hard to find. If you overcompensate and hit the 2-ball flush, it's quite possible that the rack won't budge except for the 4-ball, not even if you hit the shot hard; and again, you'll have to get lucky for the 4-ball to wind up anywhere advantageous to you. Once more, what seems like hard luck is really a common pitfall.

If you do hit the 1-ball, though, you'll smash the balls apart. Just be sure you stroke and follow through smoothly enough to get the cue ball off that 1-ball. It can stick there otherwise.

I've left the break shot of Diagram 33 for

Diagram 31

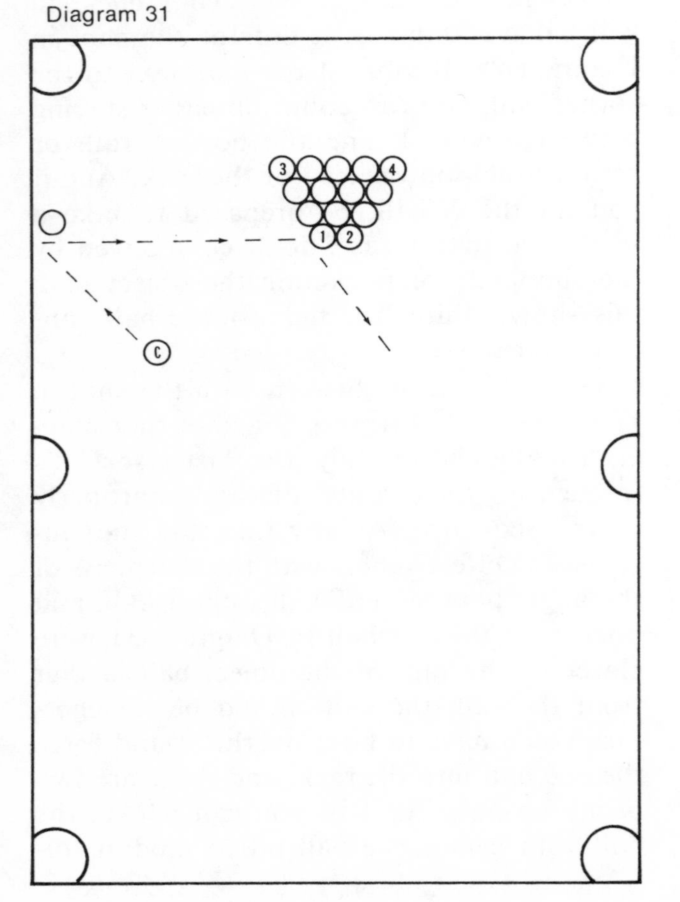

Diagram 32

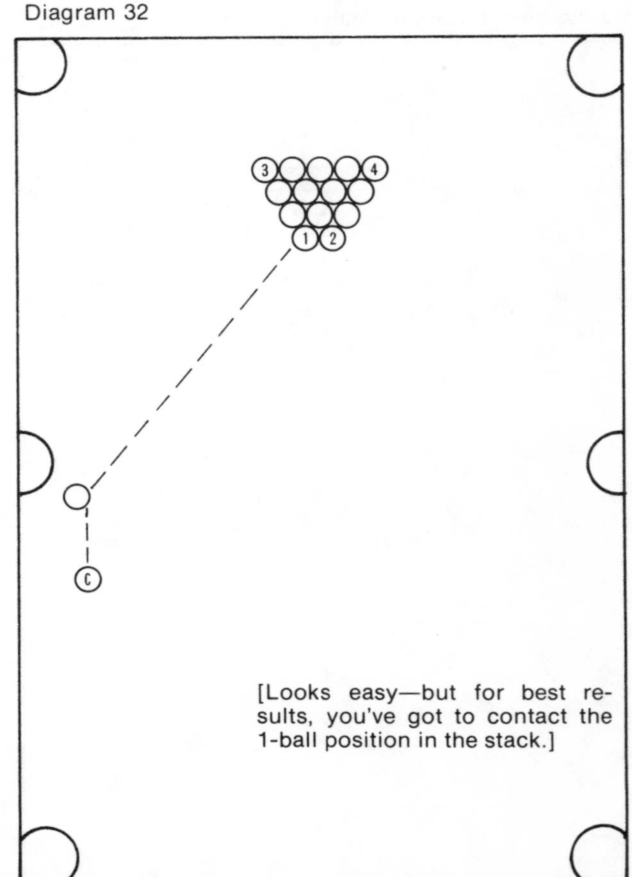

[Looks easy—but for best results, you've got to contact the 1-ball position in the stack.]

last in this section, because it's the one that seems to confuse intermediate players most. It's neither the shot of Diagram 15, where the cue ball is nearer the middle of the table than is the object ball, nor is it the shot of Diagram 20, where the reverse is true. In the former shot, you draw the cue ball; in the latter shot, you use follow. Now the two balls are precisely in line. How do you hit it?

My opinion is based far more on my observing top players than on my own playing experience, and it's this: As long as you can make solid contact with the side of the 1-ball, draw your cue ball. At the angle you see here, you could probably even afford to take a little speed off your stroke, and still bring your cue ball out safely while doing an efficient number on the bottom portion of the stack. I know the temptation is there to really rear back and potch this one, especially when things are going well for you and this shot turns up in the middle of a nice run, but don't fall for it. The game can turn fickle on you more quickly than you'd believe, and there's no surer way to court disaster than to turn lots of balls loose on uncharted trips.

Diagram 33

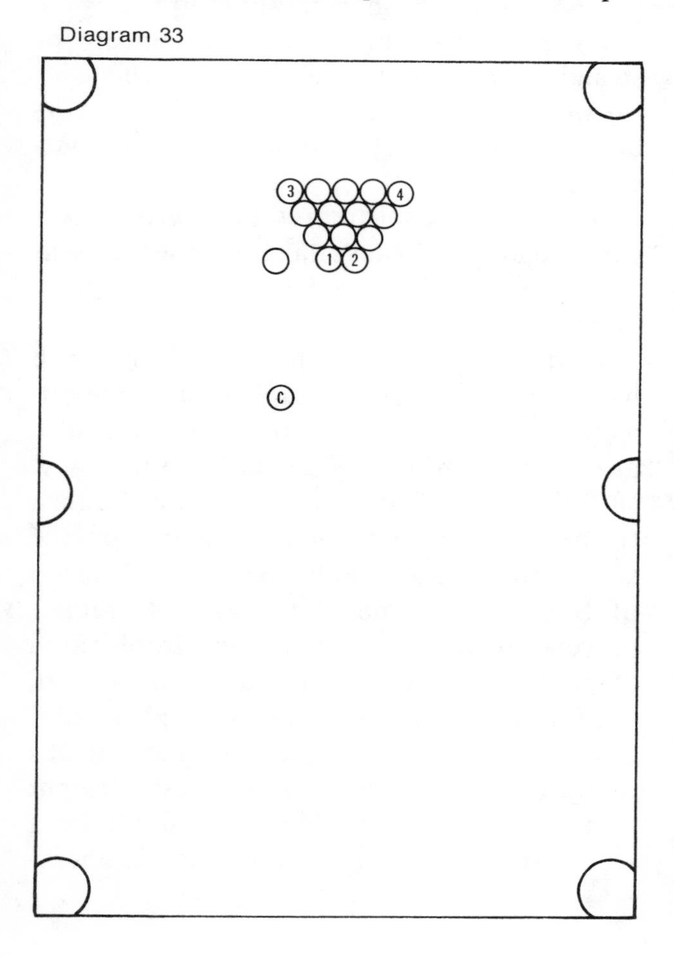

I don't want to dwell unduly on the matters of stroke and stance; all the beginners' books on pool have treated those subjects thoroughly and well. But good break shotmaking is largely a question of good fundamentals, plus the mastery of your attitude about them. The same break shot that terrifies you in the company of those other 14 balls would probably be a piece of cake for you if the racked balls weren't there. So you must bring that same nonchalance to the shot, plan it as thoroughly as you can, hit it as though the other balls weren't there, and let your fundamentals do the rest.

The fundamentals I'm talking about include a relaxed rear hand, a fluid delivery and follow-through, and a stance firm enough to restrict your motion to your arm, nothing more. On break shots (in fact, on *any* shots) that require you to cut the ball thin, I think you'll find it helpful to redistribute your weight in the opposite direction of the shot. In other words, a right-handed player cutting a ball sharply to his left should have the lion's share of his weight on his right, or rear, foot, and should lean forward to put extra weight on his left foot when cutting balls thinly to his right. (Reverse all this if you're left-handed, of course.)

Finally, while knowledge is power and all that, and the pointers I'm passing along here will complement and may even enhance your accuracy, it's no substitute for that same accuracy. Not this book nor anyone else's is going to sink the object ball for you. I strongly recommend setting aside part of your practice time for getting acquainted with these break shots, and learning what to expect from them. Don't worry about running the balls you've opened up; just set the break shot up, make it, observe the results, then rerack and set up the same shot, or another one. It will cost you a little extra bending and squatting, all that reracking time, but that can't hurt you, and it will pay you generous dividends. You simply cannot play good straight pool unless you know how to break the balls; and it's awfully tough to be comfortable with unknown quantities. That's one more respect in which the game imitates life, a point we seem to have made before.

Sequence

I know what you're thinking, as you sit there sullenly and watch a better player turn a crowded table into a desert: How come, when *he's* at the table, the object balls behave like boot-camp troopers and he has all those laughers to shoot at; and when it's *my* turn, the balls all turn to mutiny and begin bunching up like a baboon's behind during mating season?

Well, it's no accident. And it's not because the other guy is good to his mother, or because your moon (no offense) is in the wrong house, or anything like that.

What it *is* is that he understands sequence better than you. (But you and I are about to go to work on a nice surprise for him.) To the vast majority of those who sail the sea of billiards, Sequence is the siren Circe, with all kinds of sweet beckonings that lure your cue ball into doom. (That *New Yorker* address, once again, is . . .) You're not alone. Lots of players invest decades of their time in the game—yes, *decades*—without correctly solving all the mysteries of sequence.

There's a necessary bit of foreword, before we begin studying sequence: Fourteen balls, each 2¼″ in diameter, can occupy 40½ square feet of playing space (on a regulation table) in a considerable variety of patterns. I'm sure there is no pronounceable number that you can put to that.

So how can you learn straight pool sequence out of a book, when the possibility exists that you may never encounter the same situations? The answer is that pocket billiards, correctly played, not only presents recurring situations, but that is precisely the objective of the expert player: to reduce those infinite pattern options to that which is familiar and certain. Second, if you're following my advice and controlling, rather than murdering, your break shots, you're driving fewer balls out of the stack, and less far at that. So the possibility of keen similarity, if not actual duplication, certainly does exist, and we're going to talk at some length about how you take advantage of that.

Any game that depends on *improvisation* to the extent that pool does would seem to defy rules of thumb. Still, we'll begin with some generalities, and proceed to examine just how often those generalities apply.

I believe that the underlying concept of straight pool sequence is that *whenever possible*—and those are two terribly important words—you should strive to do whatever's easiest.

Now that in itself represents a gross oversimplification. So let's take a closer look at the statement as it applies to straight pool, and what it really means.

1) It means that you don't hit the cue ball hard when you can accomplish the same objectives hitting it soft. Most of what you've already read in these pages talks to that.

2) It means that you don't apply English to the cue ball when you can accomplish the same thing hitting center ball. Peter Margo of New Jersey, one of the game's premier players, even states the case geographically: "Out East, we play center ball, and leave all the fancy English to the Midwest players." I don't know how he documents that, but it's unarguable that the world's best straight pool is played in the East, so don't be a stubborn Midwesterner. I think the opera-

tive word in Margo's statement is *fancy.* English has its place in the game, but you employ it when it's *functional,* not because it's more aesthetically pleasing, or you're more comfortable hitting the ball that way, or (shudder) you took a guess.

3) It means that *whenever possible* (well, I told you they were important words), *you don't move a second object ball that is already pocketable, after sinking the one you called.* Think about that. It sounds elementary, but it has more to do with cutting the game's men from its boys than I can ever describe to you in words. Just watch the next pool game you see, and take note of how often the players scuttle their own ships by moving balls unnecessarily, even if accidentally. Master the knack of not doing that, and I guarantee you that your game will improve by a conservative guess of 50 percent, likely even more. *Please* learn this.

4) It means that *whenever possible* (w. p.), you don't choose cue ball routes that require your driving or *forcing* the cue ball, as opposed to rolling it, someplace.

5) It means that w. p., you don't drive the cue ball to a rail when you can get it to an advantageous place without using a rail.

6) It means that w. p., you don't employ two-rail routes where one-rail routes will get the job done.

7) It means that w. p., you don't employ three-rail routes where two-rail (or, sometimes, one-rail) routes will do.

8) It means that w. p., you provide yourself with a second shot that you can count on as part of all your mid-rack break shots. This is the exact same principle as the Safety Valve pass in football. I'm not talking about the specific shots we just discussed, of course, but their smaller brothers and cousins that you use to separate (a good word) smaller-than-fourteen-ball clusters. We'll get back to this.

9) It means that w. p., we position ourselves to shoot at balls on or near the rails early in our sequence. I have to be out-front enough to credit all the pool authors who preceded me for this point, too; it's mentioned in just about all the beginners' books. This time around, I want to give you the *why* behind that tip, and show you where it fits in the scheme of things.

Balls on or near the rails represent two potential sources of trouble: They may block routes that you need to move your cue ball efficiently; and they may also occupy areas into which you may need to drive more object balls on your subsequent break shots. In that case, you only end up creating more miniclusters along the rail, causing you to interrupt the sequence you originally planned and execute more break shots. Remember, the fewer times your cue ball is required to move secondary object balls, the better for you.

Don't worry about remembering all this. Nor will you have to carry my book around the table with you as though it were some kind of pilots' checklist. Take my word for it, experience and confidence will eventually cause all these considerations to come to you spontaneously, and in milliseconds. While you're still learning to put these concepts to work, your play might slow up some; but once you see that these are really the things you need to know, they'll automatically become part of your game.

Now, as to all those *"Whenever Possibles":* What makes the game of pool so intriguing and infinite is the frequency with which it will deny you the chance to take those simplifying steps. You will be forced to violate every single one of w.p.'s 1 through 9, and plenty of times, too. When you are required to do that, your success will depend on how much *control* you can retain over all the variables that confront you at that point. What the very maximum in control will do for you is that it will let you resume your simplifying process at the earliest opportunity. What you never want to do, in this or any pool game, is *guess.* I've said it before: The player who obtains the most certainties for himself is the player who figures to win.

Okay. Let's apply these principles to balls on a table, instead of merely on paper. Say that the balls have been broken, by either you or your opponent, and it's your turn to shoot and you do have shots available. Up to now, you've been treating this situation by shooting off the open balls you see, more or less taking potluck about additional shots that might come up along the way, and hopefully some of those will break up the remaining balls for you too. Have I got your game accurately scouted? Then let's see if we can get you into some healthier habits.

Your first move is to shoot *which* balls? Your first move is to shoot *no* balls, Fast Eddie. The balls have just been broken, remember, and that means your first move is to inspect the balls that are still clustered, to see if you can find any lucky stiffs (not bad, huh?). And if you should find one, leave it alone for now. We've already agreed that open shots are pocketable now, and you'll see shortly why you ought to consider taking them off first.

But do read the stack first. If you detect no dead shots, that means you'll have to use one of the balls that are loose now to break up the rest of the stack later. That's what you look for first. What I want you to do next is characterize every single ball on the table, like this:

A) Which balls have open paths to pockets, just as they lie?

B) Which balls *will have* open paths to pockets as a result of your pocketing the A-balls?

C) Which balls simply cannot be pocketed unless you alter their current position? (In other words, still unfavorably clustered?)

D) Which of the A-balls or B-balls might you logically use to move the C-balls?

And that's all. Once you've done that, you at least understand the nature of every ball confronting you, and what needs to be done to them. What's left is to decide on the sequence in which you shoot off your A's and B's, in order to move your C's so that *they* become A's and B's. Don't forget, any time *any* secondary balls are moved as another ball is pocketed, your first moves are to inspect the remaining clusters *and* to determine the answers to questions A, B, C, and D. If you can discipline yourself to go through those two exercises every time you should, without fail, you'll be a man, my son. It's perfectly amazing how easily you can forget to do either one under the pressure of a match. All but the best players make that kind of slip.

I promised you real balls on a real table. Let's apply what you've just learned to a modest run of 14 balls. Most of the nine w. p.'s we just considered will arise in even that short a run.

(And I do recognize, by the way, that a 14-ball run is not likely to strike terror into the hearts of Peter Margo; his brother-in-law Steve Mizerak, who is coincidentally the best player in the world; nor anyone else who knows beans about the game. The idea here is that this run represents the nucleus of *correct play*. That's an innocent-looking phrase, but it's actually a very rare thing indeed in pool; and all that the very best players really do is successfully apply these concepts of correctness over and over again. Thus their runs go on for racks and racks. Don't worry about how many balls you can run, for now. Focus instead on how correctly you run them. The runs that you can ultimately achieve will be dictated by how often you're able to play and your aptitudes. Leave everything else to me.)

Here we go, and I don't mind saying this again: You quickly will learn how to plan a pool pattern like this in a teeny, tiny fraction of the time it takes you to read about it here. Don't be fooled by words.

Photograph 1 shows you a layout facing me after a break shot such as in Diagram 15, my favorite. (And the inset shows you just how the balls were originally racked, to show you where the balls now open came from in the rack.) I've already examined the remaining clustered balls and found no stiffs.

Photograph 1

As you can see, I have six A-balls loose (that is, balls with at least one path open to a logical pocket). That leaves eight balls clustered, or C-balls, and the easiest ball to use to open them up (in other words, a D-ball) seems to be the 14. It now becomes a matter of playing these balls exactly as I see them now, without the need to improvise; and in order to ensure that, I'm going to arrange a sequence of the easiest shots available.

Naturally, there are specific reasons for shooting each and every shot in the way I suggest, beyond merely sinking one more ball. W. p.'s 1 through 9 form those reasons, and I'll mention the various ones that apply to each shot. (Since I'll be shooting these as softly as I can, you can assume that w. p. 1 applies in each case.)

In Photograph 2, I've rolled the 2-ball into the side pocket, following up just a few inches for position on the 11. This shot is a function of w. p.'s 3 and 5.

In Photograph 3, I've taken the 11 off. I

Photograph 2

needed to use the rail here to get the angle I wanted on the 7-ball, but the shot still employs w. p.'s 3 and 9.

In Photograph 4, I've put the 7 in the subway, a quite simple shot that still accomplishes several objectives. For the first time, I've put w. p. 8 to work. Notice that if I didn't have as good an angle on that 14-ball to break the clustered balls, I'd still have another opportunity to get one, by playing the 4-ball first. So the 4-ball has acted as a "safety valve" here, and will on the next shot too. (For those of you who don't follow football, by the way, a "safety valve" is generally a running back who stays in the backfield on a passing play, so the quarterback can dump the ball off to him if all his intended receivers are covered. In short, it's

Photograph 3

Photograph 4

a last-resort, just-in-case proposition, and I'm sure you can see the parallel to pool.)

So now I'm ready for my second break shot of the rack. I am easily capable of a stroke that will pocket the 14 and send my cue ball all the way *through* that stack of balls (and so are you; that's no sweat), and that will *probably* leave me open for shots on the left-hand side of the table. But remember, in pool, probabilities aren't nearly as good as certainties. If, in sinking the 14, I reduce my cue ball speed so as to drive the cue ball *off* the stack rather than *through* it, I will certainly have the 4-ball to shoot next (plus, most likely, other shots), and that's what I'm going to do.

Photograph 5 shows you that I haven't exactly smashed the pack to hell and gone;

Photograph 5

Photograph 6

still, there are some significant and very favorable differences now. There are two new A-balls, the 6 and the 8, and both are important. The 6 has knocked the 1 over toward the side pocket; the 8 is a D-ball as well as an A-ball, and one that should let me break up the remaining stacked balls with ease. And position on the 8-ball should follow naturally if I just play the 1, with as little cue ball movement as possible after contact. First I'll look at those last six balls; there are no combination shots in there, but with the layout I have now, I don't particularly need any. Then, even though I was saving the 4-ball, I'll play the 1, simply because I'm in such a good natural position to do that now. (By contrast, I don't need to be anywhere special to make the 4.)

Photograph 6 shows me ready to shoot the 8-ball, having made the 1. To be as precise as I can be about this break shot, my cue ball figures to enter the stack between the 9 and 12-balls, and they will break up the rest of the balls for me. So I'll pocket the 8-ball with just enough speed to move the 12 and 9-balls a foot or so, no more.

Voilà. Note, in Photograph 7, that I didn't move the 12 or the 9 very far, yet all the balls on the table are now A-balls, except for the 12-ball which is a B. I'd have to shoot either the 4 or 3 to open the 12 up for either corner pocket, but that will be no problem. Also, note that although the 5 and 6 appear to be B-balls too, they are both open for the right-hand side pocket, and that is a logical destination to consider for them because of where the 13-ball is; my cue ball is going to have to go over there anyway. The 9 is my break shot for the next rack, and that is something I want to be able to plan as early in a sequence as I can.

In Photograph 8, I've taken that easy 4-ball off, and come back off the rail a few inches for another easy shot on the 3. It looks like it would be a cinch to roll my cue ball just past the 12-ball and shoot it next, but instead I'm going to use the side rail instead and get position on the 10-ball. I know that appears to be a violation of w. p. 5, but what I'm really doing is applying w. p. 8 again, and making things easier for myself in the long run. And you'll see why in one more shot.

Photograph 7

Photograph 8

Photograph 9

In Photograph 9, the 3 has been made as described, and the cue ball easily cleared to take on the 10.

Photograph 10 shows you that I've made the 10-ball, and have used a little draw on the cue ball to bring it out of that corner area. Now I can make the 13 easily in the back corner pocket. What I want you to see here is that if I didn't have quite the shot I wanted on the 13—if, for instance, the cue ball were a few inches closer to the side rail than it is—I'd still have another chance to get good position on the 13 by playing the 12 first. So the 12 has been used as another "safety valve," and that's why I left it there. As you can see, it's the principle of good old w. p. 8 again.

As it is, the cue ball lies ideally for the 13,

Photograph 10

Photograph 11

just a few degrees removed from a straight-in shot. A center hit on the cue ball with moderate speed will advance my cue ball a few inches, for either the 5 or 6 . . .

. . . and Photograph 11 shows you that my next shot will be the 5. I'll hit it with just enough draw to bring my cue ball back where I can get a good shot at the 12 . . .

. . . which is what I have in Photograph 12. You can see that even if my cue ball were a few inches to either side of where it is now, I could obviously still make the 12 and get good position on the 6 with little trouble. Again, I'm not quite straight-in on the 12, so soft draw will move me a few inches toward center table, and a gimme on the 6.

And that's just what I have in Photograph 13. Now I can roll that 6 softly into

Photograph 12

Photograph 13

the side, with a little follow on the cue ball that puts me right where I want to be on the 9. Photograph 14 shows you that's just where I am, ready to break the next rack and start the whole process all over again.

Anything is possible, of course, in a sequence of still photographs, but let's not be cynical. I assure you that I did actually run this rack just the way you see it. Let's see what made the rack so outlandishly easy.

In 14 shots, I only made contact with secondary object balls three times: my original break shot, the 15-ball; the 14; and the 8. In each case, naturally, that secondary contact was completely by design.

In the 14 shots, I only drove the cue ball

Photograph 14

to a rail four times: on the 11, 4, 3, and 10-balls (Photos 3, 8, 9, and 10).

And in each of the 14 shots, the distance traveled by the cue ball after contact with an object ball was no more than two feet or so, frequently less.

I'm not saying I deserve Pulitzer Prize consideration for that run. My point is just the opposite: You could have done it too. Seen individually, none of those shots was one whit harder than anything that confronted you in your first few weeks at the game. What made the rack so simple was an effective analysis, and that is something you can certainly learn to do efficiently and quickly.

Again, here are your simplifying rules in a nutshell:

Separate the layout before you into the categories of A, B, and D-balls (in other words, which balls are pocketable as they lie; which will be pocketable as soon as you pocket one or more of the balls now open; and which you can use to break up the unopened balls, or C-balls). Then it's simply a matter of plotting the easiest possible route among your A's, B's, and D's, much like the connect-the-dots puzzles you did as a kid. No rule says your sequence must take the balls off alphabetically (first your A's, then your B's, then your D's); but as you become more advanced at the game, you'll recognize that the most effortless racks are those in which you do just that. Just combine w. p.'s 1 through 9 to your simplifying process, so you have specific reasons for your choice and execution of shots, and you'll be putting correct runs together almost before you know it.

Let's go through another rack, off another break shot, and see how the same principles apply. The layout you see in Photograph 15 was produced by the break shot of Diagram 23; you might note that al-

Photograph 15

though this is a break shot I generally like, the cue ball is nowhere near where I'd like to have it, and if it weren't for that easy 11-ball, this rack would challenge my shotmaking abilities right off the bat. More proof that you can't always get what you want.

As opposed to the last rack we just analyzed, there are numerous B-balls this time. The A-balls we have to make first before our B's become A's themselves are the 2, 3, 4, 11, and 12. The B-balls which could become pocketable just as they lie, if other balls were moved first, are the 1, 5, 8, 14, 10, and 9. That leaves the 6, 7, and 13 as hard-core C-balls, balls that look as though they simply must be moved from where they are now. And the best D is the 14.

Naturally we'll play the 11-ball first, and for the very reason you'd expect: It's the easiest option available. (There is an added psychological reason for selecting this shot, which we'll get into shortly.) As the shot lies, simple natural running English, the kind you get by stroking the cue ball just above its center, will easily pocket the 11 and leave me a modest angle on the 4 (Photograph 16).

What I want to accomplish now besides putting the 4 in the subway is to get reasonable position on my best D-ball, the 14. It is generally advisable to pick loose A-balls off the table before getting to your secondary break shots; but in this case, we're only talking about moving three balls, and most importantly, the area into which these balls will be moved by using the 14-ball—off to the right—is completely clear now. So the shot will get most of my work done early, and that's what we'll aim for.

Photograph 16

To get what you see in Photograph 17, I

Photograph 17

stroked the cue ball at about 7 o'clock in pocketing the 4. Now I'm ready to use the 14-ball to break up the 6-7-13 cluster you see just above it, and the 12-ball on the bottom rail there will offer me a safety valve if I need one.

Done. Now, in Photograph 18, I have no more C-balls and only three B's (1, 5, and 8-balls). Those three balls will all become pocketable in the right-hand corner pocket once I've made the 9 and 10 balls, and that is where I'll try and make them if I can because each ball can be made there without moving any of the others; and right now, the 8 and 5 are definite candidates for my break shot into the next rack. So the 9 and

Photograph 18

Photograph 19

10 are my first priorities here, and I've made each in Photographs 19 and 20 respectively.

Now I'm ready to play for the position I want on that B-group of the 1, 5, 8, which have all become A's. I can do that simply by playing the 12 with a gentle center-ball hit—and note that, once again, I have a safety valve available (the 3-ball) in case I don't quite get the cue ball where I'd like to.

As it is, Photograph 21 shows you that I'm just about where I want to be. I can make the 8-ball without touching the 5; that will make the 5-ball my break shot for the next rack, plus a natural, easy progression to get to it. In fact, the next seven shots will only require my driving the cue ball to a rail once.

In Photograph 22, we're ready to send the

Photograph 20

Photograph 21

3 into the far corner pocket. This is not a shot that beginners are used to looking for, but actually it's very simple. You must get into the habit of considering *all* feasible routes for the object balls confronting you; remember that the table has 6 holes in it for a reason. All we need do here is pocket the 3 and stop the cue ball right there.

Then we have a slight angle on the 1 (Photograph 23), just what we need to leave our 5-ball completely in the clear and give us a soft roll-in shot on the 13.

That's just what we have in Photograph 24. All we have to do is get the cue ball 12 inches or so off the side rail, and we'll be straight in line with the side pocket on the 6

Photograph 22

Photograph 23

Photograph 24

Photograph 25

. . . as in Photograph 25. Stop the cue ball dead here, and the 7-ball lines up nicely for the far right-hand corner, another easy shot . . .

. . . as in Photograph 26. Just a few inches' worth of draw here, easily accomplished with a soft stroke . . .

. . . leaving us this cinch on the 2-ball in the side pocket, in Photograph 27. An inch or two of following roll on the cue ball will leave us perfectly on the 5, as in Photograph 28.

Photograph 26

Photograph 27

Photograph 28

Once again, in shooting off the 14 balls, we touched secondary balls only once, on the 14-ball, and we did so intentionally then. We used the rail on 4 of the 14 shots (the 11, 4, 12, and 13-balls), but each of those four shots was extremely simple and the cue ball was easy to control. And again, there was no more than 18 inches' travel for the cue ball on any one shot.

Don't waste time looking for situations absolutely identical to the ones we just encountered to pop up in your next game. And there aren't enough trees left in the universe to provide the paper I'd need to tell you about all the pool problems you ever will see. The point is that these two racks conform to certain principles that will be valid in the vast majority of your opportunities at the table.

The first of these principles is that in no case did I take an option even remotely more difficult than the one I did choose. I did the easiest things I possibly could, and planned to leave myself more easy things. In the two racks, I had only one violation of any of the w. p.'s (and which one was that, students, and let's not always see the same hands? In the second rack, I let the 13-ball sit on the rail until my third-from-last shot, and that is a crime against w. p. 9; but it's only a misdemeanor, because the shot was still functional in my sequence, rather than an interruption of it, and it required very little cue ball movement after contact. I'm sure you all saw that.)

The second denominator between the effective dispatching of those two racks was the breaking of the secondary balls, and just when in my sequence I chose to do that. In the first rack, I rebroke the balls on my third shot; in the second rack, on the fourth. That is not as significant as the fact that in each case, the break shots occurred at a perfectly logical point in the rotation. I didn't have to give any thought as to what else I might do before those break shots, because most or all of the loose balls were already downstairs. I was able to break the balls into open areas, thus avoiding more troublesome clusters.

Most of the previous pool books have dwelt on full 15-ball break shots, and of course your secondary break shots are only smaller-size versions of those. But it seems to me that in games between very good players, where shotmaking poses no real problem to either, the game often hinges on the outcome of their secondary break shots. In fact, the stymies accruing to the two players out of their secondary break shots are likely to be as big a factor in the game, if not a bigger one, than are missed shots in the open. (The logic for this is simple: Very good players simply do not miss all that often, the bastards.)

If the angles and principles of full-rack break shots and secondary break shots are the same, and they are, why should *re*breaking the balls cause that much grief?

It's because you're dealing with uniformly racked balls in the first instance but not in the second. If you insist, and your equipment permits, a full rack can be made perfect for you, every ball in contact with its neighbors. You have no such luxury going for you once that original rack is broken, of course. And that's just the point: Secondary break shots are directed at clusters that have already been hit at least once. That means there is likely to be some air in there, and that can make whopping differences in the behavior of the balls. It's much more difficult to get the force of your stroke distributed out over the bunch if the balls are spaced at all, which is why I took pains to see what it would take to keep my cue ball loose each time. And if there's enough air left among those still-grouped balls, they can act like quicksand and suck your stone right in there.

So be extra finicky about your approach to secondary break shots. Try to get some fix on where the outermost balls might logically go, and be sure to plan an escape route out of that swamp for your albino. Don't trust the mere force of your shot to drive the cue ball loose; you want to know where it will go and how you get it there. And re-break shots involving a rail are treacherous.

Let's examine one more rack situation. In this case, my opponent has broken the rack successfully enough, but dogged his next shot and left me surrounded by object balls. This comes up frequently, even in pool's higher circles, and there's a reason or two for that. In fact, his having left me in the middle of things, as you see in Photograph 29, is an indication that he chose an incorrect shot that he proceeded to miss. You can tell that without even knowing which ball in the layout he actually missed, and here's why.

With this many object balls loose at once—let's say, more than half the balls on the table, eight in the case of a full rack—you'll generally do better to play your sequence *from the outside in.* By that, I mean to deal with the balls farthest from the original break area first, and close in on the balls still grouped. This accomplishes two things: It lets you save your short-shot, stop-ball opportunities for late in the rack, just when you want them most; and it pays off in better break shots for the next rack, because you're always keeping some balls in the general rack area.

My opponent obviously chose a shot near the rack to begin with, or else he wouldn't have left me where he did. As you can see, there are balls near other pockets, and one of those would have been a smarter shot. Not only would it have allowed him to begin an outside-in sequence, but it probably would have been his easiest option. That's the second point I want you to remember here: Make your first shot following a break shot, or following *any* shot that requires you to take extra aiming time, the easiest one you can possibly find. You want to be certain of continuing your run, of course, but there's a more subtle reason than that. Cinching that first ball is the best way known to man to recapture the rhythm you lost studying that last tough one. And, as you'll read in a following section, you just gotta have rhythm.

Photograph 29

Photograph 30

Okay. Now, the first thing I want to do here is get the cue ball away from that cluster and come back to it after a quick trip up the table for some of those mavericks up yonder. I'll start with the 1-ball (gone in Photograph 30), a real beginners' delight, but remember, I'm just getting back to the table after sitting a while, and I need to get my rhythm back at the same time I'm scoring. Now my white rock is loose for the other ball nearest you, the 9-ball (gone in Photograph 31), and I'm ready to get down to cases.

As you see, I've played position for the

Photograph 31

Photograph 32

12-ball, a rail-shot well worth dispatching early (haven't you been reading your w. p. 9?). In Photograph 32, the 12 is gone and I'm ready for the 13, for the same reason. Photograph 33 shows me ready for the 6, a simple but critical shot that should position me correctly for the 4-ball, the best D-ball to use to break up the rest. I got where I wanted to be in Photograph 34; notice also that if my cue ball were a few inches out of line either way, both the 5 and 10 are excellent safety valves that offer me added chances to get on the 4.

To make the 4-ball as precise a break shot

Photograph 33

Photograph 34

as I can, I note that the 10-ball offers me a certainty following the break shot if I simply get my cue ball free of the 2. So I'll draw the cue ball just hard enough to accomplish that; and no matter where the broken balls go, I'm sure of a starting point from which I can attack them.

But it turns out to be no sweat, in Photograph 35; all the balls are A's now except for the 8 and 14. They are B's, and will be freed as soon as the 15 and 7 are gone.

It should be candy from here. In Photograph 36, I've played the 5, and drawn the cue ball back just a few inches for the 3.

Photograph 35

Photograph 36

In Photograph 37, the 3 is gone, and I'm on the 7.

In Photograph 38, the 7 is gone, and I'm on the 15, which is gone in Photograph 39. They'll all be A-balls from this point on, and you should always note that point at which all remaining object balls become pocketable without further work to do. Photographs 40 through 42 show you that I've bunted in the 8, 14, and 10, respectively, and I'm ready to break the next rack with the 2.

So except for the very last shot, you can see that the last balls pocketed were those nearest the rack area, a happy circumstance that almost always provides an excellent break shot for the next rack as well as a cinch key shot to get to that break shot.

Photograph 37

Photograph 38

Let's talk a little about a less happy circumstance: What happens when you *don't* get the cue ball quite where you planned to?

It all depends on how far from your original plan you've left yourself. If you're stroking softly and smoothly as I've advised all along, and planning ahead efficiently enough, your failure to stop the cue ball on a dime should not be all that costly. Photograph 34 is a good example of how to provide yourself with just that sort of just-in-case options.

But I don't want to oversimplify this. Pool is a remarkably subtle game, and I'm well aware that just a few inches, and often fractions of inches, can turn a game around. I have been both the winner and loser in games in which the turning point had to do

Photograph 39

Photograph 40

with *which part of the pocket a ball was successfully sunk in;* and while that sounds like splitting hairs, it comes up more frequently than you'd expect. That's what makes certainties so desirable in the game.

All right, you didn't get where you anticipated, and now you can't proceed as planned. What do you do?

Well, assuming you've left yourself *something* to shoot at, you should treat this situation just as you would in life: A detour has come up, but you want to return to your original route as soon as it's feasible. Ever since I was a kid and the baseball coaches told me that baserunners who change their mind about sliding often break

Photograph 41

Photograph 42

their ankles, I've been a great one for sticking with your original plan. In pool, of course, you risk no broken ankles, but indecision can and will put you in your seat, and for many players, that is a far worse fate. So look for an alternate route that can get you back the same way you were going.

If that doesn't appear likely, reevaluate the balls—which are the A's, B's, C's, and D's left to you—and begin another plan, doing your best to stick to that plan. If you've left yourself *no* shots as a result of your miscalculations, don't get mad at yourself; that's all part of the game. Find a safety you can play and shrug it off. Keep in mind that a well-played safety will relinquish the table to your opponent for only a single turn. You can wait that long.

Since I obviously can't show you all the factors that might cause you to abandon your plan, or change your mind about it, let's settle for a look at the game's premier mind-changer, in my opinion: the thin cut shot along a rail (Diagram 34). I've seen some very good players (and a whole flock of intermediate ones) go way the hell out of their way to avoid a shot like this in their

Diagram 34: One of the game's great intimidators.

sequence, even when it was pocketable without disturbing any other balls. The psychology of the shot, of course, is identical to a weekend tennis player's running around his backhand, and a player of any consequence in either game is just going to have to get over that fear. Let me see if I can help.

In the first place, a shot like this, with the object ball frozen or close to frozen, will benefit from correct speed as well as from accuracy. Your lack of confidence in the shot will generally tend to make you overhit it; that is just what you should not do. A softer stroke will not only enhance your accuracy but it will let you maximize another advantage: Unless you're playing on new cloth, your table will quite likely have little grooves worn into the felt along the rail. And a softly stroked ball in such a groove is like a plane landing on instruments only, and just as dependable.

The second hint I can pass along for the shot is this: If your shot requires you to cut half the object ball or more, aim at a tad more ball than you normally would and favor reverse English (Diagram 35). When you have a fuller ball to shoot at, favor the opposite English—that is, English on the side of the rail in question (Diagram 36). These techniques should help change your whole attitude about this sort of shot, and mastering this shot will strengthen your game surprisingly.

At the conclusion of this straight pool chapter, I'll give you two layouts to analyze on your own, before reading how I see them (which certainly doesn't mean, by the way, that my way is necessarily the best way; we're just checking to see how well you can extend the principles you've learned).

Remember, none of us will ever live long enough to see all the pool layouts there are.

Diagram 35

C

Right-hand English

[When you have to cut half the ball—or even thinner—use outside English and aim at a hair more ball.]

Diagram 36

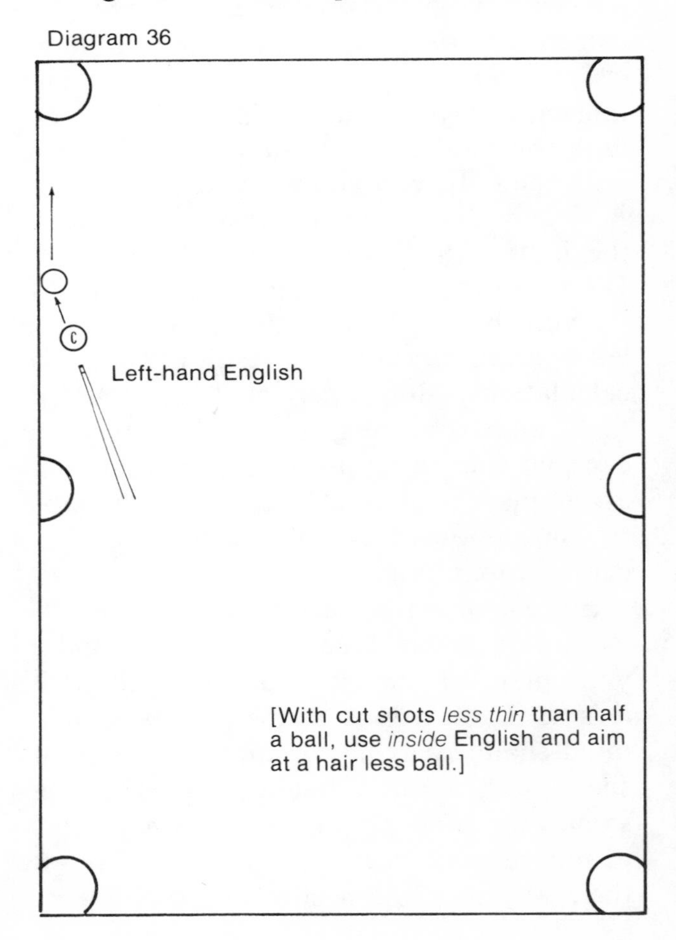

[With cut shots *less thin* than half a ball, use *inside* English and aim at a hair less ball.]

You might say that I've given you the equivalent of an *alphabet* of pool sequence knowledge. Now it's up to you to learn the *language,* and that can take you many, many moons (or it can come to you naturally. It's just like anything else). But you can't learn the language very well without learning an alphabet first.

Safeties

What do you do when there are no A-balls?

You don't panic and start looking to take a flyer, for one thing. What confronts you now is not necessarily a stymie, but rather a defensive opportunity. And any smart money player, assuming you can get him to talk, will tell you that denying your opponent a shot is at least equally important to scoring yourself.

An ideal safety, however, will do far more than simply deny your opponent a shot. It will deny him a chance to leave *you* safe as well.

Let's consider closed-rack play first. Suppose the 15th, or open, ball is unplayable as a break shot, or you've made it but still failed to contact the stack.

Diagram 37 shows you a good play from in front of the rack, and what you can expect. Be careful, though, to contact that head ball at a point exactly in line with the balls behind it. (See Diagram 38.) If you hit in that crotch between the two head balls, the chances are you will drive no object ball to a rail, and that is not only a scratch but leaves you in deep, hot water to boot. If you strike the head ball too far to its open side, you'll open that corner ball to the cue ball—just as mortal a wound.

Correctly struck, that safety will leave a corner ball down near its pocket, and the cue ball at the top of the stack.

Diagram 37

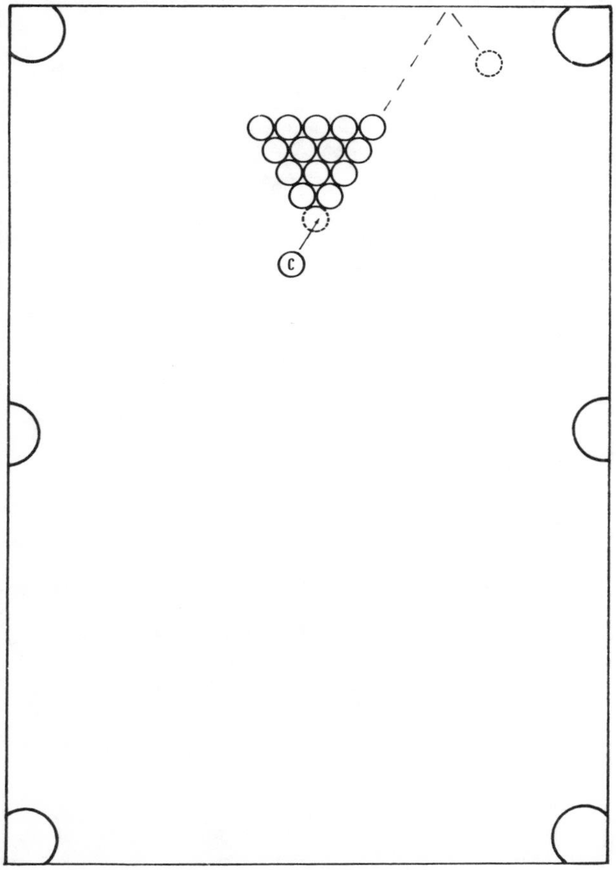

Diagram 38: You must make contact at point "x" to make the safety in Diagram 37 work.

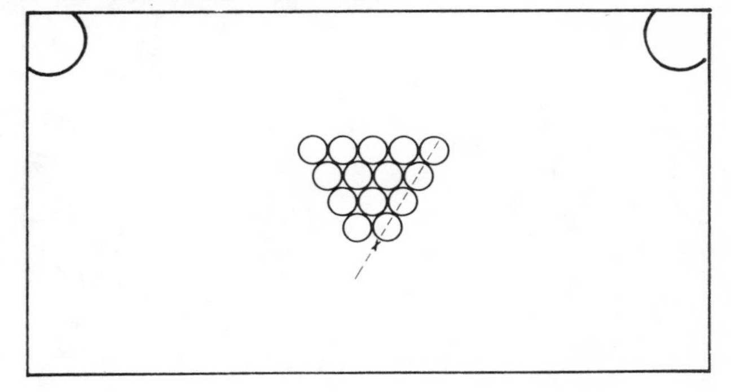

Since you've now captured one whole side of the table with that open object ball, your opponent will most likely roll out in the direction of the opposite side rail (Diagram 39). What you should do here (and it obviously works on an untouched rack, too) is play softly into the ball marked "X." Depending upon your angle into the stack, this safety has two points of aim, designated in Diagram 40. As with the last safety, you must strike your target ball in line with the ball behind it (except here you have a choice of two lines). The principal movement will come from Balls "A" and "B," and both are likely to go to or near a rail no matter where you began the shot. The speed of the shot is especially critical here; you must stroke with enough force to get A, B, or both to a rail, yet not so hard that they come off the rail and back near the stack. You can see, in Diagram 40, that if Ball B rebounds off the rail far enough, my opponent has a chance to send me up to the end rail with nothing but danger to shoot at. If Ball A comes back near the back row of the stack, he can get down to the bottom rail—not quite as dangerous a trap for me, and you'll see why, but he'd still be out of the trap I was setting for *him*.

Diagram 41 shows you the same shot in principle, at least, from behind the rack. As long as you can hit Ball A in the line shown, you should be able to drive B to a rail, even if you were frozen on the bottom rail; after all, you're only distributing the force of your stroke out over two balls. This is the easiest safety of the last three to escape, and usually ends up with a shot that challenges either of you to cut it along a rail into a far corner pocket. It's a shot that intermediate

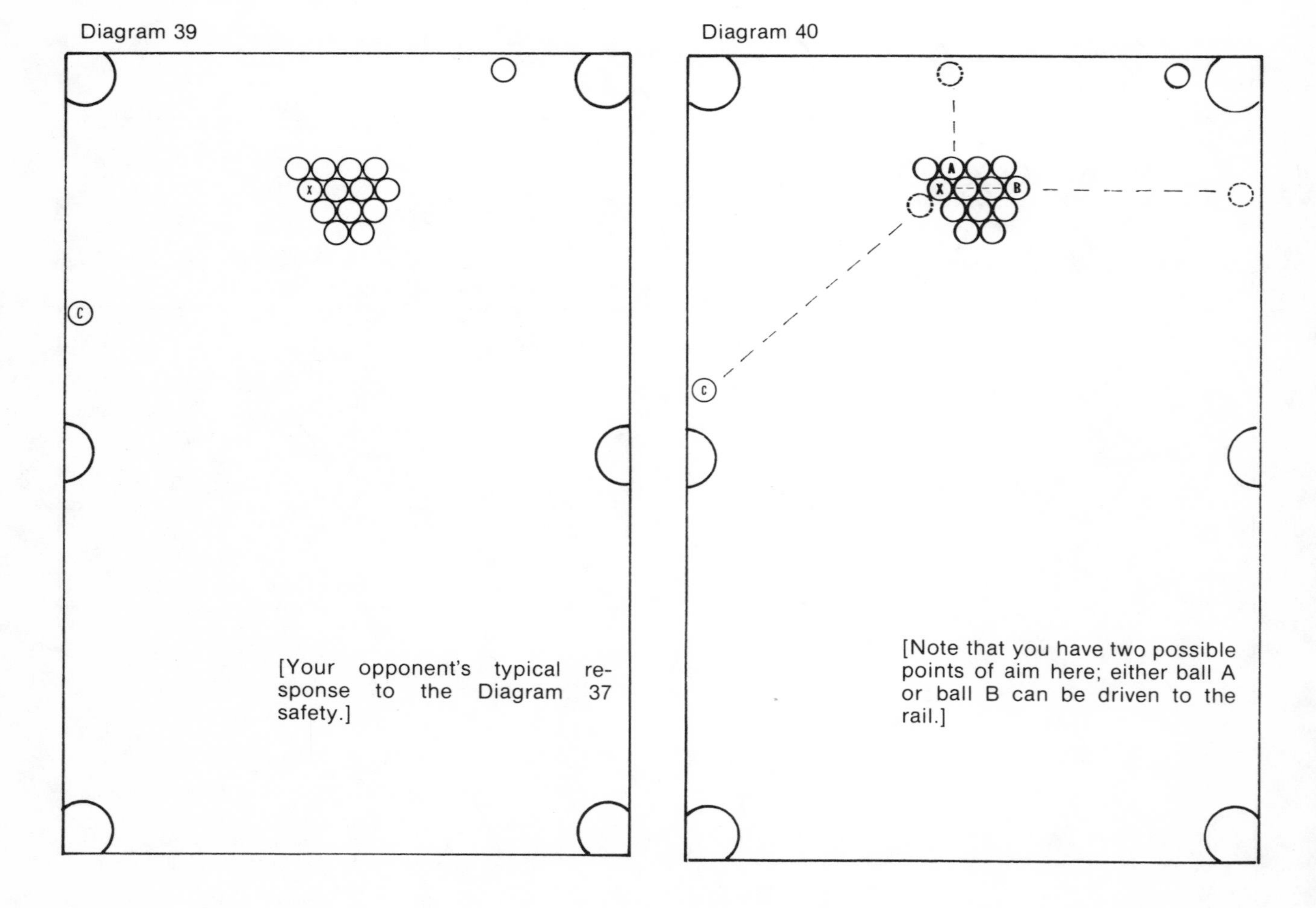

[Your opponent's typical response to the Diagram 37 safety.]

[Note that you have two possible points of aim here; either ball A or ball B can be driven to the rail.]

Diagram 41

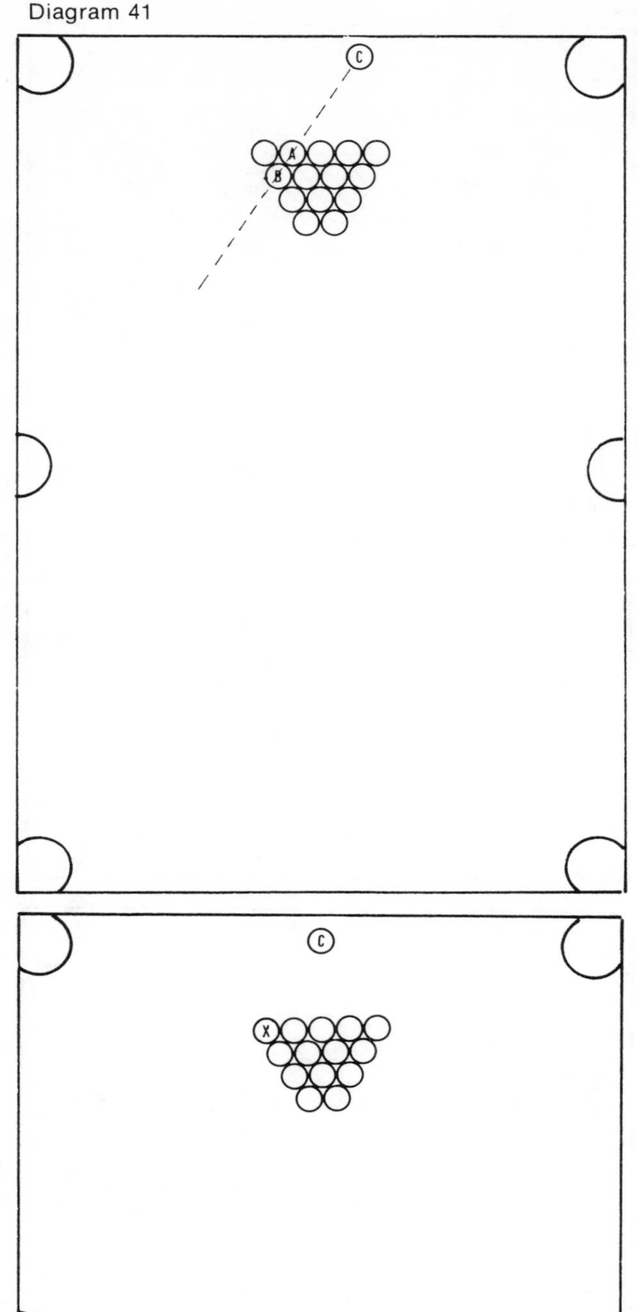

Diagram 42

Diagram 43: Rear view of the safety play in Diagram 42. Make contact in the area between the dotted lines, and kill the cue ball.

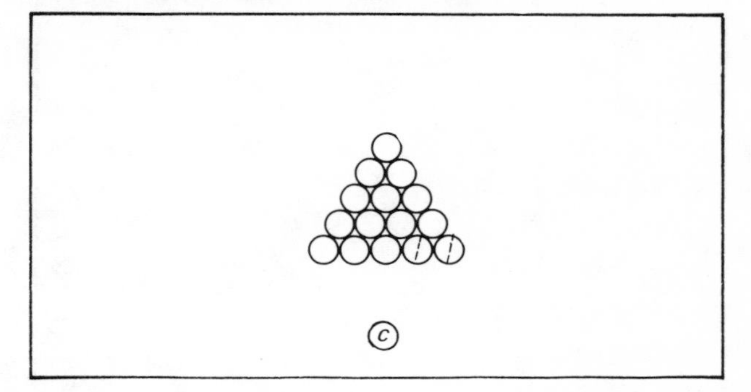

players usually want their opponents to shoot first; only the best shotmakers go after it aggressively.

You can do more damage by playing a similar safety off the corner ball, as in Diagram 42. This safety requires that your cue ball be somewhere where you can hit it low—in other words, not on or very close to a rail. You should grip your cue butt slightly tighter for this one, and jab rather than stroke the cue ball; we want to communicate nothing to it but rigor mortis. Aim at a point between the corner ball and about 1/3 of the ball next to it, as in Diagram 43. Correct kill on the cue ball will leave the mess shown in Diagram 44. I prefer this safety to the one before it because it frequently gets a ball out near the side pocket; makes it quite impractical for my opponent to try anything in that direction; and leaves him a carom, going to his left, that will at least make him think about a possible scratch in the corner if he rolls the cue ball that way.

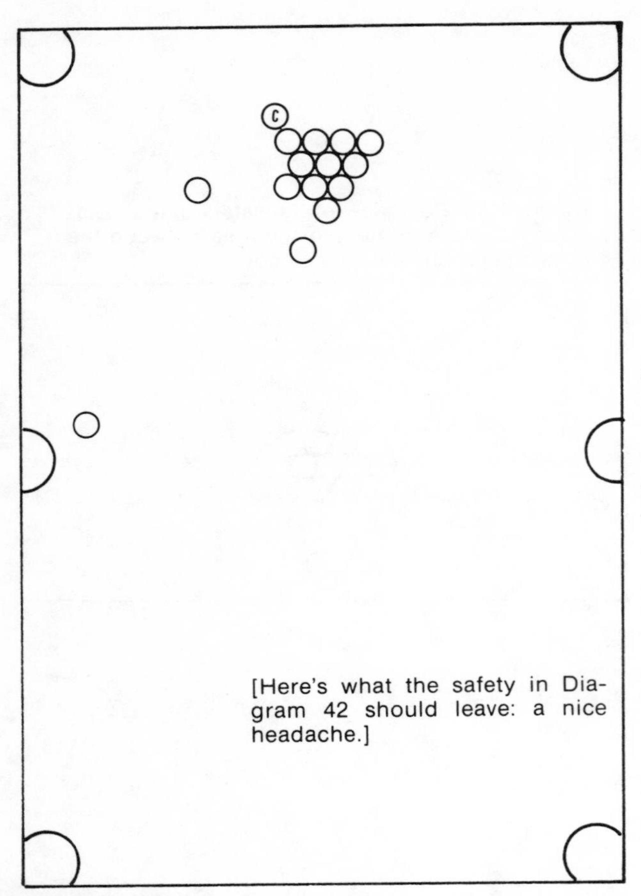

[Here's what the safety in Diagram 42 should leave: a nice headache.]

Diagram 44

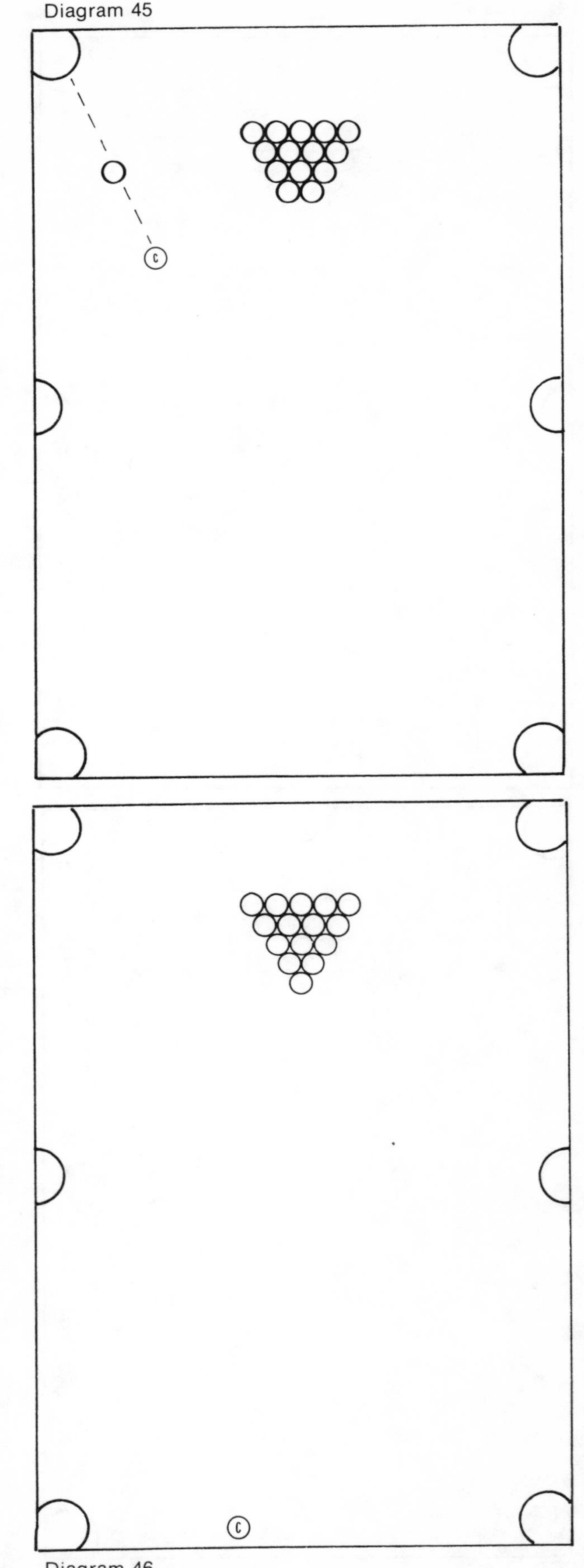

Diagram 45

Diagram 46

A move you see frequently among intermediate players occurs when the 15th ball is pocketable but breaking the stack with the shot is impossible. The player therefore announces a safety but pockets the ball, leaving his opponent a full, closed 15-ball rack to shoot at, from as far away a position as he could negotiate. There's nothing really wrong with that move, and it certainly doesn't leave any open shots. But it can be answered, often to the incoming player's advantage. Take a closer look at it.

Diagram 45 shows you a typical situation leading up to this safety: The object ball is straight-in to the corner pocket, and there's no way my opponent can both sink the ball and move his cue ball off the stack. So he pockets the ball and draws his cue ball nicely back near the head rail (Diagram 46). Fine. Except that I have an answer; in fact, a choice of answers. Which one I choose

Diagram 47

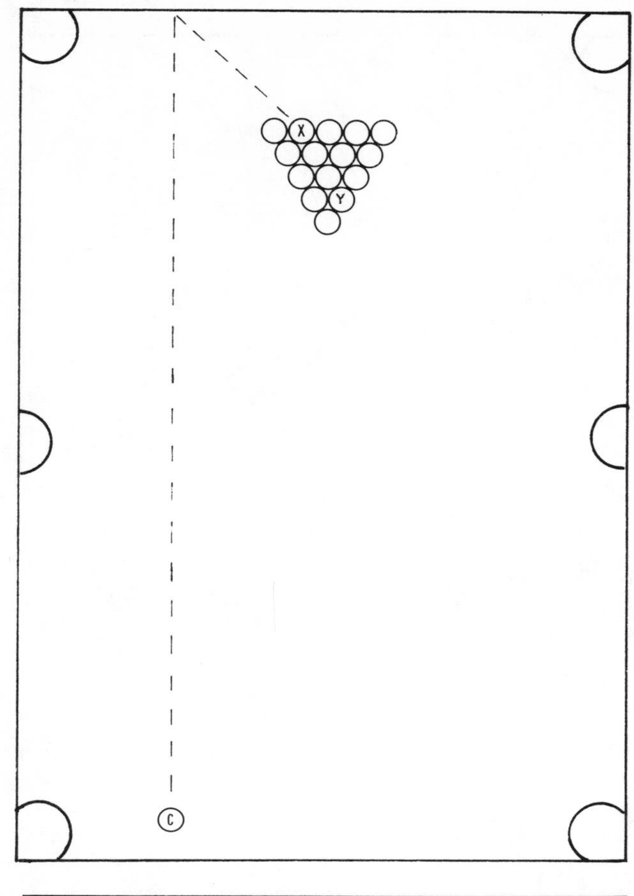

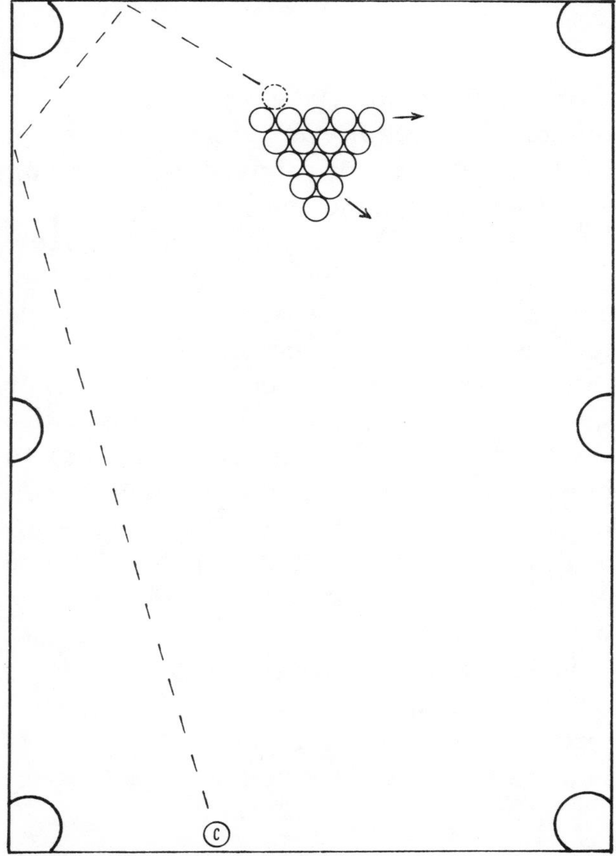

Diagram 48

will be a matter of how the game is going, naturally, because the approaches correspond somewhat to the conservative, the median-of-the-road, and the wild-eyed radical.

What I won't do—ever—is try to feather either corner ball and get back up the table. It's usually the first thing that occurs to beginners, but forget about it. It's an extremely low-percentage shot, in terms of the probability of leaving nothing open.

My conservative reaction to this leave would be as you see in Diagram 47. I've spun my cue ball off the bottom rail to make contact with the back row of the stack; Ball X is the one I want to hit. (You can't spin your cue ball enough to do that, by the way, if you start out frozen to the back rail; make sure the cue ball's center axis is available to your cue tip.) It always looks like a lucky break when you get away with this, but the fact is that you have a pretty good chance to drive the necessary object ball—usually Ball Y—to the rail, and stick the cue ball back of the stack. It takes a combination of spin control, speed, and accuracy, but that's quite attainable with practice.

The ultraconservative variation of this occurs when my cue ball is too close to the rail to let me spin it that way. Then I'll do as you see in Diagram 48, rolling *two* rails to come behind the stack and knock out a ball or two. I don't really expect to complete the safety here; it will probably cost me a point, but at least my opponent can't send me back to the head of the table quite so freely now, and I'll probably be able to get the bottom rail in my next turn.

Now for my most likely response, and it's not as hard as it looks. Diagram 49 shows you three points of aim on the head ball, depending upon cue ball position as shown, center-of-the-table being the most dangerous. I will generally give this a try when my sense of speed is close to its peak, because cue ball speed is everything here. The same

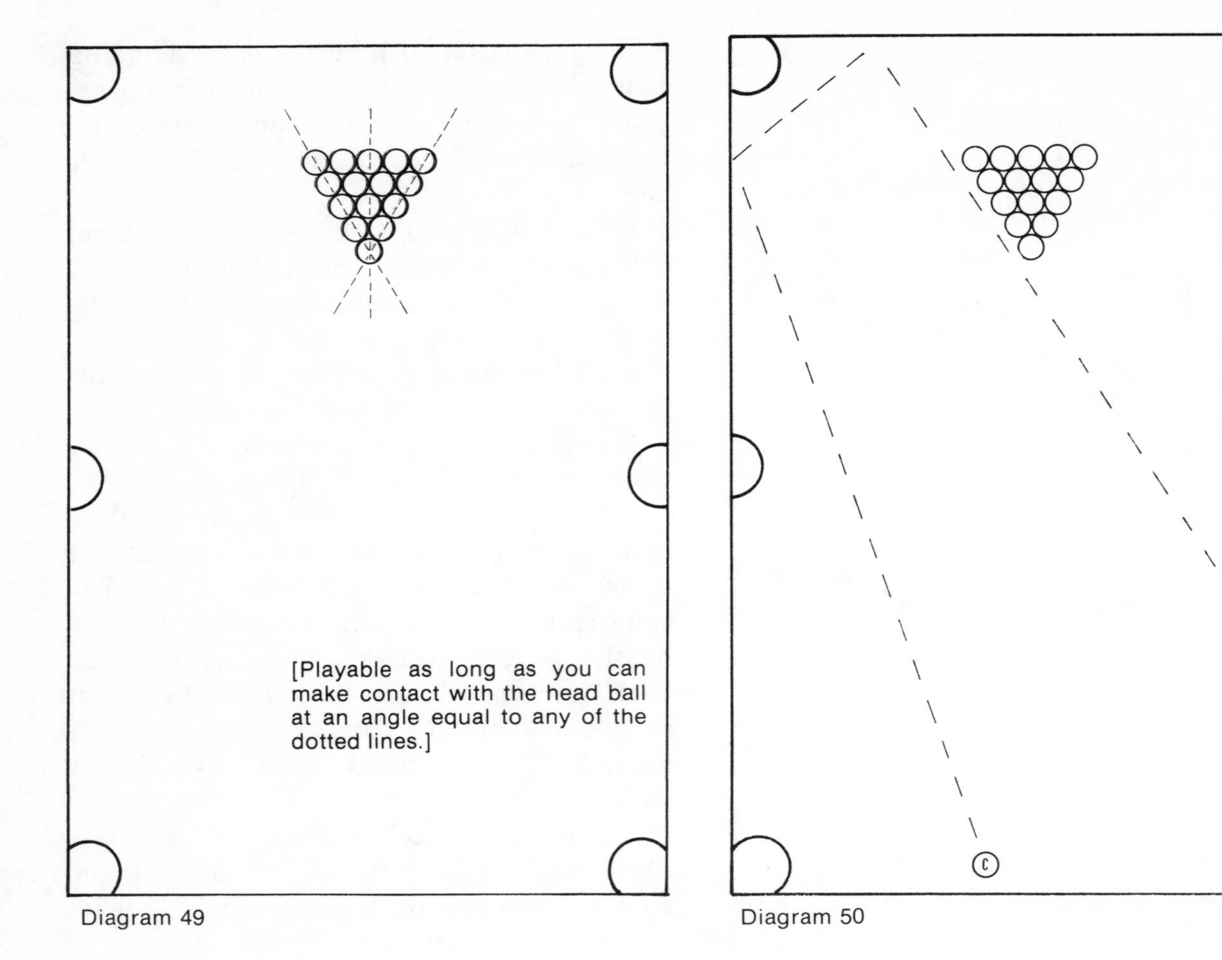

[Playable as long as you can make contact with the head ball at an angle equal to any of the dotted lines.]
C

Diagram 49

Diagram 50

speed sufficient to send either corner ball to the rail (or, from center-table position, maybe both) is the correct speed to stick the cue ball on the head ball. And if, in one of the two angled approaches, you cut the head ball a tad thinner than you really should, you can still get home free; nothing much on that side of the stack should move, and you'll still have that open object ball hidden from the cue ball's view.

There is no sane reason to take on my radical approach to this safety situation, as you can see from Diagram 50. I kind of like the purist challenge to it—perfectly executed, it leaves the stack absolutely unaltered, and as a psych, it's as devastating as a ring of shark fins in your bathtub—but it would take an extremely sociable game to bring the shot out of me.

On the other hand, the great seven-time World Champion Irving Crane will go for this one just about every time it comes up, so there you are. (It will probably serve you well to bear in mind that there is only one Irving Crane.) He feels that with his experience, in both reading the correct two-rail angles and cue ball speed, he should be able to execute this shot acceptably one out of three times; if he can't do that, Mr. Crane says, he deserves to take the consecutive three scratches and their penalty (loss of 16 points and being required to break a full 15-ball rack).

The correct speed and spin for this one are elements you can achieve only by playing, not reading. I can tell you that the shot is at its hardest if the cue ball begins near either corner pocket. But spend some time practicing this, using center-ball hits unless you really need to create the angle, and see if you can develop any consistency at it. If you can't, you can't (and few can), but it's a potentially awesome weapon for your arsenal if you can.

You can probably tell, from the choice of responses I have to this safety situation, that my opponent could have done better with the shot confronting him in Diagram 45. What he should have done is pocket the ball as called, *then* announce "Safety" and play the safety of Diagram 40. All he would have had to do is pocket the 15th object ball and stop his cue ball dead, and the shot would have lain perfectly for him, and I'd have had a lot more trouble answering.

The other aspect of safety play occurs, of course, when object balls are already open. If you're playing (and, naturally, thinking) correct pool, your ending up safe in a situation where A-balls exist but are unavailable to you is very likely to be dictated by luck, your bad or your opponent's good. The principles of advanced pool all have to do with minimizing the factor of luck, but the chances are you will never see a pool game that precludes luck completely. Even a game in which a player runs out in his first inning is likely to offer that player some lucky rolls to keep his run going. So make your mind up that luck is very definitely part of the game, and stop cursing fate. If curses could move the cue ball, I would have been a world champion ages ago, along with about ten million other players.

The objective of open-table safety play is exactly the same as before: Leave your opponent not just shotless, but answerless. Your best allies for these safeties, logically enough, are just those areas where you *don't* want to be when you're shooting to pocket something, namely, the stack and the rails.

Balls that are still clustered should be your first object of attention when you get left safe in an open table. It's quite possible you will be able to find "bunt" opportunities of the sort we just discussed, even though the clustered balls are no longer regularly

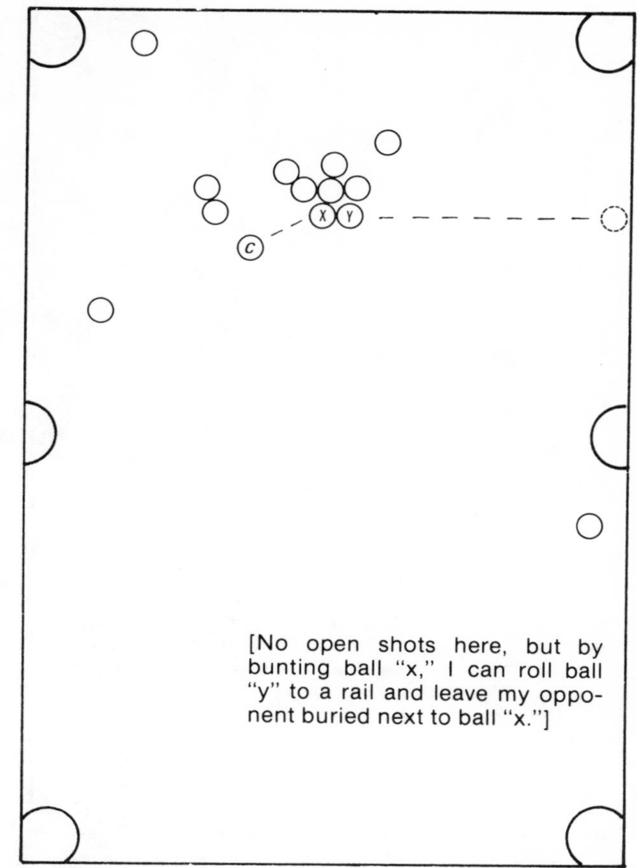
X
Y
C
[No open shots here, but by bunting ball "x," I can roll ball "y" to a rail and leave my opponent buried next to ball "x."]

Diagram 51

shaped. Diagram 51 gives you an idea of what I mean. Just as you learn to examine a stack for possible dead combination shots, you must learn to examine it to see if it offers you natural safety opportunities.

If you can't bury the cue ball in what's left of the stack, though, it's just about mandatory that you get it to or very near a rail someplace; if your opponent is to be left with any shotmaking opportunities at all, the least you can do is make him work to accomplish them. A frequent open-table safety ploy is to select a nearby object ball that is both unpocketable and near a rail, and duck the cue ball in between that ball and the rail (Diagram 52). This shot is likely to lead to a dreary exchange of bunts unless one of you can get the cue ball frozen to that rail, in which case the incoming player must involve some other rail for a legal safety.

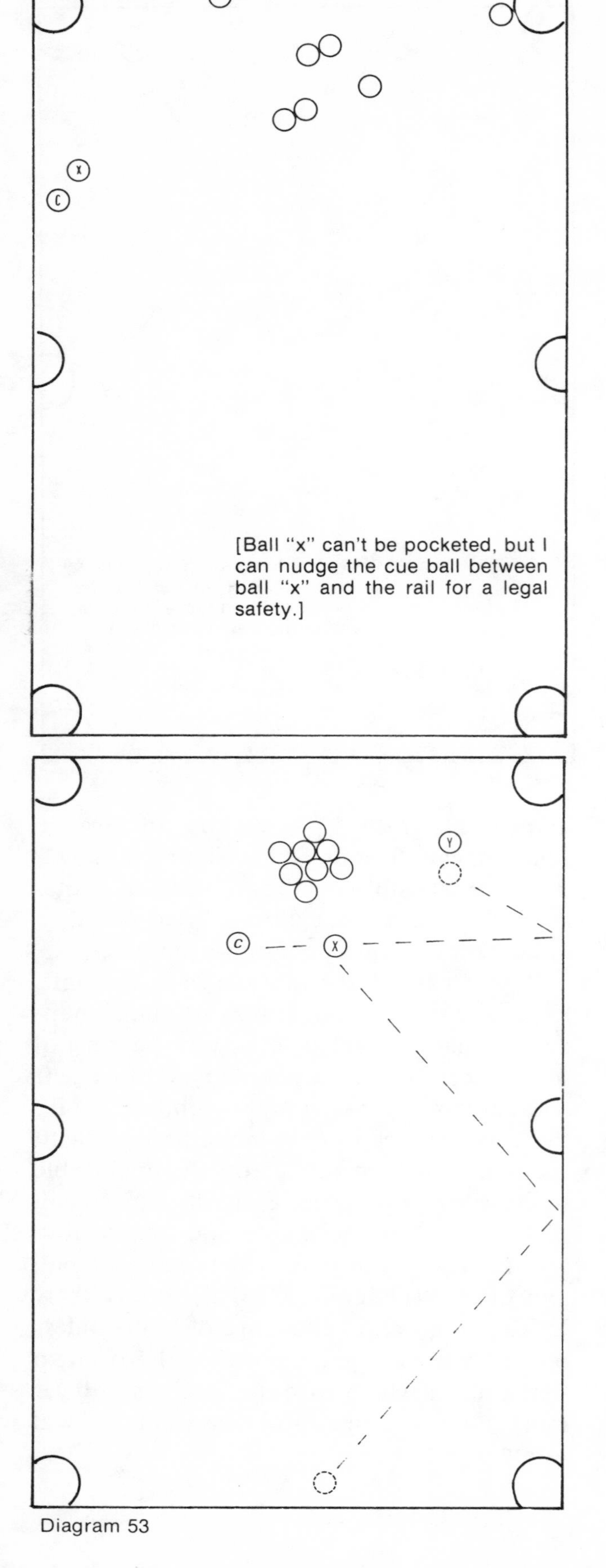

Diagram 52
[Ball "x" can't be pocketed, but I can nudge the cue ball between ball "x" and the rail for a legal safety.]
Diagram 53

Diagram 53 demonstrates a safety in which you *spoil* a shot that was previously pocketable. Touch is critical here, since the possibility exists that Ball X, if hit too softly or too hard, will become merely a second open object ball (or, worse, form a pocketable combination shot with Ball Y). But this is a shot well worth knowing; you can see how dramatically it can turn the table in your favor when executed correctly.

Diagram 54 shows the same effect—eliminating a previously pocketable ball from consideration—but this time by moving the ball itself. As the shot lies, it's only a low-percentage bank shot or just-about-impossible cut shot; the safety you see in the diagram is far better than either of those, and sends your opponent to the far country without anything to shoot at.

The only acceptable safety plays that leave the cue ball in the center of the table are those that freeze it on another object ball. Diagram 55 shows you that type of situation; you bunt the first object ball to a rail and out of play, and your cue ball limps over a few inches (if that much) to snuggle up uselessly with another object ball. This shot should be made with the shortest, softest stroke that will get the job done; its concept, of course, is quite the same as in closed-rack safeties: minimum force, minimum cue ball movement.

When no opportunities arise for you to shut your opponent out completely, you're simply going to have to decide what ball, in what pocket, represents the stiffest challenge for your opponent. I've left my opponent a side-pocket shot on Ball X in Diagram 56, but I don't think he's going to love it a lot; it's an angle he's not used to looking at, and he'll have to turn his cue ball loose for a run up the table, and he must shoot off the rail to boot.

Another safety that will at least make him think is shown in Diagram 57. This is an extremely common straight-pool ploy: chal-

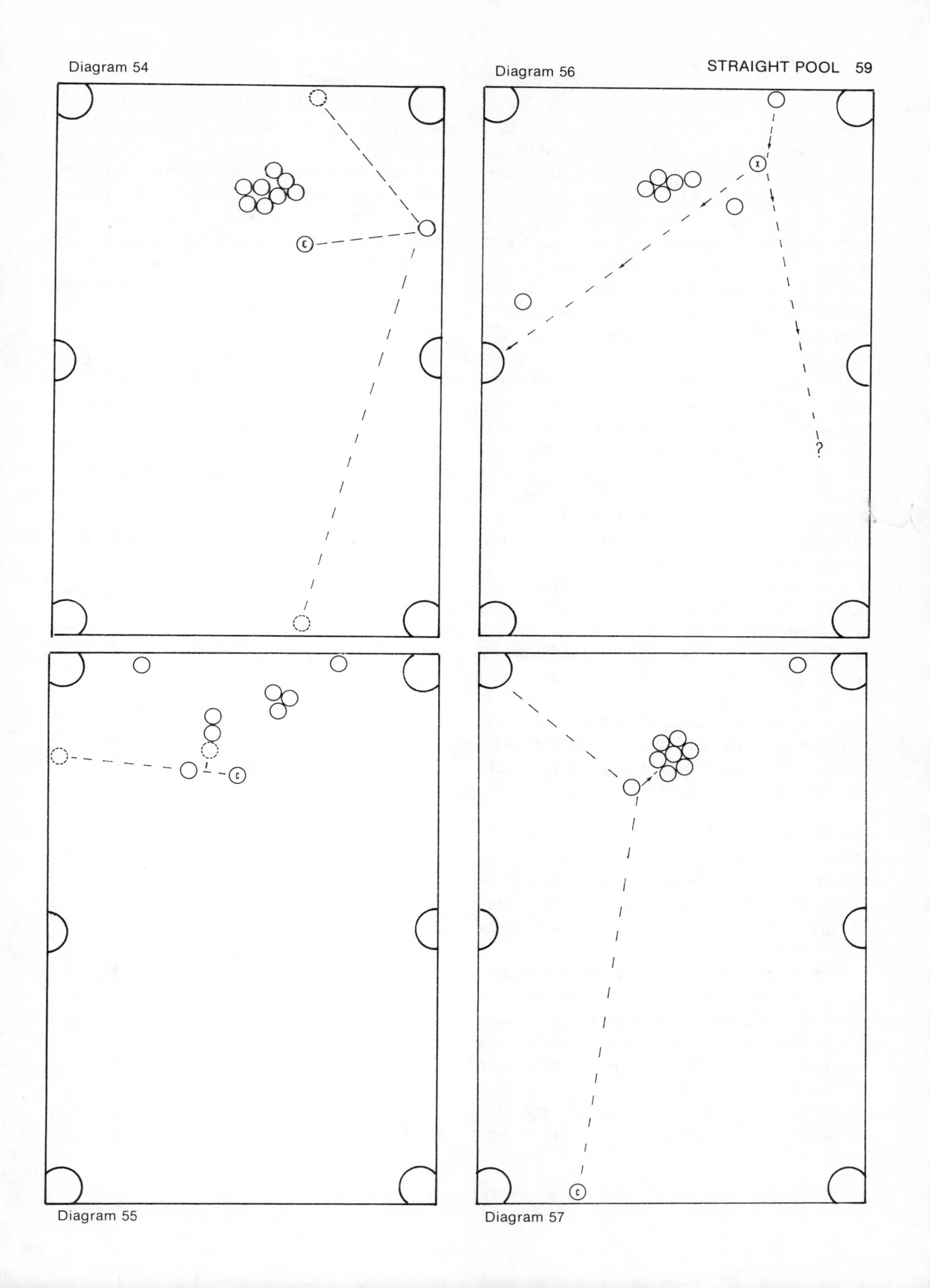
Diagram 54
C
Diagram 56
X
?
Diagram 55
C
Diagram 57
C

lenging your opponent to shoot a break shot that figures to either capture or surrender the entire rack for him. This shot depends upon how well you know your opponent's abilities. If you make the open shot too tough, he'll probably duck it; if you don't make it tough enough, he'll hurt you with it. You want to be somewhere in between, as in the diagram, to make it a tough decision for him. The more time he spends pondering that decision, the tougher the shot becomes.

Like good sequence selection, effective safeties are mostly a matter of your ability to read the balls correctly, and think defensively as well as offensively. Both come with practice and confidence. Safety options and opportunities are almost as infinite as pool sequences, but again, I've shown you some common instances that recur, in varying forms, all through the game.

And what you must always—*always*—do before playing a safety is recall whether your opponent scratched in his last turn. If he did, you can get away as easily as by touching the cue ball without moving it, and leaving him your present mess. That costs you a point, needless to say, but it takes the pressure off you and puts it back on him where it belongs. And it brings us to an entire new area of the game.

Intentional Scratches

It seems self-destructive, but actually this is one of the prize strategies that separate the advanced player from the intermediate one. Diagram 48 showed you one example of such a move.

Intentional scratches are almost entirely a matter of outthinking your opponent, since no balls are going to be moved very much. Their most valuable application, as we just noted, comes up when you're left without a shot and you remember that your opponent scratched in his last turn; the move makes good sense then, and its availability to you adds considerably to the loss-of-point-and-turn penalty he's already suffered for his scratch.

There are times, however, when it makes some sense to incur the first scratch *yourself* with an intentional foul of this type. Suppose my opponent successfully executes the safety of Diagram 40. He has opened up object balls but shut me off from them; worse yet, the only rails available to me, to drive my cue ball toward, will expose those object balls. It's quite likely, in that spot, that I'd do as you see in Diagram 58: nudge the cue ball into those clustered balls. It costs me a point, but if my opponent falls for this ruse and intentionally scratches back, I now have a chance to play off one of the neighboring object balls to that near side rail for a legal safety, one that hides the open shots and removes my scratch from the records while

Diagram 58

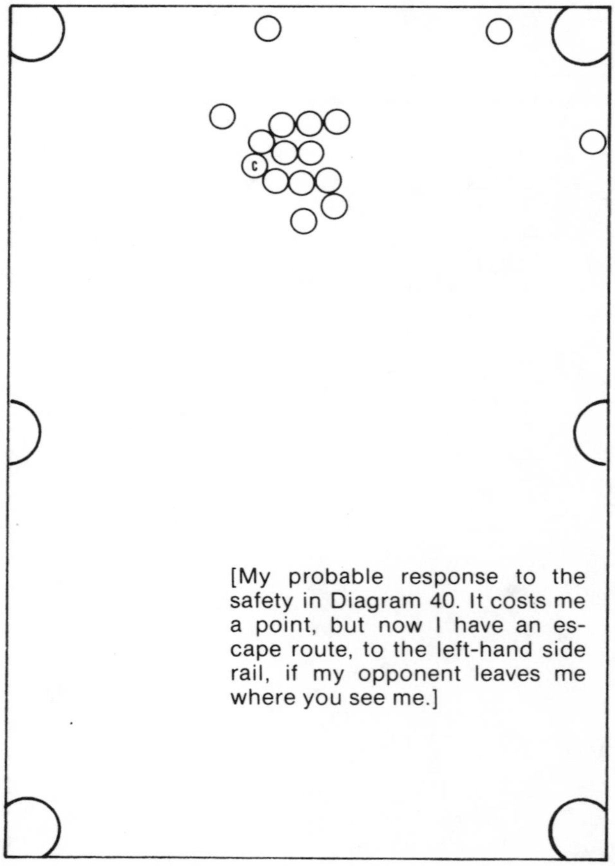

[My probable response to the safety in Diagram 40. It costs me a point, but now I have an escape route, to the left-hand side rail, if my opponent leaves me where you see me.]

preserving his. What my opponent should have done, instead of scratching back, was beat me to that legal safety, so I would still have a scratch against me.

The whole trick to intentional safety play is to see what your opponent sees. If the guy you're playing takes an intentional scratch and you have no scratch against you at the time (and remember, three consecutive scratches carries the largest single penalty in the game), you know he's got a legal safety or even a flyer of a shot in mind within his next two turns. So you've really got to think this situation through: What is he going to do to avoid that third scratch? Having determined that, you either beat him to it; alter the balls so the opportunity ceases to exist; or, if there don't seem to be any safeties available to him and you think he's going for a highly improbable shot after all, let him cut his own throat. By now, you can probably see that the art of looking ahead in pool applies to way more than just shot sequences.

If the shoe is on the other foot, and it's *you* who is forced to plan on a low-percentage shot to work your way out of an unsolvable situation, by all means try and lure your opponent into taking two consecutive intentional scratches with you. The advantages of this become clear once you've taken your flyer: If you make it, it's your table with the balls very likely open *and* two scratches on your opponent, which means that you can turn any trap you encounter right over to him with another intentional scratch, and he must respond to it at once. And even if you miss it, you can still get lucky and leave him safe, with those same two scratches staring him in the face; or, you can get semilucky and leave him a tougher shot than he'd like, made considerably tougher by those two scratches and the danger of a third.

So learn to think ahead, both with shots open and when shut off from shots. And never lose sight of your opponent's having scratched in his last turn. Your forgetting that can make a whopping difference in the game.

Rhythm

Eyesight is the first prerequisite of the game of pool. But rhythm comes second, and few players realize how close a second it runs.

I can't think of a game on earth that turns the offense over to you so limitlessly, once it's your turn. In Monopoly, the only way you can get a second consecutive turn is to throw doubles. Even majestic Chess offers you only one move at a time. But in pool, you're alone and free as long as you can keep yourself that way. No one is permitted to block or tackle you to hinder your offense (unless you play in unruly places). No one can move the balls to make them harder for you to hit. Freedom is yours as long as you put an object ball in the subway and keep the cue ball free for another shot—in other words, as long as you keep doing the same thing over and over again. And it is highly unlikely, in pool or anywhere else, that you will ever be good at executing repetitive events unless you recognize the rhythm of what you're doing.

Don't take my word for this. What I want you to do is check out what I say, the next time you have an opportunity to see an advanced pool player really hitting his stride. He's running balls, sure, but there's a lot more going on than his merely running up the score; and everything he's doing mechanically can be interpreted in terms of rhythm. Make note of the following checkpoints, apply them to the expert player you're watching, and see if I'm not right:

He spends about the same length of time over each shot (excepting, of course, those points in his sequence where he needs to think or rethink).

He takes the same number of practice strokes, before actual contact with the cue ball, on each shot (except for the toughest ones).

He hits all his open shots at pretty much the same speed.

His actual stroke differs only slightly in speed from the speed of his practice strokes. (The backswing and follow-through of the actual stroke will probably add speed *slightly*.)

His movements between shots will almost always be at the same speed. Some players are faster than others, of course, but I'm talking about an individual player's consistency here. (Conversely, one of the first signs that a player has discovered chinks in his armor is when he visibly begins to slow down between shots.) You'd never guess that physical movements that have nothing to do with the pocketing of the balls themselves could have such an important effect, but they do.

Even so innocuous a movement as the chalking of his cue will be uniform, smooth, and rhythmic, and he'll probably do it while in motion rather than at a standstill. (Cue-chalking, besides preventing miscues, is a valuable aid in establishing rhythm.)

In short, the player you're watching has become *fluid*. Although all the points of sequence we've covered thus far are occurring and being put into play by him, it's very likely that he's not giving them much conscious thought at all; his thought processes and responses have become ingrained and automatic. The term "unconscious" may come to mind, especially to his disgruntled opponent, but that is a wise word indeed. So there he marches, piling his run right up there, rhythmic as you please, higher than herbs could ever get him.

Good for him. What about you?

Well, like most other things, you can't make it happen all at once. Rhythm will occur to you only through practice and confidence. Here are some pointers for you to consider *as* you practice; they will become habitual if you are to be a good pool player. (Which, by the way, does *not* necessarily indicate that you misspent your youth. That statement is alternately attributed to Oliver Wendell Holmes or Mark Twain, and it's a safe bet that either man uttered the quote shortly after being beaten by a younger man.)

The correct situation in which to begin to infuse rhythm into your game is with shots you feel comfortable about making. Eventually, needless to say, you'll feel comfortable with a vast majority of the shots you see; for now, let's consider those shots that correspond to the easy end of your shotmaking spectrum.

Your rhythm should begin even before your practice strokes, in the manner in which you address and assume a stance for your shot. I'm not saying that you have to choreograph your moves in this regard, but you should try to get down the same way as much as you can. If you look around next time you're in a billiard room, I think you'll see intermediate or beginning players who look like they're bobbing for apples while getting into position. Their heads will come up for two or three last-second looks before they're finally down, and I'll bet that they had middling success with the shot in question. Not only did they fail to achieve their rhythm from the outset, but those bobbing heads are a good indicator of indecision, and that's poison.

In watching Mosconi play (and how I wish all of you could have), one of the *added* joys—even after the ungodly shotmaking and position play and other surface things—was the man's remarkable grace. Mosconi is not tall, and was never slender, but you never saw anything as fluid in your life as Willie Mosconi assuming a shooting position. It almost looked like he was parodying himself, it was so perfect, and I know others noticed it too because you could actually hear a giggle or two.

When baseball hitters hit a slump, the first thing their coaches look for is not their swing, but their stance. Stance is just as critical in pool, and for the same reason: It's where your rhythm begins. I'm not going to tell you *how* to stand; all the other pool books do that. I'm just saying that getting into that stance can be a subtle, yet valuable, aid to you. Strive to do it the same way each time, however you do it.

Practice strokes have been covered elsewhere, too; all the experts say no more than three to five, except on shots hard enough to require more, and that certainly needs no verification from me. What I'd like to add is that those practice strokes should approximate the speed of the stroke you're planning (and have mentally rehearsed, right?). It is not imperative that your practice strokes match your stroke speed *exactly;* I think you'd find that difficult to achieve anyway, because of your added backswing and follow-through. But I don't want you to stand there idly sawing wood just because you were told to; these provide a dress rehearsal for your stroke, and deserve that kind of attention. The habit will pay you back well.

So concentrate, until you no longer need to, on taking the same number of practice strokes, at least on your shots of average-or-greater ease, and make them a clocking of the speed for your stroke. Watch good players, too, the best you can find; you'll see testimony to the effectiveness of this.

Unless, that is, you catch somebody like Richard Lane, a super straight-pool player from Texas. Lane spends a period of time just short of his entire summer vacation on his tougher shots, and some less tough than that, including just about all his break shots. (He is, however, considerate enough to move spryly in between those interminable shots.) It takes a world-class player to set the man down; still, it's intriguing to wonder if he might not be even better if he spent less time over the cue ball? Richard Lane is smart enough to answer that one without any help from me, but you can be pretty sure that that has been suggested to him before, quite likely from a far better player than I. It just makes sense.

The next focal point of your pool rhythm is the transition between your last practice stroke and your actually hitting the cue ball. To go back to those apple-bobbers in your room, another thing you'll see them doing is rushing their strokes on tough pressure shots, especially when they're stroking from over an object ball. The first couple of their practice strokes might be fine, but suddenly there'll be this little flurry of activity. Some very good players do the same thing, simply because there are few players alive who can't be reached by pool's special pressures. And that's all it can be, in explaining that break from rhythm; since the little flurry of strokes adds absolutely nothing to the shot, whether successful or not, it can be due only to what's in the shooter's head.

Each player develops his own abilities, and tolerance, for the game's pressures, naturally. It's a matter of the peculiar combination of concentration and relaxation, and we'll be talking about each. And one good checkpoint for your own progress is, are you letting any shots intimidate you into rushing your stroke? *Your last practice stroke should always be the same as the rest.* The immediate benefit of this is that your actual stroke has a planned beginning, middle, and end; all are imperative for both rhythm and an effective swing, whether in pool, tennis, baseball, golf, name it.

Now for the stroke itself. You've seen to it that you've made the necessary pause after your last practice stroke, and that is the last thing I want you to think about. Go right ahead and hit the cue ball exactly as you saw yourself doing in your mental rehearsals. It should not be necessary for you to think about any of the various aspects of your stroke, and may well in fact be harmful (unless, of course, you hit a slump, in which you should take some practice time to analyze *everything*). Take a backswing exactly like the one you saw yourself taking; hit the ball at just that rehearsed speed; follow through with the same smoothness. The first key to executing a smooth, rhythmic stroke is rehearsing one. Then just do it.

That brings us to your movement between shots. I'll assume that most of you have seen *The Hustler;* remember their first game, in Fats' first turn at the table? Paul Newman's line was something close to, "Look how he moves, like a *dancer*." The author of that line, Walter Tevis, knows his pool. Good players have a rhythm so highly developed that they do in fact seem to be moving in a highly disciplined, almost choreographed way; and that's a critical part of what makes them so good. When a player like Lou "Machine Gun" Butera flies around a table at his well-known rack-a-minute pace, he is literally and figuratively stepping to a different drummer; that is the tempo the game suggests to him.

I can't encourage you to play that fast, and I tend to doubt that he would either. What makes more sense by far is for you to find a playing speed that feels comfortable, and do your best to stick to it. As I said before, when a player breaks his rhythm between open shots, it's usually an indication of trouble. Concentrate on playing without pause, as long as things are going according to plan for you.

The key word there is *open* shots. Certainly the game is going to make you stop and think; after all, I've already advised you to re-examine all layouts following break shots, and that's only one reason for interrupting your rhythm. Any time something does not go as you rehearsed it, or something happens that you could not possibly have rehearsed, that's a valid reason to break your shotmaking rhythm and take time to re-examine or remake your plan. And as we pointed out in the section on Sequence, your first shot following such pauses should be the easiest one you can find that will lead you to another. Your rhythm should come back to you like Poe's raven.

Even in your short runs, try to move between shots at a consistent rhythm. The longer your runs become, naturally, the more you'll become aware of your rhythm during them. Don't slow down, unless you have a good reason to—and don't speed up, either. A good run really gets your adrenalin flowing if you're at all into the game, and your rate of play will automatically increase to some degree. But don't let yourself get carried away, because too much added speed in your rhythm invariably leads to mistakes, frequently quite simple ones.

Now and then, you'll find a between-shots dawdler who has become a top player in spite of that. The fabulous Luther "Wimpy" Lassiter is no speed merchant; Al Miller of Wisconsin has been denied entry to tournaments because of too-slow play; and there are a few others. As fine as these players are, I think it's fair to say that they are exceptions to the rule.

In the early 1960s, Chicago's city champion was a player named Mike Stichauf, and he made Richard Lane look like Beep-Beep the Road Runner by comparison. Without exaggeration, it took Mike a full 15 minutes to run a typical rack, despite the fact that he played excellent sequences and seldom had anything all that challenging to shoot at. He just liked to think about what he was doing. He went undefeated in city tournament play for close to three years, not only because he was quite good, but because his opponents were usually close to coma by the time he sank game ball. Mike had a second quirk, to go with his Gregorian-chant type of rhythm; while the balls were being racked (this was round-robin play, with all games refereed), he would come over to you and explain, in excruciating detail, how and why he had chosen that last dreary rotation of balls. That is not exactly what you have been waiting to hear when you are fourscore balls behind and your buns are beginning to feel as though they had been shot with Novocain. Mike Stichauf was a modest, sincere guy, and I don't have any doubt that he meant those mini-lectures well. But between the lectures and his slow play, you suffered only slightly less than Dustin Hoffman did at the hands of Olivier. Still, this was tournament play, and you had to be polite.

He still *is* a modest, sincere guy, as far as I know; the reason I said "was" is that he doesn't play pool any more. He was told by no less a player than Mosconi himself that he would never be first-magnitude unless he developed his rhythm, and that prophecy proved correct. Which will hopefully lend you some idea of just how critical rhythm is, at all levels of pool. As a final example, the game has been popular among show business personalities for years and years. And the best players from those ranks include Jackie Gleason, who originally did Broadway musicals; Jerry Ohrbach, who still does them; and Fred Astaire, who also had a nodding acquaintance with rhythm.

Concentration

I'm going to go out on a limb and say that by now you have probably realized that the game is somewhat complex.

I've told you before that pool thinking, correctly learned and applied, will become an extremely fast process for you, and it will. Provided, that is, that you don't introduce extraneous things to think about.

The reason good pool concentration doesn't come easy is the structure of the game itself; as we noted in the early paragraphs of the last section, you're totally alone at the table. There is no opponent to preoccupy your thoughts, and therefore you're apt to wander onto some totally irrelevant areas, maybe even at important, *really* important points of the game. The best players don't do that, of course, but only a few get to be best, at anything.

Be honest, now; are you not currently guilty of talking yourself out of some shots, every now and then? Not just because you came upon a shot that intimidated you to some degree, but because your head was not really there? Maybe you were thinking about the game two tables away, or grades, or the job, or adultery in your heart, or whatever. Isn't it true that your game has been invaded, at one time or another, by completely unrelated thoughts?

See how well we know one another already?

The thing is, it clearly won't do. Surely you recognize, without any encouragement from any expert, that pool demands concentration. Catch-22 is that the game demands way more concentration than you think you're giving it. And you have to accomplish this almost pure level of concentration at the same time as maximum physical relaxation. It's a very advanced form of patting your head while rubbing your belly.

But you can do it. It relates absolutely and directly to how good a player you want to be, and how much you really want it. The game is rated by its champions to be no more than 20 percent physical. Now, there's no question that you do need a respectable portion of that 20 percent to get anywhere in pool; but I can't help you much there. I can't do much about your eyesight (I wear glasses of the Coke-bottle persuasion myself), nor your head-hand-eye coordination, which is all that pool really is in the physical sense. The basics of shotmaking can be learned in a few weeks if you have any aptitude at all. But no matter how mediocre or spectacular a shotmaker you are ever to be, you've still got a big fat rich 80 percent of this glorious game to which to apply your good head. And a good greedy share of that 80 percent will bring you through scrapes where your share of the other 20 percent would not have been enough by itself.

One of my pet theories about the game concerns why so many top players were phenomenally good when phenomenally young. It seems to me that when you're younger, you would by definition have fewer distracting thoughts available to you simply because your memory of things is smaller. Which makes it far, far easier to put more and more of your concentration into the game. Put that with the good eyes and hands of a kid, and a pool player is born.

It's also a pretty fair psychological guess as to why the game attracts its sad share of super-playing unworthies. Lazy, unsubtle folks are the very people who are most likely to have nothing much going on in their lives, thus in their heads, any more important than that next lone shot; and therefore they enjoy far fewer distractions. In that sense, the game has truly been its own worst enemy, advertising itself to and through the wrong kind of players, making bums out of too many people. If you haven't guessed by now, I love this game, but only as a game. As a be-all, end-all lifestyle, I find it rather dumb.

The point is, the correct principles of the game are available for you to learn at any age. I think that the biggest problem facing you by far is concentration. You're attacking an inert ball, with a minimum of physical activity. The game's real power clearly will emanate from your head.

And about the most I can do for you here is to remind you that the problem does indeed exist: Pool needs the firmest, most highfalutin' kind of concentration you can muster. It's up to you to deal with your own head.

I can give you a hint there, though. Like most things that are hard to find, this one is literally right there under your nose: the cue ball. The albino. Kojak. The king of Siam. Your li'l ol' pal the round white rock, who grants some dreams but takes others away, representing purity.

The second-best pool book you will ever read, and one that I recommend almost as enthusiastically as I do the first, is Gallwey's *The Inner Game of Tennis*. Yes, tennis. If you don't play tennis, skip chapter 5 of that book, but just about every other single concept translates beautifully to pool. And Gallwey, and Tutko, and many other prominent psychologists are convinced that in all games played with a ball, the ball itself can provide the player with a brilliant point of focus for his concentration.

Let's make a modest revision in your mental rehearsals before stroking. The chances are that you've focused more of your attention in that rehearsal on the object ball and its path to the hole. I don't know what the precise ratio is, but you've been watching the object ball more than the cue ball, in those rehearsals. And, for that matter, after your stroke itself.

Why?

You already *know* where you want the object ball to go: in the hole. The pocket, despite what you occasionally hear from grumpy players, will not move. It's a fixed target. What's far less certain is precisely where the *cue* ball will go, even if you're planning to stop it dead. So why not dwell on it a little more? See the cue ball going just where you want it to before your stroke; then, follow it there after your stroke. It gives you a far more worthwhile object of your attention than those invading daydreams; more practically, your concentration on the cue ball will increase your cue ball control by an eye-popping margin.

I believe that the majority of players look at the object ball last at the moment of stroke, and I do too. But whereas most players will follow the object ball with their eyes *after* contact, *then* look back to check the cue ball's path, I prefer to follow the cue ball all the way. There's no point to my watching the object ball, when you come right down to it; I can't do anything about it anyhow, and I've already rehearsed its destination. If I follow the *cue* ball instead, and it goes where I've seen it going, the object ball automatically will be in the subway (unless, of course, I've simply *seen* the shot incorrectly in my rehearsals and proceeded to execute it that way. Which does happen. I told you I had clay feet. Why else do you suppose we're getting along so well?)

I've had pretty fair success with that technique. The reasons I think following the cue ball only has helped me are these: My concentration is vastly improved, I can plan my sequences much more precisely, and it helps me keep my head down.

Try it. It couldn't hurt. If it's not for you, at least be aware of the dire need to focus your concentration. Pool and kibbitzing go together like Damon and Pythias, and that means you've got a noisy little world outside your head to go along with that universe of thoughts you've got inside. Shut it all off, Fast Eddie. Think white. The game will reward your pure thoughts.

And don't let lack of confidence steer you into any mental rehearsals in which you actually see yourself missing the shot, not in mid-stroke or any time else, because that is very likely to be just what you do, just as you saw it. Ever notice a good player miss and then nod his head vigorously? That's exactly why; the player has done what he just saw himself doing, and it's like being told "I told you so."

In talking about break shots earlier, I proposed that during the actual stroke you might consider the word "flow" as a mantra. I used that term in the most respectful way, because what hypnotism, TM, the relaxation response, and other meditative forms actually do is allow you to bypass consciousness for a while. Which is exactly the state from which you would benefit most while pocketing balls. *Your conscious work concerning the game should be accomplished between shots, not during them.* Eddie Robin, a very good billiards player, became a Scientology "Clear" and *then* he became a national champion, and that's no coincidence.

Relaxation

So much for your head; what about your bod?

Well, it *should* be another aspect of what we've been talking about all along: *fluidity*. I started out by suggesting that you hit the balls more softly, so as to increase your smoothness. Throughout the book, we've seen the benefits of fluid, continuous thinking ahead of yourself. Rhythm and fluidity are just about synonymous, right? Well, I think you'll find it impossible, in any physical endeavor, to be fluid and rigid at the same time (unless you count sex, and there you are again, Fast Eddie, with lust in your soul when I want you thinking pool). Contract the muscle of your choice, keep it that way, and try to accomplish any natural movement smoothly. Other muscles will usually begin to tighten in sympathy, either slowing you down drastically or making you jerky. Now *relax* and try the same move. Feel the difference?

The reason for this section in the first place is that relaxation in pool is admittedly easier to talk about than achieve. And, again, your powers of relaxation, just like those of concentration, largely have to do with what's in your head. Because concentration and relaxation would seem to be at odds with one another; yet I think you'll find that in pool, they actually feed each other.

You can test this quite easily. Next time you miss a ball, in practice or otherwise, think of me and freeze (as people often do). Aren't you tight someplace, right this second? Most likely, in your butt hand, but maybe in your back or neck or legs or gut or all of the above? Some of that will be an involuntary reaction to your seeing the missed shot on its errant way; but the chances are that some of it was there for your stroke too.

I've seen the game played at the highest level the world has to offer, and I can't think of a single level at which you totally get away from the expression, "He choked." Ring-around-the-collar runs rampant in the game, or at least its reputation does. Everybody is accused of choking. You can still turn up guys who'll swear that Mosconi choked. *Mosconi!* For me, it was like being told there was no Santa Claus.

It's certainly true that the vast majority of players do choke to some degree. At least, that's what they do emotionally. What they do physically is *clench* something, somewhere in their bods. That has to happen first.

Let's check the basics of your game and see if we can help you let go.

Begin with your stance. As I've said, *how* you stand doesn't concern me a lot as long as your stance isn't actually wrong, and other books have instructed you well on that. If they've omitted anything, it's the importance of being comfortable in your stance. There is no point in imitating the stance of anyone if that stance doesn't feel as good to you as it looks good on the player you're emulating. It's just that the stance of your choice must accomplish two things: balance, plus the opportunity to keep your cue level. How low you should be in that stance has to do with the characteristics of your own body, more than with any advice I could give you. I do think that the ability to get down *good* and low—but comfortably—is a decided advantage. With the exception of Luther Lassiter, most of today's really fearsome money players get way the hell down there. Jim Rempe, Jim Mataya, Jack Breit, Bill Incardona, Richie Florence, and lots of others all carve clefts into their chins. But you be content with getting as low as you can in comfort.

Comfort is the key, simply because you can't possibly be relaxed unless you're comfortable first. It can be a factor of your balance as well as your stance. You can inadvertently put that front foot down somewhere you usually don't and wreak havoc with the shot, if not your whole game. It's because your misstep altered your balance, which made you uncomfortable, and unless you stopped right then to check everything out, it was discomfort cutting into your shot, nothing else.

Good balance feels good, both in your body and in your head. It's probably the first ingredient of pool confidence. Your balance, whatever foot position you use to achieve it, should be enough that you could resist a theoretical push on your shooting side. Leave your elbow free enough that you can take your cue back and stroke forward in a level plane, and you have the fundamentals of a perfect stroke. And the ultimate starting point was relaxation.

As to relaxation of the stroke itself, it's quite similar to the point we began with in the book. Just as the correct speed for any given shot is the minimum speed that will get the work done, the correct tension for you to apply to the cue butt is the *minimum* tension with which you can still control a beginning, middle, and end to every stroke. Too light, of course, and you'd have lots of mini-javelins in your game, but I don't think you'll have to worry about gripping the cue too light. Too *tight* is much more common, and that's what you want to watch out for.

As you probably know by now, you can't draw the cue ball unless your butt hand is relaxed. But it's more important that that: The same cue ball, stroked in precisely the same spot at the same speed, will react in two quite different ways when stroked first with a relaxed hand and then with a clenched one. Try any medium-hard shot both ways and see.

And then, start working on a lighter grip. That's where your touch for the game will come from. If you've ever heard a pool player praised for his "soft touch," the words refer to more than his cue ball control. If you can efficiently execute your stroke with a grip of a third less tension than you were using before, you can expect your cue ball control to increase by at least that much, quite likely more.

The starting point here, again, was relaxation. It is not possible to hold your cue lightly with an unrelaxed hand.

Yet despite all this logic, all but a handful of players on earth could still trace missed shots to something that was clenched. They all do it, and it's hard to say why, because when you get right down to it, hardly anything that's good in life has much to do with clenching.

Ever been on a bad blind date? I'll bet my case cheese that you spent a good part of it clenching. (To be fair about it, your date probably did too.)

Ever been late somewhere when it really mattered whether you were on time? Terrific clenching spot.

Been to a dentist lately? The very words probably made you clench just now.

Sometimes the humor goes out of it. Show me a case of hypertension and I'll show you a postgraduate clencher.

Clenching. Who needs it? Boxers, maybe, and other physical endeavors that involve normal muscle contractions. But at the pool table, it's the last thing you want to do, and it's no bargain anywhere else.

How do you stop? Largely with your head. Physically, I've had some luck with a technique that involves consciously relaxing the base of my spine and the base of my tongue. I find that if I'm relaxed there, everything else falls into line. You may have had an Army sergeant or other mentor who suggested that you maintain sphincteral tightness, but that achievement won't do you a bit of good in the game of pocket billiards. Nor, in my experience, away from the game either.

As for your head, I think relaxation has a lot to do with your perspective on the game. You may be overestimating the importance of a given shot to the entire game; you may be overestimating the importance of the game itself.

Regarding the first, every pool game in history that went two or more innings can be traced to the losing player's miss at one point or another; but that hardly means that the game hinges on *every* ball you shoot, unless your opponent is the obnoxious sort who is always a threat to run out. He's probably something less than that. And since you've got the table all to yourself, why not keep it a little longer? You'll do that once you've convinced yourself to shoot the balls you know you should, rather than simply the ones you fear least. Don't let the balls make up your mind for you; they are unqualified to do that. Select the right shot; hit it with the most level, relaxed stroke you can; if you miss, you miss. You'll get another chance.

And when a missed shot *does* cost you the game, what happens then? The San Andreas fault will not let go (not yet, anyway), nor will any other natural disasters occur. Banks and schools will still be open on the next available day. It's just a game, and despite your loss in it you may still be pretty sure that somehow it will still get to be tomorrow.

I can hear those who know me sniggering at this point, so the rest of you might as well hear it from the horse's, er, mouth: I was a cue-buster of the first stripe for a good many moons. What got me over it, and it was no cinch, were the simultaneous realizations that the cues were both good and expensive; turning them into driftwood still did not put the missed ball in the subway; it really didn't make me feel any better, even though I thought it would; and what it did make me feel and look like was the village idiot. So I stopped. Sounds simplistic, I know, but you can see only what you let yourself see.

I'm not so hypocritical as to suggest that I oppose the playing of pool for stakes. All I'm saying is that the stakes should not only be affordable, but *comfortable,* in that they create no artificial pressure that will detract from your enjoyment of the game, win or lose. Personally, I generally play with guys my speed, or slightly better; I try to handicap the game, when necessary, as fairly as I can; sometimes I win, sometimes I lose, but in neither case does the GNP move in the slightest.

It's also quite possible, and highly recommended, that you relax when your opponent is at the table too. Or at least, to do that until game ball is within reach in your next inning, at which point you could be forgiven if you began to psych yourself up instead. The price good players pay for being that good is that they never let up on themselves in the chair; the game is always within their single-inning capabilities, and it must be a never-ending pep talk. (I wouldn't know.) But I think they'd still be more comfortable relaxing.

Put your cue aside, for one thing; find a place to lean it where it won't fall. (If you hold on to it, it will only offer you another clenching opportunity.) Try to learn from what your opponent is doing, rather than hating him for it. (It's a good idea to forget whom you're playing. My opponents all seem to.) There is growing support for the technique of concentrating on your breathing as a technique of relaxation; at the table or in the seat, this will also help keep your mind from wandering. It would be great if you could train yourself to think about a breath or two every time a negative pool thought popped into your head, especially when planning sequences.

Relaxation will help you play better pool, simply because you're enjoying it more. Or maybe it's the other way around. It doesn't really matter.

Psyching

Yes, of course it exists. Scandalous, I know, but remember that the game is 80 percent mental according to its experts, and I'm afraid that makes it all too vulnerable to all levels of psyching.

At the low end of the scale, we have out-and-out distraction, such as moving in your opponent's view. Distraction is most commonly known as sharking, and on the intellectual scale of psyching, I'd say it's Stone Age stuff. (That, after all, is when sharks evolved.) But there are surely more subtle things to be done than that neighborly wave of handkerchief or cue stick.

Why do them at all? I applaud your purist view, but the fact remains that they are there, all those psychs, and the chances are excellent that some will be used on you. So be prepared. It's a cruel world for innocent things.

Psyching is not exclusive to pool, either. Bobby Fischer has said that his favorite moment in chess is not checkmate, but rather that point at which he crushes his opponent's will. Fine talk indeed.

Bearing in mind just how fragile pool concentration can be, here are some examples of pool psyching that I find tasteful and acceptable, provided they are never done to me:

1. Theory challenges. Pool players generally take inordinate pride in their shot selection, whether they're any good at it or not. You can interrupt a serious pool player almost any old time to challenge his selection

of shot, and he will ignore the fact that you're interrupting him just to defend his choice. So you've broken both his concentration and his rhythm, you bounder.

2. Ask relevant questions. Similar to 1, but harder to detect. Let the guy tell *you* why he chose a certain shot, instead of telling him he shouldn't have. He will proudly share his wisdom with you, then return to the table for a diamond-and-a-half miss.

3. Ask irrelevant questions, such as, "How's your wife?" Unsubtle but effective.

4. Luther Lassiter used to have a shaft with a red ferrule (although I don't think he uses it any more). There is nothing illegal or unsportsmanlike about that in the slightest way, except that you could drive yourself good and bonkers just sitting there thinking *"Why?"*

Along similar lines, Bob Meucci, one of the game's more creative cue-makers, once told me a guy ordered a cue with a little bell in it, that would tinkle on contact. The owner would get used to it in no time, of course, but his opponents must have thought that the Chinese water torture was being reborn.

5. The Stichauf-type lecture between racks (see section on Rhythm). I think your big problem here will be in bringing this off with a straight face.

6. Body English. You really may be insecure enough that you have to jump around like that to steer a ball in; but in my experience, you see more body English on shots that fall than on shots that don't, and therefore one can't ignore the psyching possibilities in this. Body English says to your opponent, "Woops, I think I missed," and if you *don't* miss, the anti-climactic effect on your opponent can be brutal, because he clenches and fumes and thinks, "Shoot, he thought he missed and I guess I did too."

There are some skilled practitioners of this. Ed Burton of Oklahoma City, better known for games other than straight pool, misses a ball about every third Michaelmas, but he leaps, twists, and pirouettes like Nijinsky to the strains of *Spectre of a Rose*. Dave Lipner, a very good straight pool player from New Jersey, earns more aerobics points in a 100-ball game than you or I would in a two-mile jog.

7. Kingpin Mizerak has a cute little bit wherein he announces his next shot while the balls are still rolling, and before he has even arrived to inspect the cue ball's next position. It's much like running backwards for the last 10 yards of a 90-yard touchdown run; he denies you the teeniest fantasy that he might be stopped.

It is also likely that few players in history were able to get out of the chair any faster than Miz does on an opponent's miss. Valeri Borzov, the Soviet Olympic sprinter, wasn't that fast out of the starting blocks, and everybody said he cheated. Mizerak is not seated during a pool game all that frequently to begin with; but in the first millisecond in which he detects that an opponent's shot is going to miss, he roars out of there like he had just sat on a whoopee cushion. He has retained this remarkable capacity despite varying stages of plumpness. I've never played the gent myself, but I imagine it must make you think something like a monstrous "*Uh*-oh."

I see no reason why you cannot add these techniques to your own repertoire, allowing that he's Steve Mizerak and you're not. Weigh this carefully.

8. Any and all psyching ploys practiced by the author.

The W. P.'s Revisited

Let's return to the table.

Your w. p.'s will always serve you well in helping you simplify the game, and that's what advanced play is all about. The more religiously you adhere to them, the better your results should be. But w. p., remember, stands for "*W*henever *P*ossible," which obviously means that they're not always going to be possible. Before we conclude this straight-pool chapter by turning you loose to think your way correctly through two racks, it probably would be helpful to review the w. p.'s and examine both typical violations and their consequences, and typical exceptions to the rule.

We'll skip over w. p.'s 1 and 2 (shoot soft, avoid unnecessary English); they are so fundamental to the game as to defy diagramming or examples. All I ask is that you always bear them in mind.

W. p. 3 deals with the importance of not moving secondary object balls that don't need to be moved. This will come up as early in the game as on your first shot following your opponent's break; chances are you'll have a long shot to deal with, and another shot or two available once you've made that long one. There will usually be something you can do to use one of those open balls as a D-ball, to open or partially open the remaining clustered balls and launch a good run . . . provided that you don't miss *and* you can leave your early open shots as they lie.

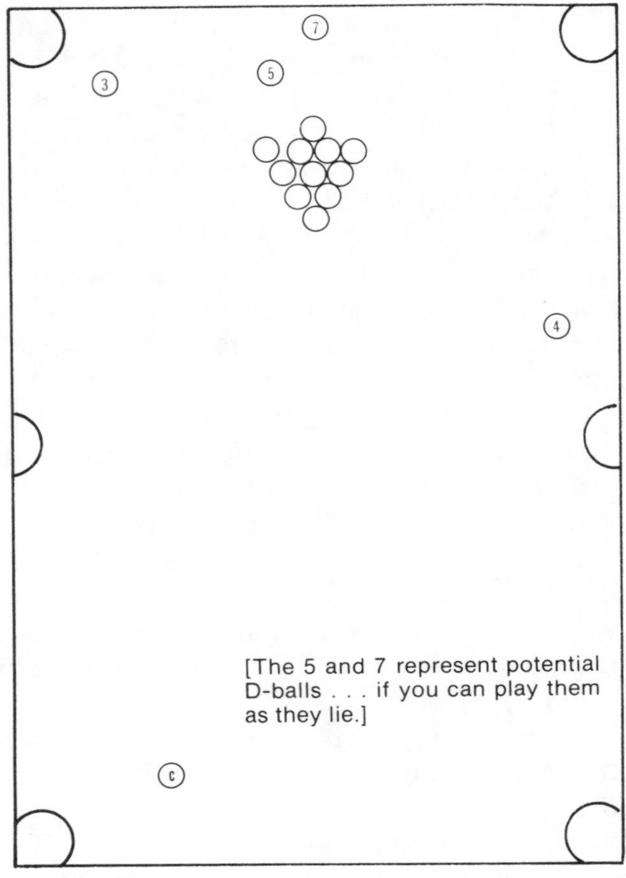

[The 5 and 7 represent potential D-balls . . . if you can play them as they lie.]

Diagram 59

In Diagram 59, the balls have just been broken at the outset of the game. This is a reasonably typical leave, with two long shots available right now and a rebreaking opportunity in those loose balls behind the stack.

Of course the 3-ball is easier to pocket in this spot than the 4. But your angle to the 3-ball makes it quite likely that you'll move one or both of the loose balls down near the bottom rail too. And unless you can be absolutely sure of where the moved object ball *and* the cue ball will end up, your chances are excellent for obliterating your secondary break shot opportunity and shutting your run down at 1, hardly a critical factor in the game.

Since pocketing the 3-ball nets you the *certainty* of that one lone point, wouldn't it be smarter to shoot the 4, which will cough up *three* certainties if pocketed with correct speed? Individually, it's a tougher shot than the 3, but you're supposed to be looking further ahead than that. Pocketing the 4 will leave your cue ball near the middle of the table, with a near-straight shot on the 3 and easy access to either the 5 or the 7. The 5-ball, of course, is a D, and if you like your position for it following the 3, the 7 will even act as a safety valve. If you decide you don't have the break shot you want on the 5 going right, you can still use the 7 to position yourself on the 5 going left; it's a D-ball in either direction. If you either overcut or undercut the 4, too bad, but you don't figure to leave very much; the cue ball will be very near the stack. The only danger here, and I think the benefits make it a worthwhile risk, lies in leaving the 4-ball very near the pocket—"hanging"—if you miss; correct cue ball speed is a partial insulation against that (even though the possibility can never be *completely* eliminated).

Here's another common example of the exact same principle. Diagram 60 shows you a set-up with some of the object balls already off the table; the shooter needs only pocket the 1-ball and follow out for position on the 2. That will lead to the 3, or the 4, both good D's. But in Diagram 61, the player has nudged the 3-ball on his way out, even though there was plenty of room; this will often be a matter of a hair too much speed, because speed unquestionably affects pool angles. At any rate, you can see the dismal consequences, even though he barely

Diagram 60: All we need here is position on the 2.

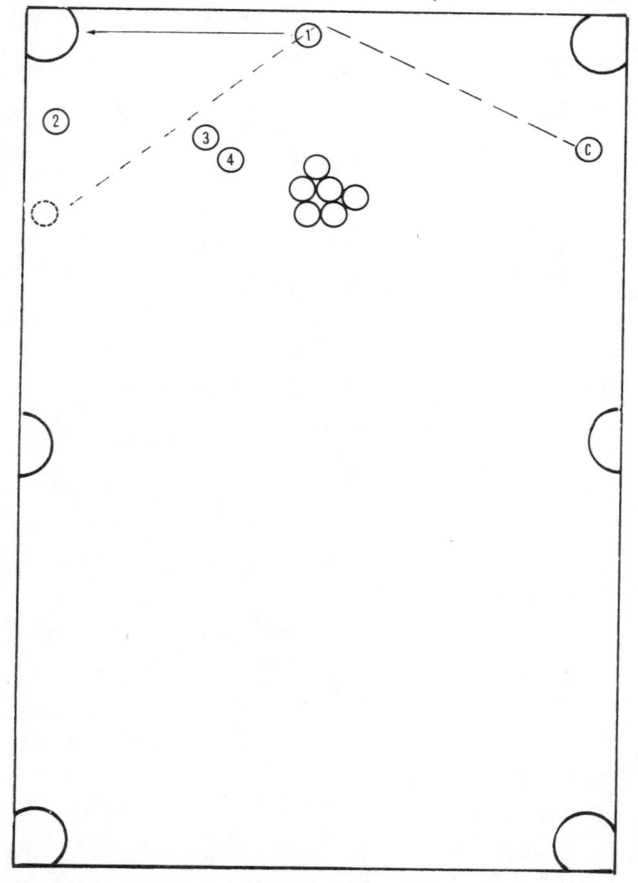

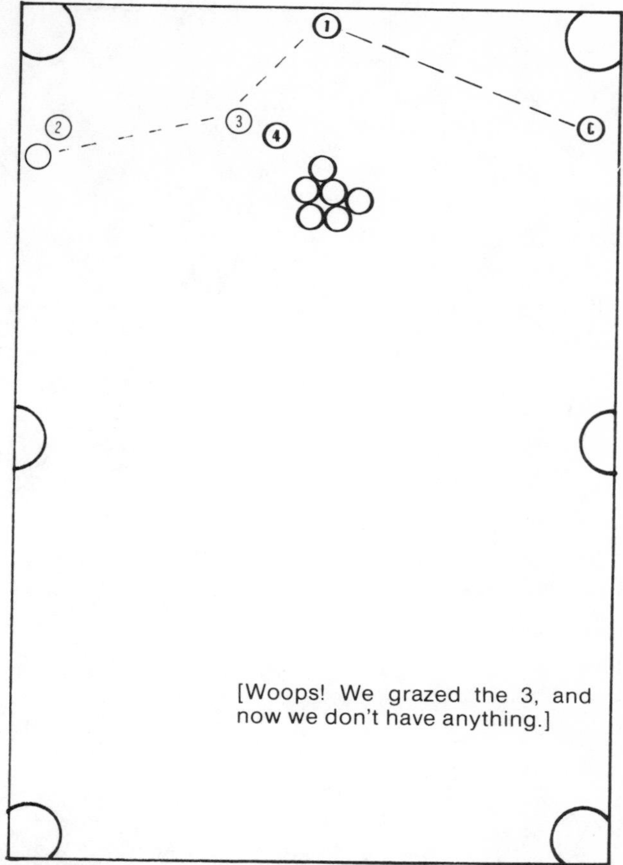

Diagram 61

moved the 3 an inch: no shots *anywhere*. Touching a secondary object ball without purpose made all the difference. Even the most subtle violations of w. p. 3 can turn a game around. You'll see this in the next game you watch, regardless of how good the players are.

Diagram 62 offers a reasonable example of the rape of w. p. 4, don't drive the cue ball when you can roll it. Only a thin rail cut shot on the 1 stands between the shooter and a very good key-ball/break-ball duo, the 2 and 3. This is as good a time as any to pass along a simple, single-sentence tip that can improve your overall game virtually overnight: *learn to stop overhitting thin cut shots*. The vast majority of pool players think that because a thin object ball hit is required, it will take increased cue ball speed to get the object ball where it's going.

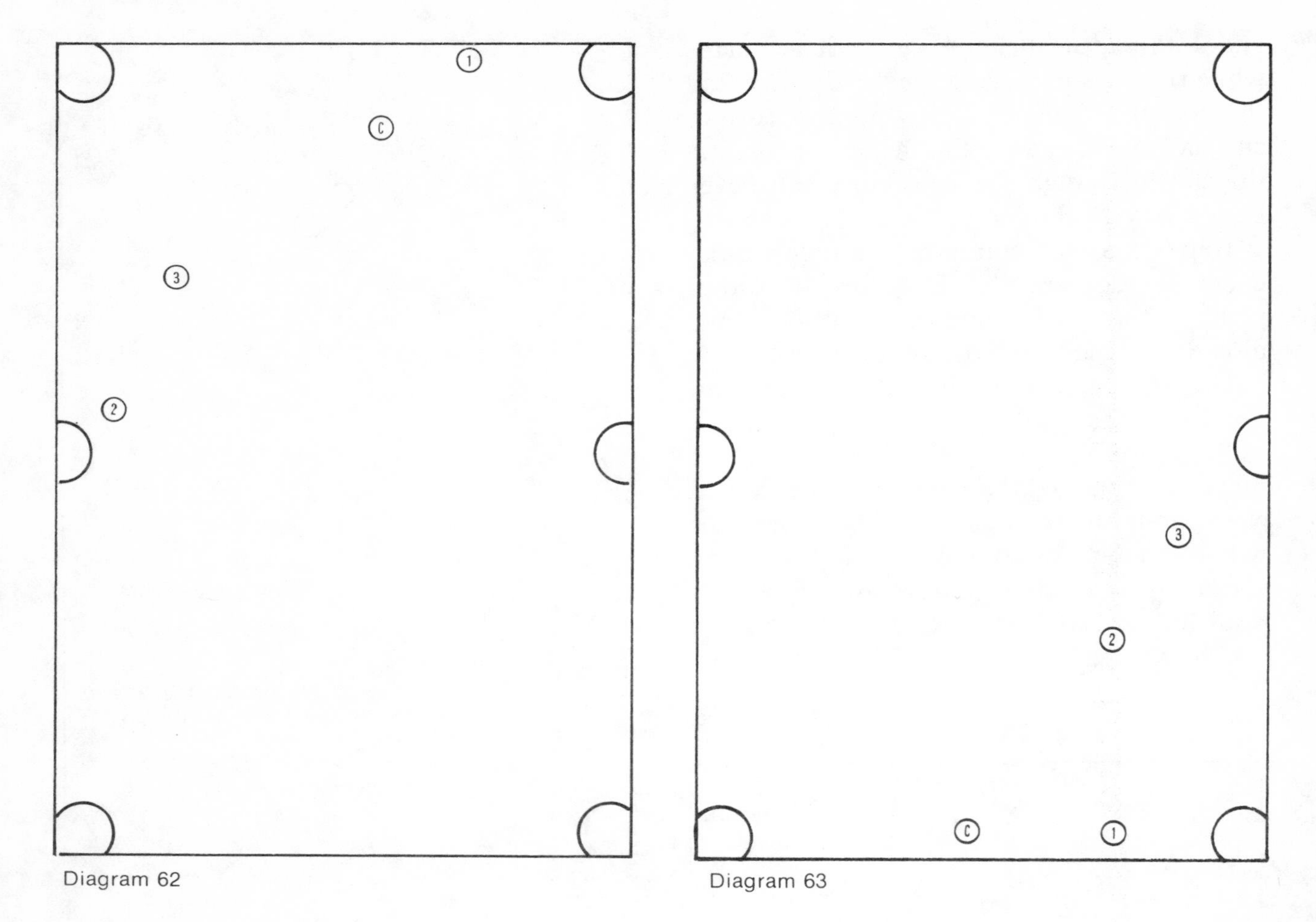

Diagram 62

Diagram 63

That is simply not true, except for the very thinnest cut shots in the game, those close to 90°, where the actual point of contact between the two balls is in fact slightly smaller than on other shots. But most thin cut shots require no more than medium speed to make them, and if you can master this you will enjoy both increased accuracy and cue ball control, plus the confidence that comes with them.

With respect to Diagram 62, what most players will do here is drive their cue ball up and part way down the length of the table, trying to pocket the 1 and get position for the 2 in the corner. It takes a polished player to merely roll the 1 into the corner and stick around for the 2 in the side instead, but that's the right shot. The other way, you're sacrificing accuracy, begging the 1-ball to hang because of overspeed, and not even insuring good position for the 2 in the corner. Roll the stone. Don't drive it. It will reward your gentleness. And make it a point to practice soft-hitting thin cut shots. You'd be surprised at how little speed it takes to get the job done.

Diagram 63 shows you the work of a player who's been minding his w. p.'s & q's, so to speak; those last three balls lie pretty near ideally, with an easy shot on the 1, followed by natural position on the 3, and a subsequent break shot on the 2. But oh my stars and garters, look what happened to him in Diagram 64. No position, no break shot, no *shot* for that matter, and how did he wreak this havoc? Well, by hitting the 2, of course; but he wouldn't have hit the 2 at all if he had avoided driving his cue ball to

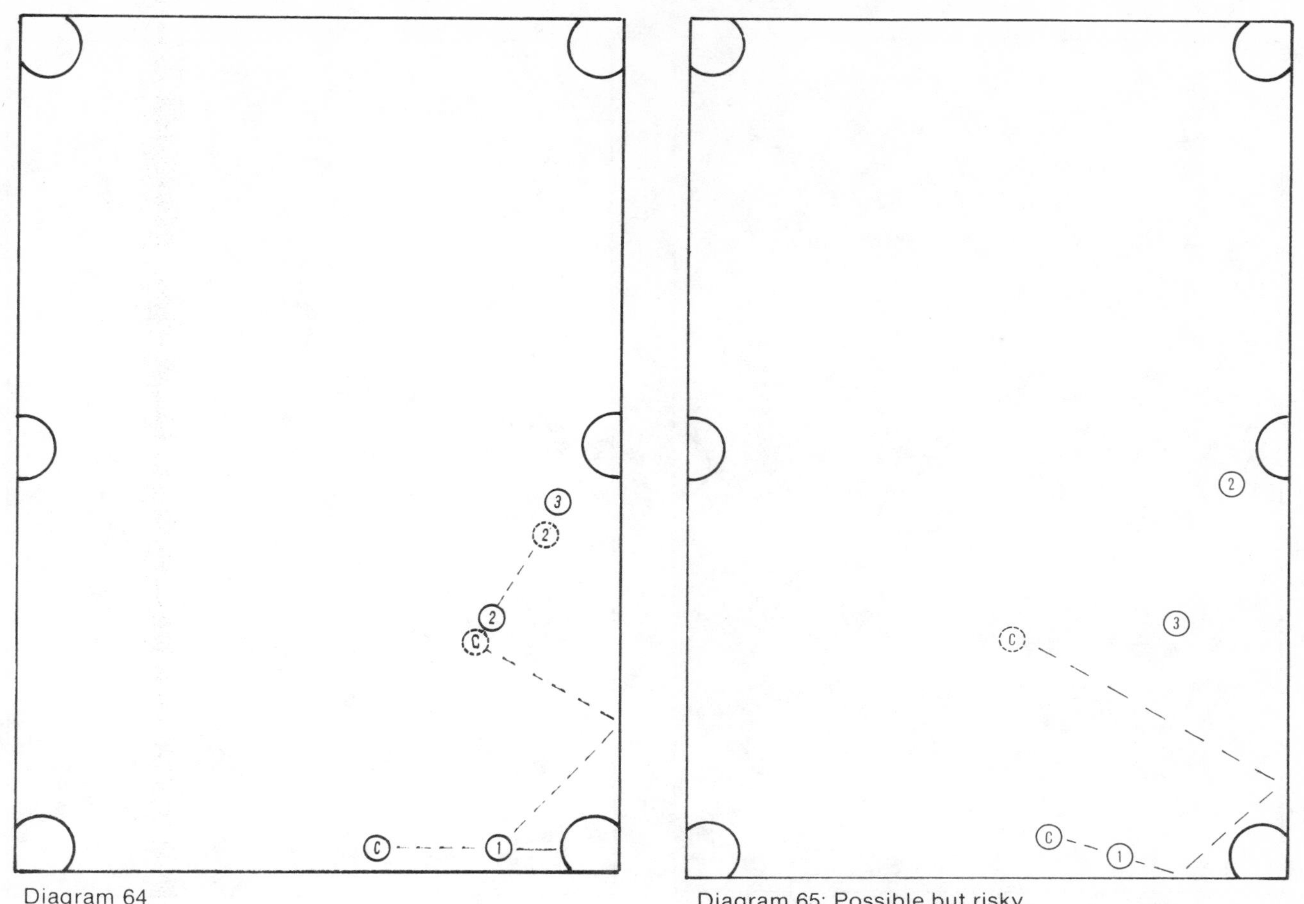

Diagram 64

Diagram 65: Possible but risky.

the rail. He misread the angle of the cue ball off the 1, or applied a tad more spin than he meant to, and cue ball action off a rail will amplify those kinds of errors. Our player has pillaged w. p. 5 (don't go to a rail unnecessarily) and justice has been sure and swift in this case. All he had to do was pocket the 1 with a soft, firm draw, and he'd have easily cleared the 2 for position on the 3. This is not a rare mistake by any means; learn to watch out for it in your game. The rails can be your good friends in advanced pool, but for some stuffy reason they insist that you use them correctly before they accept your friendship. Most of the game's bad luck seems to accrue to shots where the cue ball comes off at least one rail. It's downright spooky.

If you buy that, it shouldn't be any trouble to sell you on w. p. 6, choose one-rail routes rather than two-railers. The shots in the game that make best use of two-rail cue ball routes are those involving pocketing at the head of the table. In that instance, going two rails with the cue ball makes sense, because it creates a natural angle toward the center of the table. But back at the business end of the table, there are recurring two-rail route situations that can give you fits, especially those where the object ball is near a pocket and not quite straight-in with the cue ball (Diagram 65). Most players will elect to drive the cue ball through the object ball and off those two rails to come further up the table. There's no question that that can be made to work, but it takes more cue ball control than you think; the reason for that is that rails take the most wear down there

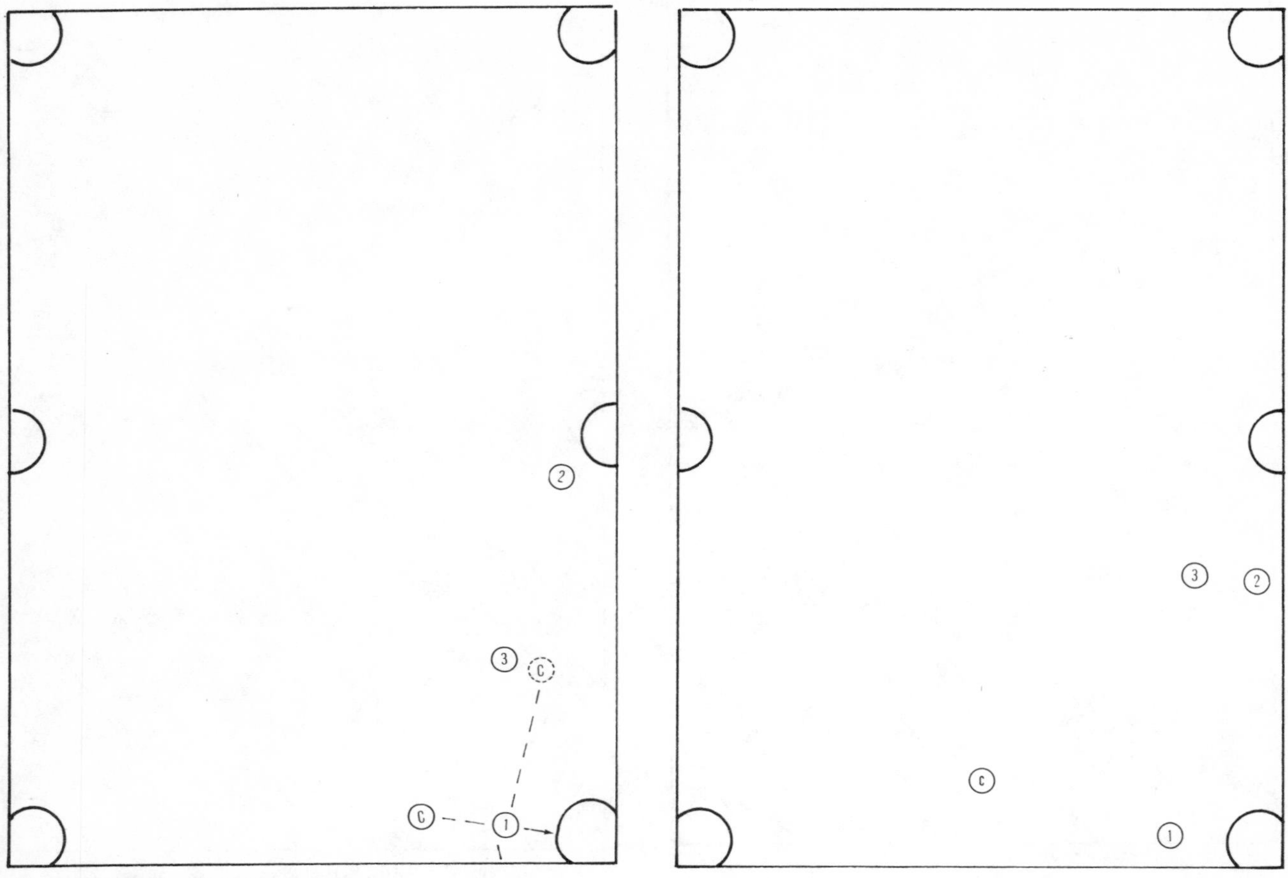

Diagram 66: Possible but safe.

Diagram 67

near the pocket, and are therefore at their least predictable there. You may well get a far sharper angle than you bargained for, if the cue ball skids at all.

Unless you're backed up against a rail (and the cue ball isn't, in the above diagram), you don't have to risk that. You can chop a shot like that in, dead center ball, no wrist action, no follow-through, so the cue ball goes to the bottom rail with no English whatsoever; that is a shot the rail can respect, and your reward is a prim, predictable cue ball path out of there, parallel to the side rail (Diagram 66). Any time you can choose between this shot and Diagram 65's shot and still accomplish what you want to, go for 66.

Players who *choose* two-rail routes when they don't have to, and there are more of them than you think, are often players who use too much English as well, thus incurring double jeopardy for crimes against w. p. 6 *and* w. p. 2. It's a case of one bad habit feeding on another one, and these players pay some wicked dues, in the forms of exotic scratches, open-table stymies that should be photographed and placed in a time capsule, and all kinds of sundry cue ball surprises.

Here comes Fancy Dan now, in Diagram 67. He's going to finesse the 1, get on the 2, and roll it up in the head corner, following right past the 3 for break-shot position. (At least he knows enough not to force his cue ball for position on the *other* side of the 2; that would be carnage against w. p. 4 into the bargain, and the game is not lenient with triple offenders.)

The catch is that he couldn't resist that pretty little *two*-rail route down there in the

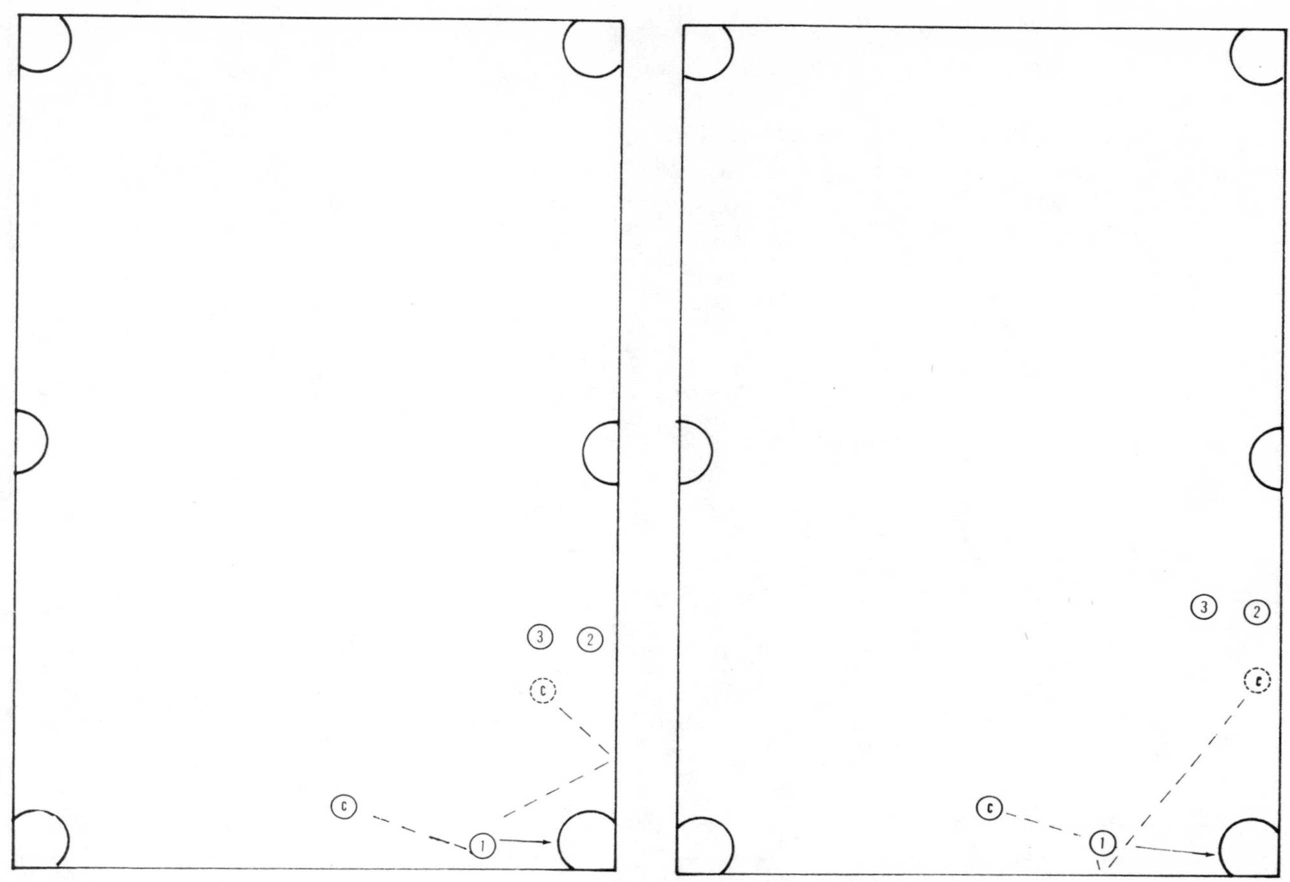

Diagram 68: The uncertain way.

Diagram 69: The certain way.

corner, as you see in Diagram 68. So he goosed up for some extra left-hand English, more than he needed, which caused him to overhit the shot and spin right into the Twilight Zone there where he can't use the 2 to get on the 3 anymore. It's not a total disaster; he can still pocket the 3 for position on the 2, but it's a far inferior break shot to the one he could have had. And you want to try to avoid giving away edges like that.

Diagram 69 shows what he should have done: little or no English, just a gentle stroke, above-center hit on the cue ball, nice pure follow-through, and a *one*-rail route. That way, the cue ball is moving *toward* the angle you want, rather than counter to it; and as long as your speed is okay, you can't go wrong.

Here's another common two-rails-instead-of-one error, in Diagram 70. Players will frequently spin their cue ball two rails behind the break ball they're trying to leave. But they're risking hitting that ball on the way out, or going too far for a really efficient break-shot angle, due to the increased speed and spin they've employed. This shot should be played off the bottom rail *only* wherever you can, and it will be possible, as in Diagram 71, whenever the angle to the bottom rail off the key ball is generally parallel to the side rail. Just add a modest amount of reverse (right-hand in this case) English to negate your angle, and your cue ball will walk right out there for a short, sure break shot.

The *three*-rail cue-ball routes that w. p. 7 wants you to shun generally begin with a thin cut shot into either corner pocket from behind the stack (Diagram 72). It looks like you won't be able to hold your cue ball in

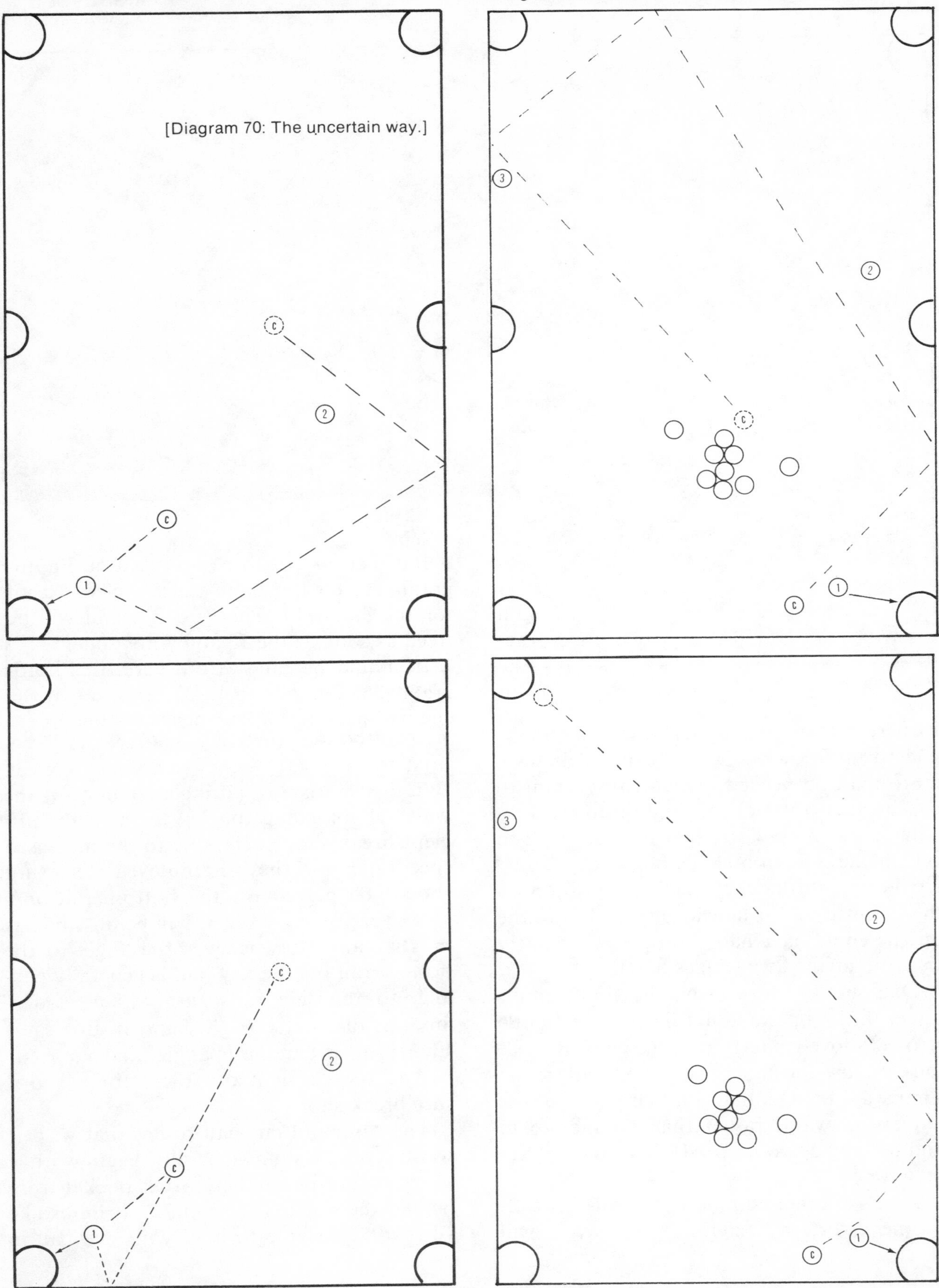

[Diagram 70: The uncertain way.]

Diagram 71: The certain way.

Diagram 72: Here's the shot the way you see it.

Diagram 73: Here's what can go wrong.

the area because of the angle, and because of that, normal speed will carry you uncomfortably far up the table; so you'd better drive your cue ball three rails and get back down to the balls that way.

Which is quite possible, of course, but it takes an expert to spot all the things that can go wrong with the shot, and that's why the shot should be left to experts.

Pitfall 1: you never get to the second rail (Diagram 73). This happens (and it happens a lot) when the player misreads his angle off the rail, his cue ball speed, his hit on the cue ball itself, or a combination of those. What happens is that the player creates a shorter angle for himself with his violation of stroking fundamentals, and the cue ball never gets the natural running English he was planning on and rehearsing to complete the angle he wanted. The cue ball actually curves into the corner pocket here (if that's any consolation), because of the shortened-angle effect.

Pitfall 2: you have a wreck with that 2-ball up yonder, that you never thought would even figure in the shot. Ah, but that 2-ball is in effect "bigger" than it looks; it's actually three balls wide, in that it can be contacted at either of its extreme edges or any point in between them. And if you do complete this unhappy little billiard and touch that ball at all, you're an odds-on favorite for punishment. (Diagram 74.)

Pitfall 3: you don't quite make the third rail, because you didn't read the angle of your shot quite right and that straggling 3-ball up there gotcha (Diagram 75).

You get the idea. Pass up this shot unless you read it as an absolute must; and in that case, make sure you chart the course of your cue ball as thoroughly as you can. The highways are fraught with marauders out there.

To replace the shot with something of value, I refer you back to w. p. 4, why drive when you can roll?, and the latest nugget of

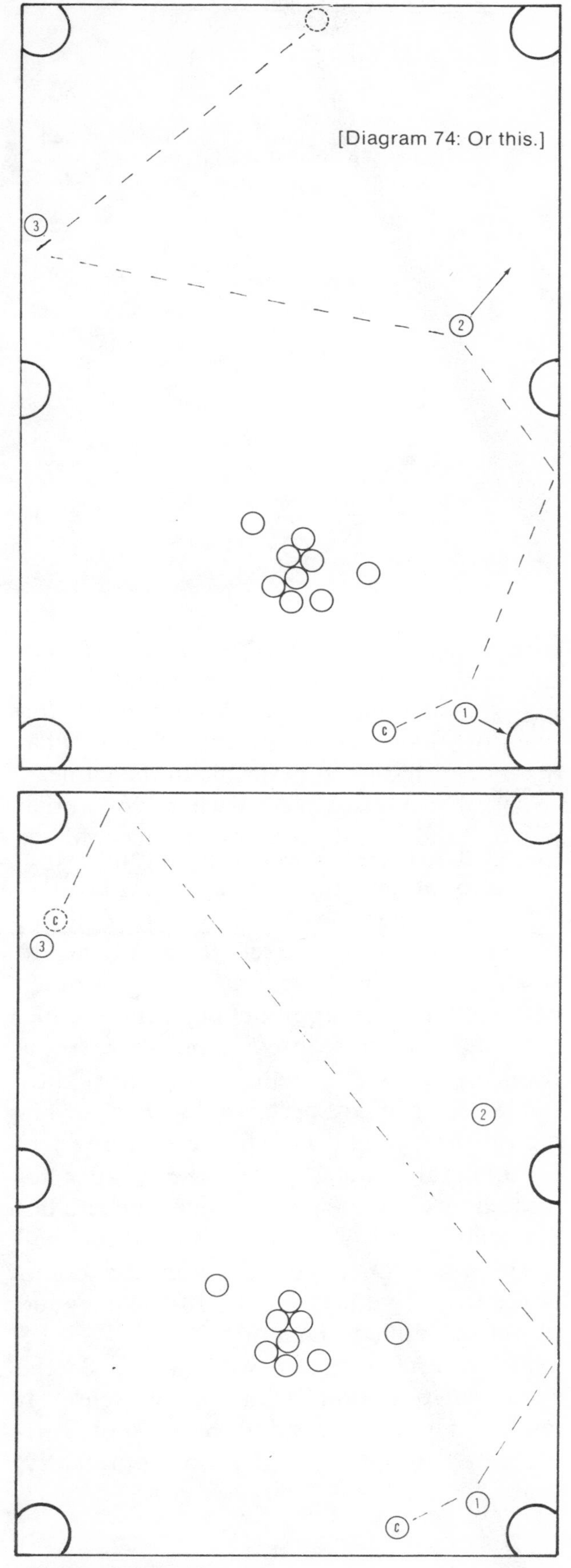

[Diagram 74: Or this.]

Diagram 75: Or this.

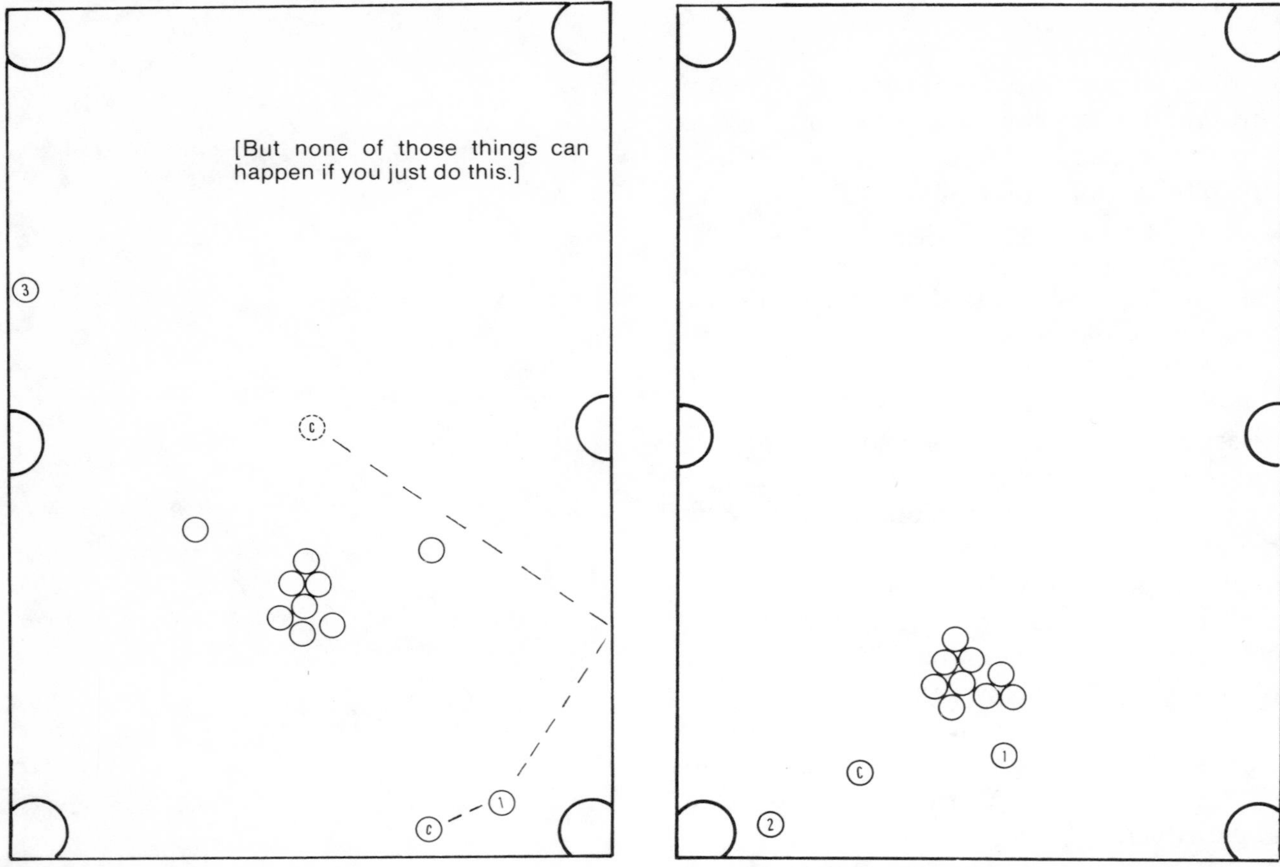

Diagram 76

Diagram 77A: Good safety valve.

knowledge I offered a few paragraphs ago: Learn to hit your thin cut shots more softly.

Take another look at Diagram 72. If our player can instead muster the confidence to *roll* the object ball, he actually has a much better chance of approaching center table, and in a lot more predictable way. Some reverse, or "kill" English, and a slightly tighter cue grip are permissible when the angle on the cue ball is extremely thin. There is minimal danger here, the chance of scratching in the opposite side pocket, but you can guard against that with cue ball speed alone once you develop the confidence to roll your thin cuts. Just like a good player has done in Diagram 76.

We've already seen why w. p. 8, the safety-valve notion, makes good sense. It lets you hit your secondary break shots softer, more smoothly, and more confidently, besides offering itself as a certainty. Remember, of course, that your break shot has to be in a direction *away* from your safety-valve ball (Diagrams 77A and 77B); otherwise you have no assurance that nothing will come between the two of you.

Obviously, the most logical type of shot to select for a safety-valve ball is one that can be pocketed easily from just about anywhere, therefore a ball near a pocket. Advanced players, however, are able to preserve safety-valve situations out in the middle of action, and the balls they save for this function are even more versatile, because multiple pockets are available to them. It makes for some of the prettiest, most effortless sequences you'll ever see in the game, but it's nothing you'd ever fall into through serendipity. That ability, when shown against you, is an unmistakable sign

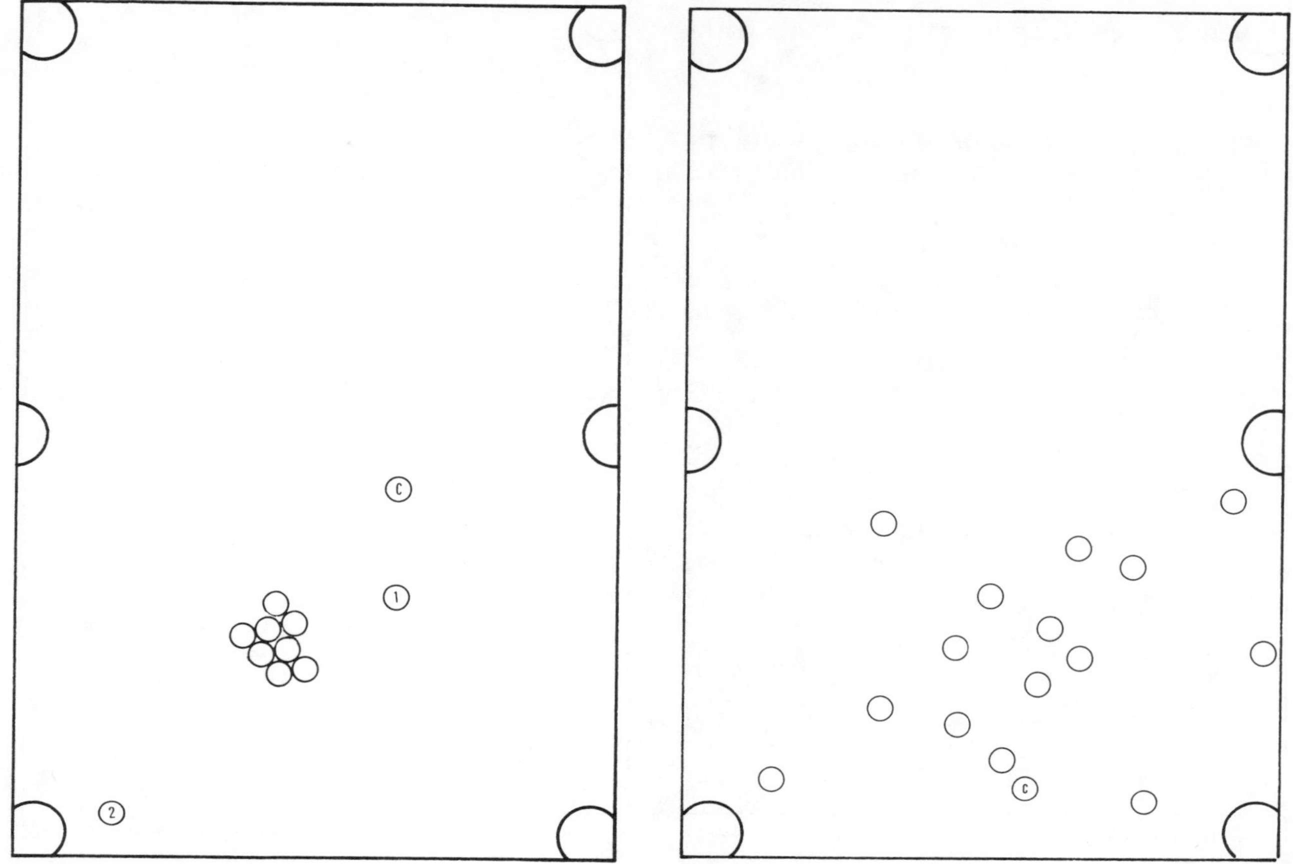

Diagram 77B: Dumb safety valve.

Diagram 78: An open rack.

that you've got some meaningful competition.

We can take a look at one example of that. Diagram 78 shows you the balls blasted to hell and gone, all A's and B's, nothing but multiple shots everywhere you look. The kind of rack, in short, that drives many intermediate-and-sometimes-even-better players into incoherence, because it's a lot harder than it looks. With all those loose balls occupying all that space, how are you going to move your cue ball around? Haven't you been reading your w. p. 3? We don't want to move open balls, and that's all there seems to be. So whither?

Well, first go to Diagram 79, which is the same layout with clues added. The four balls marked "X" have in common that of all the remaining balls, they are nearest the four corners of the table, or, for lack of a more convenient term, they are "cornermost." There will always be balls you can designate this way, no matter how many balls are left or how they lie; and which ones they are is quite important, because of the individual two-ball relationships between them.

I think you'll find that if you can plan and execute sequences involving the consecutive pocketing of cornermost balls, the results will please you. You'll be working from the outside in, which is always recommended, and you'll be observing w. p. 3 devoutly. Like every other aspect of the game, this will not always be possible for you to do, but try to make it happen whenever you see the opportunity.

Diagram 78 represents that kind of opportunity, and Diagram 80 shows you how it should be exploited: the entire rack run

Diagram 79

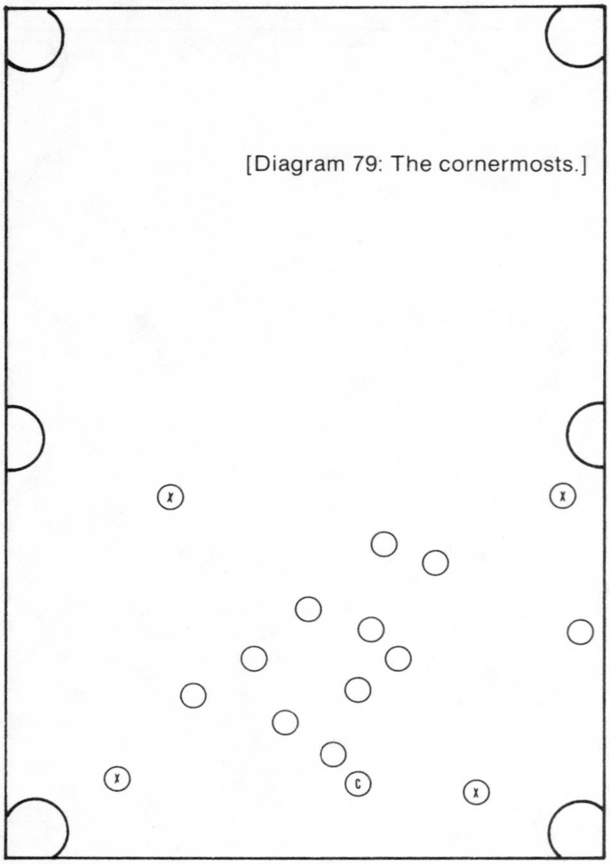

[Diagram 79: The cornermosts.]

Diagram 80

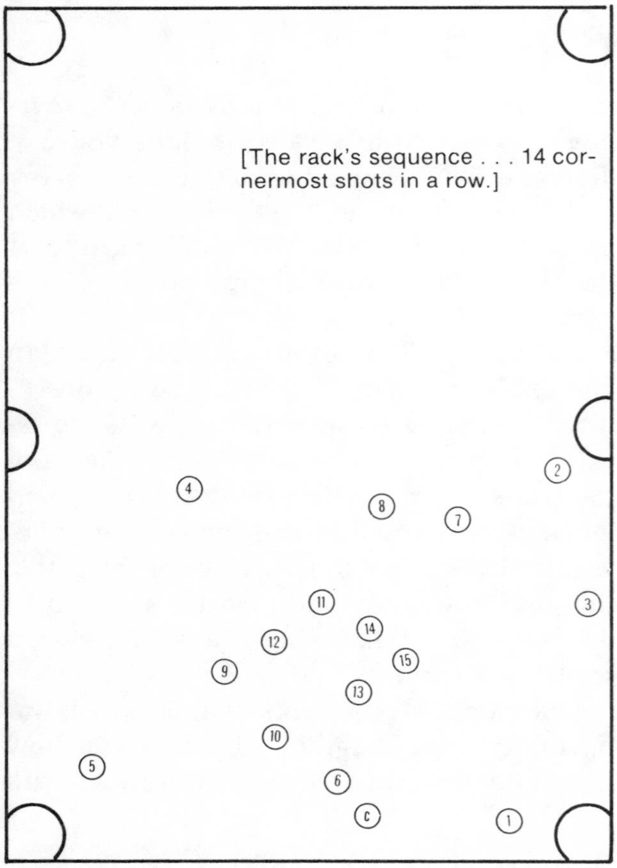

[The rack's sequence . . . 14 cornermost shots in a row.]

Diagram 81

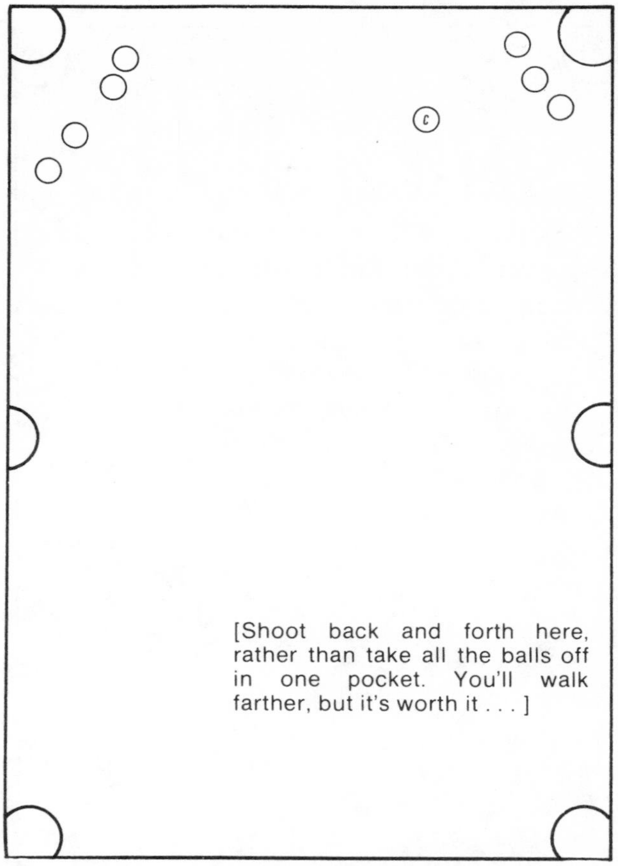

[Shoot back and forth here, rather than take all the balls off in one pocket. You'll walk farther, but it's worth it . . .]

Diagram 82

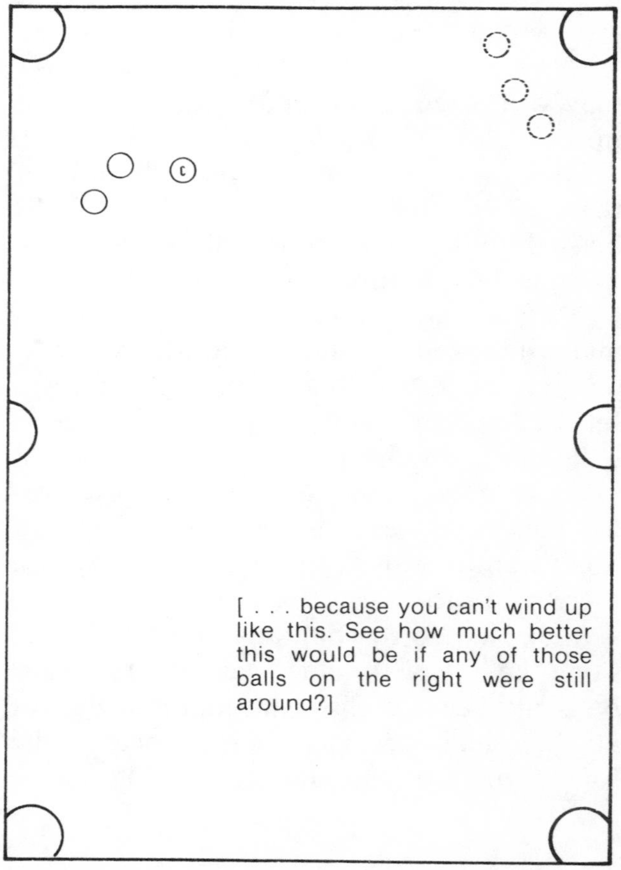

[. . . because you can't wind up like this. See how much better this would be if any of those balls on the right were still around?]

without ever touching a second ball, simply by shooting a cornermost ball every shot. The balls are numbered in rotation to show you how the principle extends. Each ball, at the time it was struck, was cornermost relative to the rest of the remaining balls. Thus the player recognized a two-ball relationship between cornermost balls in each case. Learn to look for those relationships and where they might lead you. Chances are it will be into an excellent sequence.

This is nothing more than a highly advanced extension of the safety-valve principle. What we left alone, and saved till we needed it most, was our critical key-ball/break-ball sequence from the 9-ball on up.

So look for "Corner-To-Corner" possibilities to get you started when you're stuck for planning a sequence. And as long as we're bandying idioms about, another safety-valve premise you should learn is something I call "One From Column A, One From Column B" (and no, it doesn't mean that an hour after trying it, you feel like playing again).

In Diagram 81 you see a very happy state of affairs: the cue ball midway between sets of A-balls for either corner pocket. The temptation is there to pocket balls consecutively in one corner, then come back and get the rest. Resist the temptation staunchly. You're much better off taking one from the right, then one from the left, then back again. That will offer you multiple safety-valve opportunities. If you took off all the balls on the right, for instance, and you got slightly out of line pursuing the balls on the left, as in Diagram 82, you'll wish you had left something on the other side. (While we're about this, keep in mind that when multiple balls are available to the same pocket, as in Diagram 81, you'll do well to shoot the middle balls in the row first. It will increase your cue ball options later.)

That leaves the oft-taught w. p. 9, get balls off the rail early. Diagram 83 shows

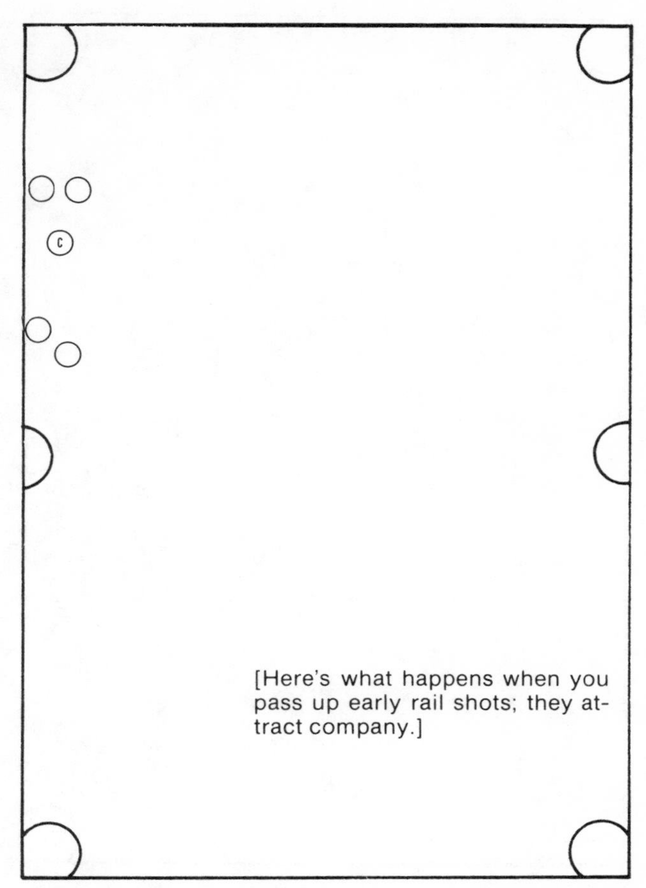

C
[Here's what happens when you pass up early rail shots; they attract company.]

Diagram 83

you a typical penalty for violation, and a mild one at that, because the balls you see are still pocketable even though they'll restrict your cue ball and decrease your options. A setup like you see here should be treated in the manner of One From Column A, One From Column B. But it's equally likely you'll suffer the boils of Diagram 84, where you'll have to rearrange your entire sequence to break up those miserable little bunches, with neither offering any safety-valve possibilities to the other until broken. Get to know your along-the-rail cut shots, thin and otherwise, so you can hit them confidently *when* you should as well as where you should.

Time to get down to cases now. Let's take a look at two separate racks, and you plan them this time. Each will be presented to

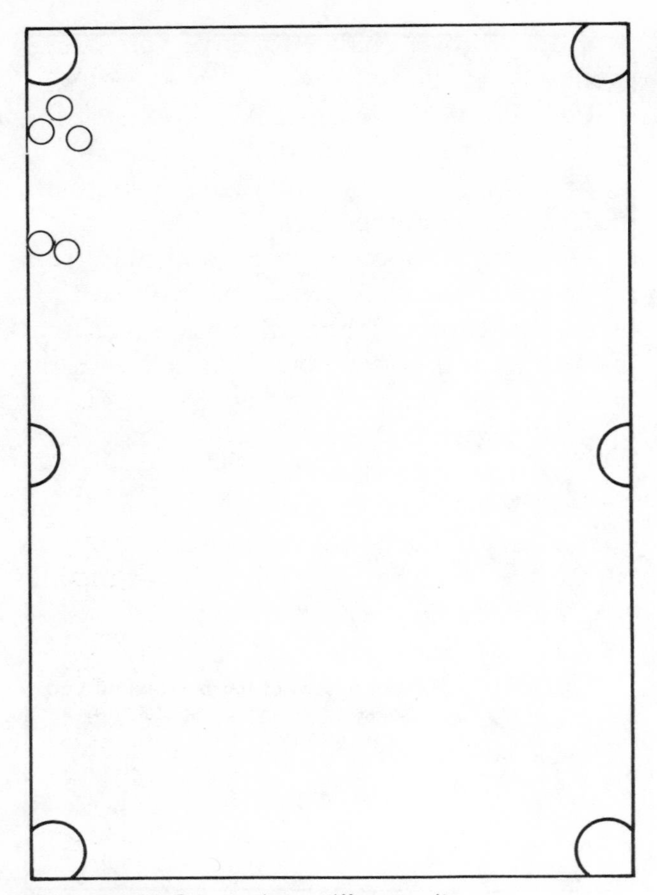
Diagram 84: Same crime, stiffer penalty.

you in a full-page photo, to give you the fairest view of the layout I can in a two-dimensional realm; you should be able to tell which the A, B, C, and D-balls are. For this first rack, to help you get used to the process, the camera will "walk" you around the table and show you which balls comprise your correct field of view as you go along. You can tell which balls were the correct shots merely by skipping a photo ahead, but don't do that. Take the photos one at a time, decide *which* the correct shot is, and *how* you play it and *why* you should play it that way. Words describing what I want you to see in the pictures will follow, of course. But at this point in the book, we've talked about everything you need to know to think these sequences through correctly. Be creative and have fun. And naturally, any workable solutions that occur to you as alternatives to mine are equally valid, as long as they're well thought through.

My Solution

Since there are no remaining clustered balls, that eliminates C and D balls from consideration. So I designated the balls this way:

A—10, 2, 12, 13, 15, 14, 8, 7, 9
B—1, 11, 3, 4, 5
C—None
D—None
Best next-rack break shot—15

Photograph 43

Photo 44—A chance for a very easy first shot, and the added opportunity to deal with my near-rail balls early. Roll the 10 in and get position for the 12 and 13.

Photo 45—Getting from the 12 to the 13 will be candy. Then I want the 2 out of there, which will make an A-ball out of the 1.

Photo 46—With those two cinches gone, I can now use the 2 to both free the 1 and get on my last rail ball, the 7. Gentle follow will do it.

Photo 47—After pocketing the 7, both the 9 and the 1 represent simple stop-ball opportunities.

Photo 48—And they lead directly to a straight-in shot on the 4 in the side. Remember, all six pockets count when you plan a sequence.

Photo 49—Straight-in shots galore once the 4 is gone: the 3, 11, and 5 are all simplicity itself.

Photo 50—No more than six inches' draw off the 5 will give me a reliable back-corner pocket shot on the 8 . . .

Photo 51—which I hit with center ball or maybe a tad of follow, depending on the precise angle, for an angle on the key-ball 14 . . .

Photo 52—and the 15-ball to break the next rack.

Now that wasn't so bad, was it? As a matter of fact, and in case you didn't notice, that solution involved running the rack without ever touching a second ball, and that's the ultimate stage of simplifying the game.

Let's try a rack that involves rebreaking the balls this time.

First, naturally, I checked the remaining clustered balls, and found no dead shots. Then I made the following ball designations:

A—1, 5, 9, 8, 12, 3, 15
B—6, 10
C—4, 14, 13, 11, 7
Best D-ball—15

Photograph 53

Photo 54—Observing my credo of cinching the first ball following a break shot, I rolled the 3 in, with just enough follow English to get an angle on the 5. This is as good an opportunity to get to my D-ball, the 15, as I could ask for. All I have to do is play the 5 softly, and the 1-ball will be my safety valve for both this shot and the next.

Photo 55—Here's where I got to for my break shot, not bad at all. To be dead certain that I have the 1-ball, if nothing else, after this shot, I'd punch the cue ball here, not trying to drive it far at all.

Photo 56—I have no C-balls left following the break shot, therefore I need no D's either. The A's are now the 1, 6, 10, 9, 7, 8, 12 and 13; the 11, 14 and 4 are B's. The best break ball for next rack: the 7. The 1 and 6 are adjacent cornermosts. So I'll

Photo 57—The 1-ball is gone, using one rail (not two) to move the cue ball up table.

Photo 58—Ditto the 6 and 8. No rails needed here, just a few inches' draw.

Photo 59—The 8 and 9 are neighboring cornermosts too, and represent a good unimpeded chance to get to your last rail ball as well. I needed enough draw to leave me a modest angle on the 9.

Photo 60—The 11-ball changed from a B into an A when I made the 6 earlier, and I got natural position on it by using gentle draw on the 9.

Photo 61—After the 11, I have the 10, and that will make my last two B's, the 14 and 4, into A's.

Photo 62—All the rest can be played as cornermosts now. From the 10 to the 13, off one rail . . .

Photo 63—From the 13 to the 12, with just a few inches' draw . . .

Photo 64—From the 12 to the 14, the same way . . .

Photo 65—From the 14 to the 4, the same way . . .

Photo 66—And an ideal break shot on the 7.

The transition between the 8 and the 9 might possibly have escaped you, but this rack was only slightly harder than the last. Those were 28 awfully easy shots you just figured out, Fast Eddie. You're really getting too good at this. Maybe we should try some eight-ball.

2 Advanced Eight-Ball

Just as the game of pool is underrated by those who don't know it, eight-ball is underrated by those who do.

Forget that it's often the first formal pool game you learn. Forget that you see it being played by kids and beginners a lot. It's really a subtle, deceptive game that, when properly played, borrows from whatever skills you have for any other pool game you know. And none of these skills counts more in eight-ball than what you know about straight pool.

If two good eight-ball players go head to head, the better straight-pool player between them should win, in the long run. There's really only one distinction: In eight-ball, you blast the balls open to begin the game. That fact alone makes it totally infeasible for me to take you through typical patterns; there is no such thing. What we will do is see how straight-pool principles might be applied to any given layout.

I've always thought that an interesting proposition for two *expert* players would be eight-ball played according to the rules of straight pool: all balls called, *including on the break;* safeties off the opponent's ball would be perfectly permissible, legal and aboveboard. I think the resulting game would show you some mind-bending moves.

But with or without any innovations from me, I do think that eight-ball may well be pool's game of the future. The game needs lots of exposure, and eight-ball is the ideal game for the tube for the same reasons it's attractive to kids and beginners: It's quick and simple to understand. Virtually all the major sports have undergone rules revisions within the past few years to help accent *scoring,* in whatever form; that is what fans want to see. And pool is no different. Straight pool potentially can keep one player at the table longer than any other form of the game, but it also has the potential to bring both contestants to their knees and produce a long, slow, dull defensive struggle. The masses just won't embrace that kind of game; pool purists might, but people on the fringes of the game would not see the same beauty. It happened to Mizerak and Lassiter, two of the finest players of all time, at the U.S. Open in the early 1970s. One year after playing one of the greatest pool games *ever*—with no TV present—the same two played two of the epic stinkers in tournament billiards history, with ABC-TV cameras and Mosconi himself as color commentator looking on aghast. The big eye hasn't helped us much since.

But eight-ball is doing just fine. In the bar-table form of the game, entire leagues have sprung up in locations all over the country. Whole tournaments have been devoted to it. There are even a few experimental special sets of object balls for Tournament Eight-Ball (seven yellows, seven reds, and, of course, The Emperor Jones). Women's leagues and most of their tournaments play no other game that I know of. Unlike nine-ball and one-pocket, which we'll get to, eight-ball can be enjoyed with family or friends in the complete absence of stakes. (You *can* play nine-ball or one-pocket sociably, I guess, but it kind of reminds me of basketball without hoops.)

It's a nifty little game, in all its forms, and our chances of making you better at it are just as good as our chances of improving your straight pool. Maybe even better. And your first step is simply to respect the game.

HOW TO BREAK

First things first; there's a correct way to *rack* the balls for eight-ball, which you see in Photo 2–1. The 8 is racked in the middle, of course, but also note that striped and

Photograph 2–1

solid balls alternate around the perimeter of the rack. No two are together except in the fourth row. This is the fairest way to rack; it ensures that neither player will get any *added* advantage out of the break (or disadvantage out of not breaking).

But the break in eight-ball is certainly an edge, and here's how you maximize it.

The blast-break to be used here, as well as all forms of Rotation, should be hit with all the speed you can *control.* Note that I did not say, "all the speed you can produce." Anybody with reasonably quick hands can give the rack a real wallop if he wants to; despite all the leaping and twisting you often see with the stroke, the rest of the body doesn't help the arm all that much. Quick hands are the only important prerequisite to breaking the balls well. And breaking them well means much more than breaking them hard.

Uncontrolled speed actually does some brutal things to your break. At the very outset of your stroke, your practice strokes lose rhythm because you're dwelling on all that force you're about to summon. Ditto your mental rehearsals; they suffer because instead of seeing and feeling control and smoothness, you're thinking power. The arc in your backswing will be tremendously exaggerated, making it much harder to keep the actual stroke level. You'll be less accurate in hitting the cue ball where you want to—dead center—and at that peak speed, your unwanted, uncontrolled English will be magnified many times after impact. You probably will be less accurate about hitting the head ball in the rack where you want to—right on the nose—as well.

That's what you're sacrificing when you just rear back and fire. What you get in return is a *possibility*—no more—that some of the object balls will roll a few feet farther, which is no guarantee that they'll fall someplace as a result. And worst of all, your cue ball is probably flying around like a balloon with its air just released, with up to 15 balls moving around simultaneously. In short, you have nothing going for you at this point but Dame Fortune to help you sink a ball and get a shot at a second one. Don't trust the lady all that often. She has this way of wetting down your chalk.

Rhythm and concentration will help you control the speed you need for the break. Hit it hard, sure, but be certain that your stroke has a beginning, middle, and end, and not the brute-strength herky-jerky lunge you see all the time. Tighten your grip on the butt *slightly,* but no more than that. Then stroke the thing smooth and pure. You'll get maximum impact as well as control if you hit the cue ball dead center; it will arrive at the stack with no natural spin of its own for the balls to absorb, and remember, with that kind of impact, any English at all would be tremendously increased.

If your stroke is level, a center-ball hit on the cue ball that sends it into the head ball dead-on (you should be breaking from dead center behind the string) will produce this effect: The albino will be rejected in the direction of the middle of the table, *and it should die there.* Don't mistake this for the force-follow effect, in which the cue ball makes contact, backs up, and then plows in again for little secondary spurts. It happens when you hit the cue ball either too high or too low; it's very dramatic to see and probably makes you think of spectacular Freudian things too, but it's still uncontrolled and dangerous. The center of the table is where your rock will be safest from all those flying missiles, and if you've stroked the break correctly, you're a favorite to make something and have the rest pretty well open. And you can make that a mighty big edge.

PLAYING THE GAME

To begin with, let's assume that in this and all the other forms of eight-ball we'll discuss, you and your opponent have agreed to "play honest"; that is, each player must try to hit his own ball before making contact with any other. (Make sure you have this in the clear before you begin playing if you don't know what your opponent is accustomed to, because plenty of players prefer the opportunity to play safe off their opponent's ball. This seems like the embodiment of the proverbial "dirty pool," but actually it makes for a much more scientific, defensive game. The reason we're passing over such a game here is that it increases the options of each player so dramatically as to defy diagramming.)

Let's play our way through three racks, one relatively simple, the next somewhat more challenging, and the third with added problems to solve.

Photograph 2–2 shows you the balls well broken but nothing made. It's your shot, and your choice of stripes or solids too. Which do you begin with?

Neither. What you do before you do anything else in eight-ball is to check out the 8-ball. Is it an A, B, or C-ball (since you're obviously not going to use it as a D)? In Photograph 2–2, the 8-ball is an A, available to the left-hand corner pocket.

Now is when you begin to choose between the stripes and solids, and the right way to do that is not necessarily to pick out the simplest shot immediately available. What you look for now is which set of balls offers the most logical path to the 8-ball, just as the balls lie? All the balls in the photograph seem to be A's, except for the 5, and that's part of a simple combination shot.

A good player could run out this game by

Photograph 2–2

choosing either stripes or solids in this case, but I think that same good player would be much more likely to choose stripes. The reasons are these: Although the solids offer three quite easy shots in the head corner pockets (5–2, 5, and 1), position on the 1 will be somewhat tricky; so will transitional plays from the head of the table to the foot, for the remaining solid balls; and most importantly, the 11 and 12 balls offer a more natural key-shot sequence to get to the 8, and the striped balls lie so as to lead the player right down the table with minimum effort.

So you begin with the 9, instead of that big fat 5–2 combination. The 9 is actually only slightly harder than that anyway. Roll it down the table and hold your cue ball there for a side-pocket shot at the 15 (Photo 2–3). Do the same with your cue ball for the 14 (Photo 2–4), and follow for the 10 and 13 (Photos 2–5 and 2–6). Follow a foot or so for a negotiable angle on the 12 (Photo 2–7), and play position using one rail, not two, for the 11 in the side (Photo 2–8), which leaves you ready to pop Othello into the subway via the corner (Photo 2–9). All you did there was play good straight pool: You used the rails only as strictly needed, you never touched a secondary object ball, and your sequence was nothing more than seven cornermosts in a row. You can see that by reexamining Photo 2–2.

Let's try something a little tougher. In Photo 2–10, you have more than mere A-balls to consider. The 8-ball is definitely a

Photograph 2–3

C. If you went with the solids here, even though the 5 is a cinch in the side, you'd have to contend with two B-balls, the 4 and 6, and a C, the 3. And you don't have a really good D-ball except for the 4, which is only good if the other guy moves that 12 for you.

If you take the stripes, you still get a C, the 10. But you can move it with the 12-ball, a good D-ball that you can play position for whenever you wish and may even be able to play with a safety valve behind it.

So take stripes. Both a solid and a stripe fell on the break, and you can get out here by playing six cornermosts in succession: the 14 (gone in Photo 2–11), the 15 (gone in Photo 2–12) with enough follow for an angle on the 13, the 13 (gone in Photo 2–13) with enough follow for an angle on the 12, the 12 (gone in Photo 2–14) softly enough that the 11 acts as a safety valve. In Photo 2–14, the balls are now open enough for you to win, shooting the 11 in the side (Photo 2–15), then the 10 in the corner (Photo 2–16), then the 8 in the opposite corner.

I have not deliberately oversimplified these racks. The fact is, eight-ball frequently can be won from the break, assuming that the break leaves you something to shoot at. It's not that hard to break the balls apart; that depends as much upon a smooth level stroke as it does on brute strength. And following the break, you generally can put a game plan together, despite the fact that there are all those balls all over the table. Where the game gets tied up in knots, more

Photograph 2–4

often than not, is *after* the balls are broken, by the players' incorrect shot selection and /or failure to execute their plans. Because the game begins with a freewheeling break, the temptation is there to keep clobbering the balls willy-nilly all game. But don't do that. Give this game the precision it deserves, and it will reward you.

Let's consider one more rack, this time without giving you your choice of balls. You've made a solid and that's what you'll have to play. As you can see in Photo 2–17, you'd have a lot more going for you if you could shoot the stripes instead, but that situation comes up all the time and it's just part of the game.

As it is, most of your balls are B's. From where the cue ball lies now, only the 4-ball is cleanly pocketable. Even the 8-ball is a B. There's no point in waiting for your opponent to clean house to open the way for you, so let's see what you can do on your own.

You did catch one break: The major stumbling block facing you is also the easiest to move. That'd be his 10-ball, hanging in the left-hand corner pocket. Let's see if there's a way to concede him that ball *and as little else as possible.*

Start with the 4-ball. It's a long shot, and the accuracy for it won't come to you from my book or anybody else's, but the fact is that it's not that hard. Just shoot it smoothly, without forcing the cue ball anyplace, the same way you've been doing all along. A smooth stroke and follow English

Photograph 2-5

should bring you off one rail—not two, now—and straight down the table in the direction of the 7 (Photo 2–18). The 7 offers you an excellent dual chance: knock his 10 in legally, and at the same time play an effective safety between another of his object balls and the rail. See where the 11 is? If we can get between there and the bottom rail, while pocketing his 10 and replacing it with your 7, the game will be turned in our favor.

That's just what happened in Photo 2–19. You got lucky and made your 7 follow his 10 in, so it's still your shot. But you can see that even if your 7 was still standing where the 10 used to be, the game would still favor you by far. All your balls would be pocketable, and he'd have three B-balls to deal with (15, 11, 14).

As a reward for your prudent shot with the 7, you're got a chance to run out. The 3-ball is your best key to the 8 now. So play that easy 5–6 combination and get natural position on the 2-ball (Photo 2–20). The 2 will lead you down to the 5 (Photo 2–21), from which you can get position on the 3, using how many rails, Fast Eddie? That's right: one. In Photo 2–22, you're ready to shoot the 3 with a little follow and get position on the ebony fool in the side (Photo 2–23). You win again.

What you learn here hopefully will keep you from making too many mistakes, but it won't keep you from missing. What I want you to learn is to think your way through each new situation confronting you, each time you come to the table. Misses are part

Photograph 2-6

of the game; the guy you're playing will miss shots too. And whichever of you is better at *recouping* his misses will win. Generally speaking, there should be *some* plan available to you that will advance your cause, even if it's nothing more than leaving him the toughest shots possible. And if he does trap you sufficiently that you can't win the game, then he deserves the win himself. There's always the next game. Don't give up, and above all, never stop thinking.

Put the object ball in the subway and put the cue ball someplace beneficial. That's all that every form of pool known to man comes down to. If you could do that every time, you'd send Mizerak, his immediate family and in-laws, and all his fellow players to the rack. Nobody can do that every time, of course. But you'll be surprised how your chances of accomplishing correct moves increase as long as you keep thinking about what those moves might be.

Last-Pocket Eight-Ball

Here's an advanced form of the game that makes even greater use of your straight-pool skills. In this game, you must sink the 8-ball in the same pocket in which you made your final object ball, whether it was a stripe or a solid.

On the surface, it would seem that all you need to modify in your thinking is the relationship between the 8-ball and your last ball preceding it. Instead of establishing that your last ball will lead you to an open shot on the 8, you must establish a two-ball but

Photograph 2-7

one-pocket relationship between them. Choose a plan that will win for you, rather than one that first lets you pocket all your object balls and then lets you tend to the matter of the 8.

This seems self-explanatory, but last-pocket is a deceptive game for that very reason. Once you're ready for your last object ball, and hopefully the 8 after that, you're actually quite vulnerable. Now I don't want you to create any fear of the situation in which you address the last two balls of the game; after all, it means that you've got first crack at winning the game outright. But I do want you to understand that should you miss that last ball—or worse, make the last ball but miss the 8—you're really not even a favorite to win the game any more.

The reason for that is that your opponent would then have an unmistakable picture of what it takes to leave you safe. He can arrange his entire remaining sequence around that; he may even legally abandon that sequence in favor of driving the 8-ball someplace where it's no longer compatible with the last object ball for the pocket you intended.

Photograph 2-8

Photograph 2-9

Photograph 2–10

Photograph 2-11

Photograph 2-12

Photograph 2-13

Photograph 2-14

Photograph 2-15

Photograph 2-16

Photograph 2-17

Photograph 2-18

Photograph 2-19

Photograph 2-20

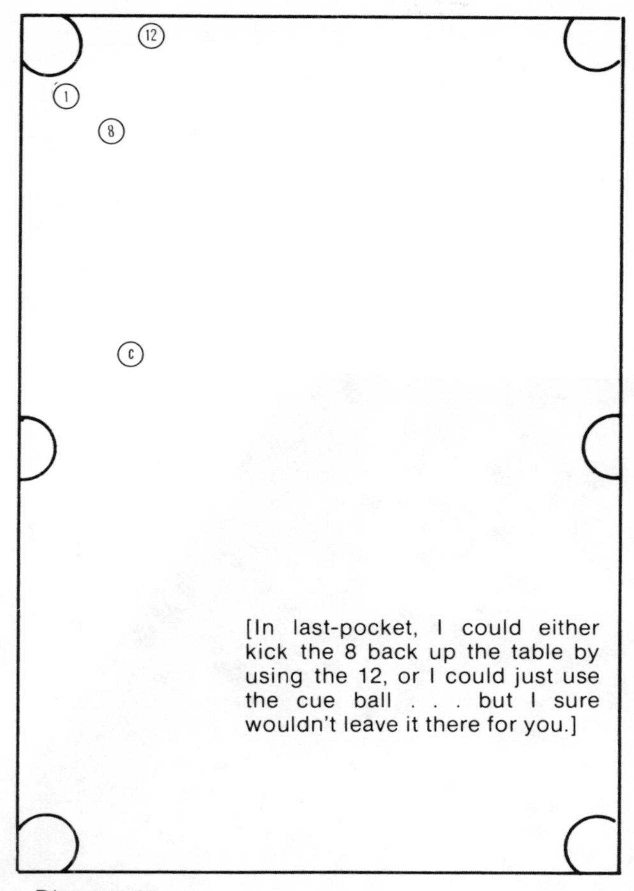

12
1
8
C
[In last-pocket, I could either kick the 8 back up the table by using the 12, or I could just use the cue ball . . . but I sure wouldn't leave it there for you.]

Diagram 85

Diagram 85 shows you what I mean. If you had just missed that 1-ball and left me nothing I liked from among my remaining stripes, you can be sure that I'd move that 8-ball up to the other end of the table. The most you could expect then would be a tough bank shot on the 8, once you pocketed your 1 where you originally missed it. In the diagram, note that I could move the 8 either with one of my own object balls, or I could use the cue ball directly; and naturally, I'd take appropriate cautionary measures to be sure that I didn't accidentally sink the 8 someplace, which would cost me the game. So even though you *appear* to have the upper hand in the game of Diagram 85, it isn't necessarily that way at all.

It's even worse to make your last object ball and then miss the 8. Unless you leave it *very* close to the pocket where you aimed it, leaving you without a second opportunity is quite a simple matter; it requires only reasonable thinking and care on your opponent's part.

And whatever else you do, do *not* formulate a sequence that saves your last object ball and the 8-ball for a side pocket (unless both balls represent absolutely cinch shots that you can be 100 percent sure of making the first time). If you make your last object ball in a side (or if your opponent manages to make it there for you legally, a smart but rare move) and then fail to make the 8, Helen Keller could play you safe for the rest of the game. Which, of course, gets back to your vulnerability once those last two balls are left.

If the shoe is on the other foot, and it's your opponent who has failed to get out, your first priority should be defense rather than offense. Try to win the game yourself, sure, but choose patterns that shut your opponent out in the event of a miss. Most last-pocket games allow you and your opponent to go for the same pocket if you both happen to sink your last object balls there; in that case, it becomes increasingly tougher to play your opponent safe, since you're trying for precisely the same kind of position. So choose shots that you can be sure of.

That situation produces some of the longest last-pocket games, simply because each player is afraid to leave his opponent anything. So the two bunt the 8-ball around defensively; or if either player does get a shot, he'll probably hit it with some extra speed to make sure the thing doesn't stick around if it misses. Another long defensive struggle situation occurs where one player is going for a corner at the foot of the table and his opponent wants the opposite corner pocket at the head of the table. The game then becomes something like one-pocket with the table turned sideways, and in that case I think you'll see a lot more games that are not won by one player as much as they are lost by the other.

Photograph 2-21

Photograph 2-22

Photograph 2-23

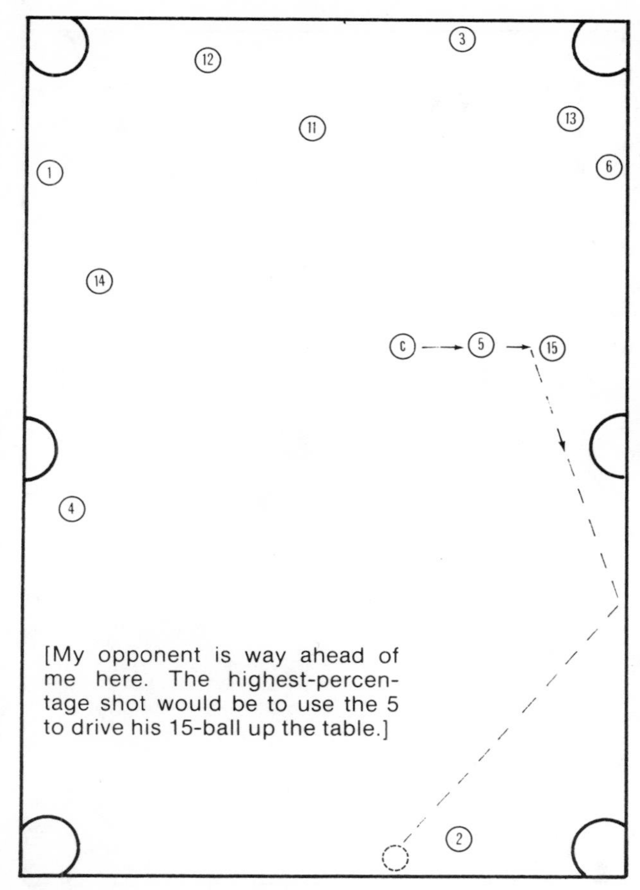

[My opponent is way ahead of me here. The highest-percentage shot would be to use the 5 to drive his 15-ball up the table.]

Diagram 86

Alabama Eight-Ball

In this game, the player shooting the solid balls is required to make his 1-ball into a side pocket, and his opponent must pocket his 15-ball in the opposite side pocket. The players may agree before the game as to which side pocket gets which ball, or they may simply play first-come, first-serve, with the player who pockets his side-pocket ball last being required to take the side pocket in which his opponent did not score. If the 1 or 15 is pocketed anywhere else, it is respotted at once and the shooter's inning ends.

Again, this game favors the better straight-pool player. Making your ball in the side pocket first makes you a considerable favorite to win the game, and you should plan a sequence that lets you do that as early as you possibly can. The longer you let it go, the fewer object balls you have available to lead you logically to a side-pocket shot. And as before, saving your side-pocket shot for last is absolutely suicidal.

In fact, if your opponent gets his 1 or 15 out near a side pocket, you should immediately begin looking for moves that will clear that ball out of there, even if it means passing up a chance to score yourself. Presumably, you're playing by rules that prohibit you from shooting directly at your opponent's ball; but you can use your own object balls to accomplish the same thing, and naturally your opportunities for such a move are at their greatest early in the game, when most of your object balls are still available.

Even though shots are available to me in Diagram 86, I'd be much wiser to play one of my object balls into my opponent's 15 and drive it where it can't be pocketed in the side. My 1-ball is not readily available for pocketing in the side, or else I'd choose a more aggressive sequence. But in the layout you see, my opponent definitely has the edge, and I want to take that edge away.

In racking the balls for Alabama, incidentally, the 1 and 15 balls should occupy the slots immediately behind the 8-ball.

The Bar-Table Game

Bar pool is really a game unto itself, and it has its own following too. You see nine-ball played on the smaller, coin-operated tables, and occasionally two very good players will square off for bar-table one-pocket, but eight-ball is easily the predominant game. Bar-pool leagues are proliferating around the country, and eight-ball is the only game played.

Many competent players on regulation tables cross over to a bar table and promptly get their clocks cleaned. You will not see the reverse of that occurring very often, because bar players are generally far more aware of how different their game really is. Many of them would be mediocre at best on a standard table, but almost all of them are smart enough to know that.

You hear about some pretty impressive scores being run up over bar-pool games, too. Frankly, playing pool for stakes with a stranger in a bar is my idea of tugging on Superman's cape, but I'll leave that up to you.

As for the game itself, what you have is 15 standard-size object balls occupying, typically, 16 square feet *less* space than they would on a regulation table (most bar tables are 3½′ × 7′; the regulation pool table is 4½′ × 9′). So it gets *awfully* crowded, and cue ball control becomes your most valuable ally by far.

And that brings us to the cue ball. The coin-operated nature of the game makes it mandatory that the cue ball be of a different size than the object balls; that way, pocketed object balls stay down, but a scratched cue ball comes back to the players. And that size imbalance makes a world of difference in the game.

To begin with, it takes a really expert stroke to draw the cue ball. Since the cue ball is bigger, the object balls offer less mass to absorb the force of your stroke; in addition, you're contacting those object balls at a point above their horizontal axis, and all that can make backspin pretty scarce. On all shots, the cue ball's momentum will tend to carry it through the object balls, and you must adjust your game accordingly.

I'm not saying that the cue ball *can't* be drawn on a bar table, but I do think you'll find it considerably harder. It would be much more practical to plan sequences of follow-English or stop-ball shots (the latter is considerably easier than drawing the cue ball). And since you have all those balls in that little space, you can count on negotiating lots of B-balls and C-balls too. As in conventional eight-ball, you'll be able to think out some sort of correct sequence; but you can generally count on several turns at the table for both you and your opponent. If a player runs out from the break against you, you can be certain that it wasn't dumb luck.

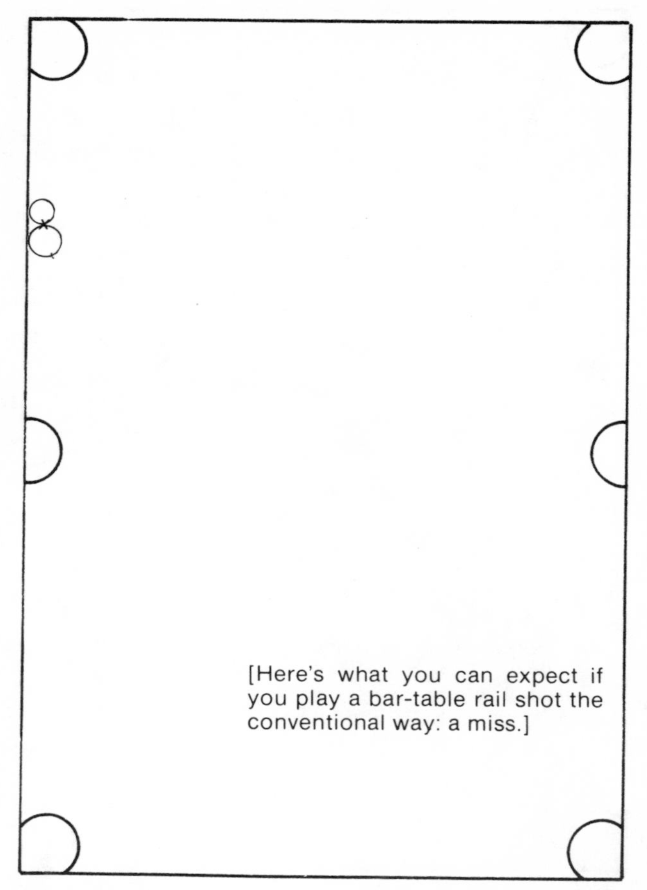
[Here's what you can expect if you play a bar-table rail shot the conventional way: a miss.]
Diagram 87

Also, with that outsized cue ball, shots where the cue ball is frozen to a rail are a completely thankless proposition. You'll see some *very* good players stopped by this kind of shot, or they may play around it completely.

Diagram 87 shows you why. Since the cue ball is larger than the object ball, the correct point of aim is no longer that point at which the cue ball touches the rail and the object ball at the same time. That will only deliver the point of contact marked X, and that point is not going to pocket the ball for you.

An advanced bar-table player will solve the problem as you see in Diagram 88: hit

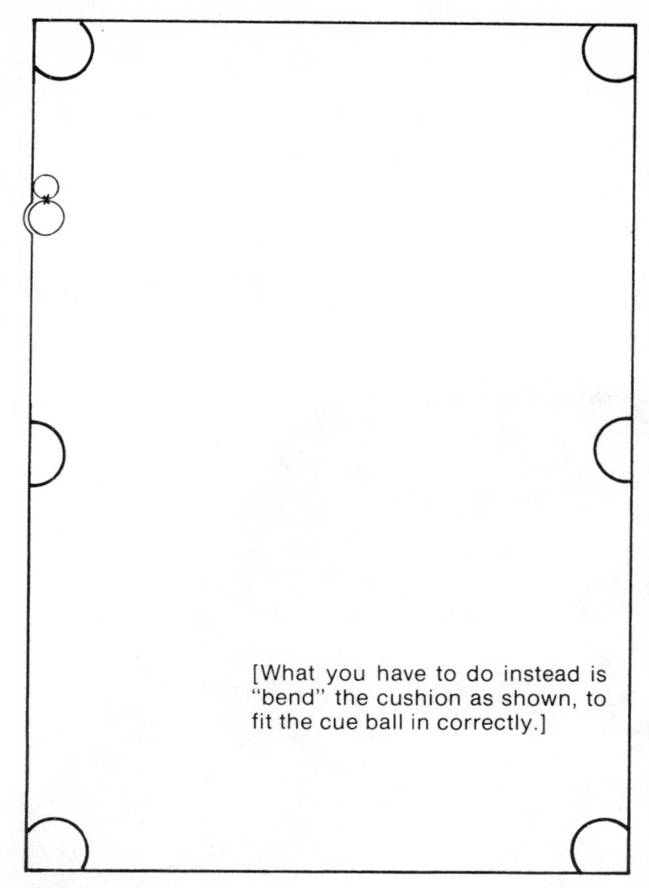

[What you have to do instead is "bend" the cushion as shown, to fit the cue ball in correctly.]

Diagram 88

the rail a hair in front of the object ball, with added speed, so the cue ball can contact the object ball at the same time it's being absorbed by the rail. Not easy, but you can learn to do this.

The good news concerning the bar-pool game is that within the past few years, that outsized white rock is becoming harder to find. Lots of proprietors have opted instead for a cue ball that still differs in size from the object balls, but not nearly as markedly. It's bigger, so every aspect of the game we've talked about here must be kept in mind; but with practice, you'll find that bar eight-ball can be mastered along more conventional lines. Your first objective should be to check the size of the cue ball available to you. Whatever the case, your success at the bar-table game depends on your abilitv to simplify things for yourself. In that sense, and probably only in that sense, bar-table pool becomes akin to all other pool forms.

Two for You to Solve

Just as we did in straight pool, let's see how you would think your way through these two racks of eight-ball. In each case, you have your choice of stripes or solids; and just for an extra tad of discipline, assume that in the second photo, the game is last-pocket too. My solutions follow the photos.

Photo 2–24 might have fooled you somewhat. If you chose the solids, you'd have your choice of four very easy shots to begin with (the 1, 2, 5, and 7); and indeed, a competent player could win this game outright shooting either stripes or solids. I chose stripes here, even though my opening shot, the 9-ball, is slightly tougher than any of those solids. Still, once the 9 is gone, the rest of the stripes arrange themselves in a quite logical sequence, and in my opinion, the 15 and 12 offer better keys to the 8-ball than any combination of solids. As Photos 2–26 through 2–32 show you, the winning sequence (after the 9-ball) is 10-11-14-13-15-12-8 in corner.

Similarly, Photo 2–25 shows you two easy shots on striped balls (the 15 and 14) to get you started. But solids offer a better long-range proposition, especially for last-pocket. I'd get those long shots out of the way first (the 2 and 4 balls, Photos 2–33 and 2–34), and the rest is really pretty smooth sailing. The complete sequence, Photos 2–33 through 2–39, is 2-4-5-1-3-7-6-8 in the same corner as the 6. Again, any other progression you saw that would work, in either of these two racks, is just as valid as mine.

Photograph 2-24

Photograph 2-26

Photograph 2-27

Photograph 2-28

Photograph 2-29

Photograph 2-30

Photograph 2-31

Photograph 2-32

Photograph 2-25

Photograph 2-33

Photograph 2-34

Photograph 2-35

Photograph 2-36

Photograph 2-37

Photograph 2-38

Photograph 2-39

3 Advanced Nine-Ball

Nine-ball is a shotmakers' delight.

To be sure, there are finesses to the game, especially when two good players get together; you'll see safeties, snookers, and especially carom shots. But it's still basically a game of shotmaking. That's why kids take to the game so well. They're able to both pocket the ball *and* move their cue ball all over the table; successful nine-ball is no more than a combination of those two abilities.

The game has a pressure all its own, too. With the exception of tournament play, nine-ball is just about senseless to play in the absence of stakes, and you'll find an uncommon number of players who can clear the first eight balls with consummate genius and then have trouble dropping the 9 into the Grand Canyon. Ring-around-the-collar not only grows here but flourishes. Correct me if I'm wrong, but I can think of no other form of *any* sport where you can do the majority of scoring and still lose.

There isn't much I can do for either your shotmaking skill or your attitude about that lone money ball. Since the game begins with a free break, as eight-ball does, there is no such thing as a typical pattern either. Nine-ball demands that your cue ball do some traveling, far more than in other pool games. And the A-B-C-D categorizing of object balls won't work, because you don't have that kind of choice going for you here; your shot must begin with the lowest-numbered ball.

So nine-ball is pretty much apart from other pool games. There are a goodly number of players, especially in the South, who play nothing else. But the game does offer certain principles that you can learn, and they'll enhance your game considerably if you can bring the necessary physical tools, shotmaking and the ability to move your cue ball with control.

HOW TO BREAK

You hit the break shot precisely as you do for eight-ball: Start from dead center of the string, and hit the head ball—the 1-ball—right on the nose. But the break in nine-ball is more formidable than in eight-ball, something you might want to remember when making the break part of any handicap-game proposition.

As you probably know by now, the balls are racked as in Diagram 89, diamond-fashion, with the 9 in the middle, and the 1 up front. But see those areas of contact marked "X"? They represent the caroms between the balls that flank the 9 and the two balls just behind it. Now those caroms do not line up for either corner pocket; in fact, if you inspect a nine-ball rack before breaking, and find all balls correctly frozen to each other, the caroms in question would appear to have those outermost balls heading to a point at least half a diamond away from the pocket.

So how come those two balls to either side of the 9 are the balls most frequently pocketed on the break?

Well, the fact is that the rack may well *not* have all balls frozen. As we noted in the straight pool chapter, it's simply not that easy to do on a frequently used table, because the balls tend to settle into low spots in the cloth. And any air within the rack will restructure those two caroms for you.

On the other hand, those two outermost balls can be made out of a perfect rack too—if your hit on the rack is perfect, which isn't quite as easy as you think. This is another peculiarity of nine-ball, arising out of the unique way in which the balls are racked. I can't tell you why the following should be true, from any legitimate standpoint of physics, but it is: The top six balls of a nine-ball rack, when perfectly struck, tend to stay together for a fraction of a second before they begin to mushroom. That fraction of a second is enough time for the balls to move to a point where the "X" caroms are aimed considerably closer to the pockets than they were. But this effect, remember, takes place only when you hit the 1 absolutely dead center, so you'll need accuracy as well as force.

Thus you can score out of an imperfect rack or a perfect one, with those outermost balls, and you have seven other balls in some kind of flight too, vastly increasing your providential possibilities. A good nine-ball player absolutely *expects* to score on the break, and it would probably be a good idea for you to stop thinking of this phase of the game as sheer luck.

Diagram 89

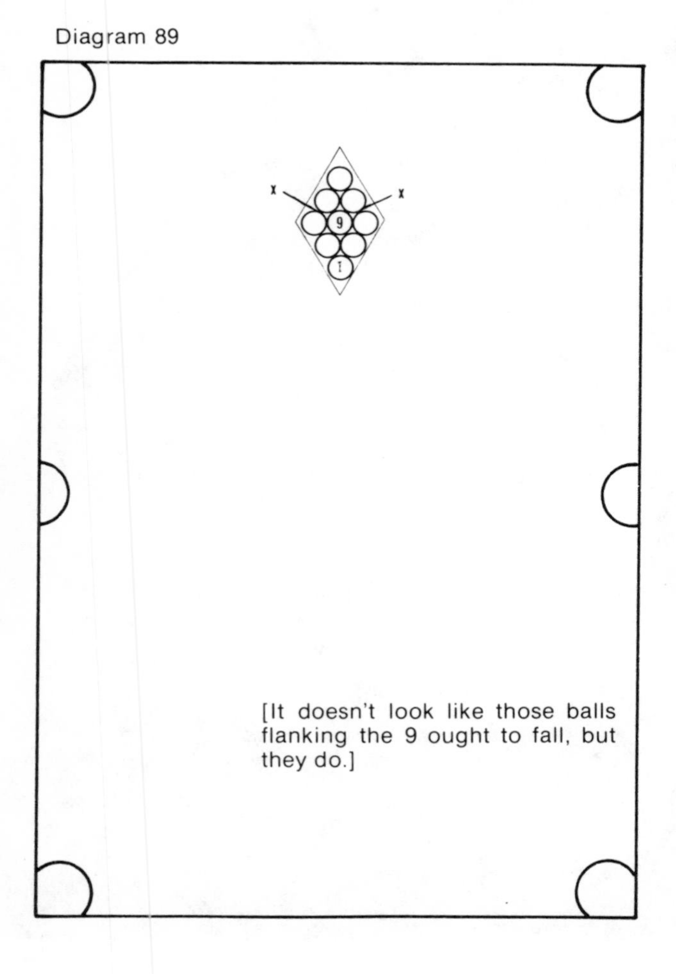

[It doesn't look like those balls flanking the 9 ought to fall, but they do.]

Again, I advise all the speed you can *control,* rather than all you can produce. In an ideal break, just as in eight-ball, your cue ball should limp back to center table and suffer cardiac arrest there.

PLAYING THE GAME

Nine-ball rules do not vary as widely as those of eight-ball, but they do vary, especially as to the fate of object balls behind the string after a player's scratch. However you and your opponent choose to play, let's assume that if either of you fails to contact the lowest-numbered ball first, the opponent may opt to have the errant shooter fire again if he prefers that to trying the resulting shot himself. It's the only fair way to play.

Now running nine balls in rotation is not wildly difficult to do, and when good players are in action, nine-ball is frequently won right from the break. This is more a function of the players' skill than it is testimony that nine-ball is an easy game. It is not. In the random breaking of the balls, stymies to running out the complete game will occur a lot more often than you think, considering that you're blasting a mere nine-ball rack to smithereens out over all that green. No one keeps statistics on this, but I would estimate that when two intermediate players play nine-ball, the remaining balls after the break create sequential problems at least half the time. Those problems take the form of multiple balls along the same rail, miniclusters, or balls blocking the path of other balls to a

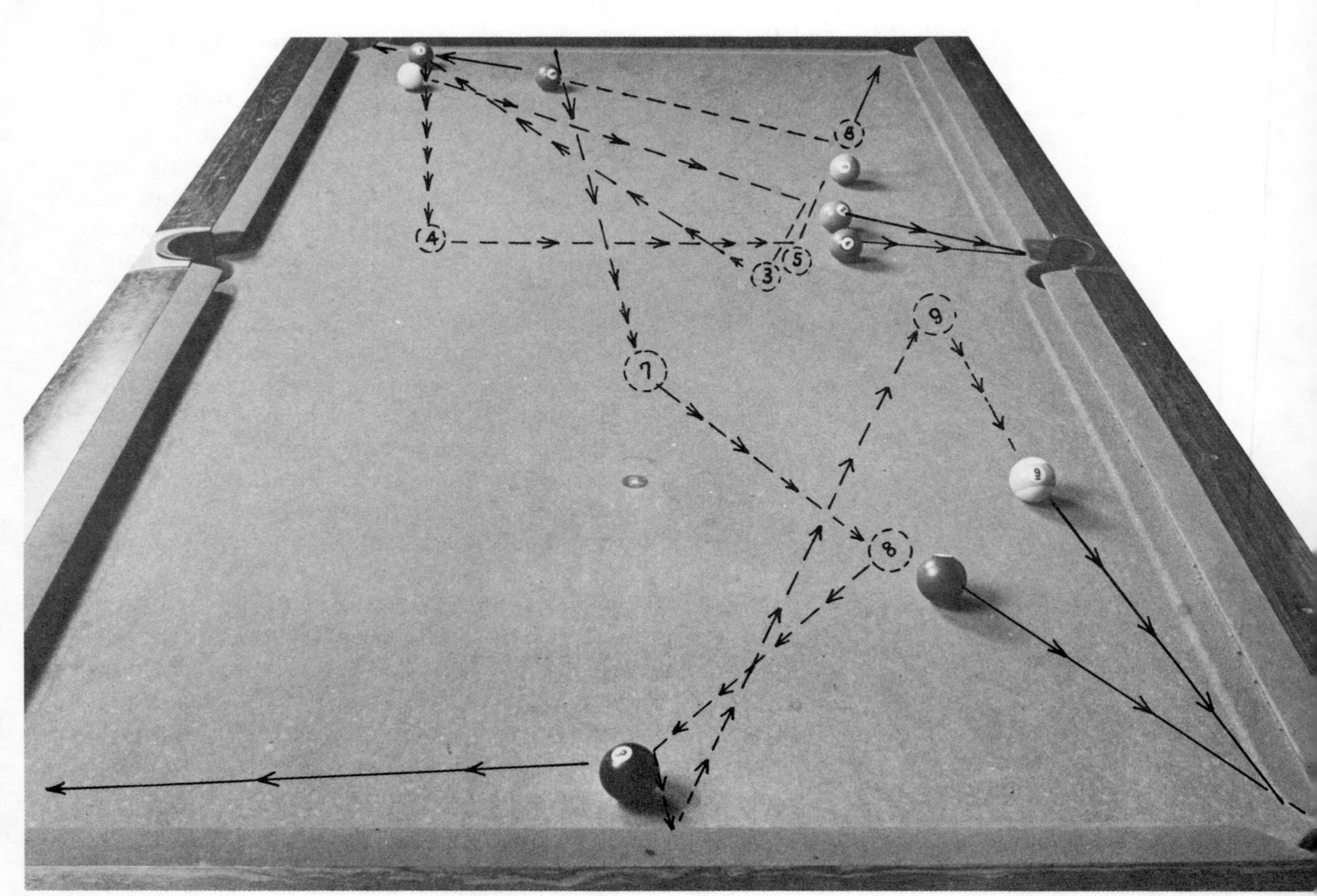

Photograph 3-1

logical pocket so that what you have is a long, quite improbable combination shot.

Not even the best players can convert such problems to run-out opportunities all the time. But once the balls are broken, you'll very seldom see a good player choose to blast away and trust his luck. Instead he'll think something out, and so should you.

Let's examine some open racks first, racks in which the balls are pocketable in rotation as they lie. Then we'll take a look at some of the more common problems. Keep in mind that I'm still advocating the minimum force necessary to get the job done, as well as all your w. p.'s; but the game of nine-ball simply (a) requires added force on a sound majority of shots; and (b) offers mandatory sequences that will make most if not all of your "Whenever Possibles" impossible.

Photos 3–1, 3–2, and 3–3 show you three nine-ball layouts, with the correct cue ball path in each case indicated by the dotted line, the object-ball paths by solid lines. Photo 3–1 is self-explanatory, a simple exercise in the making of eight relatively simple shots plus as little cue ball movement as we can get away with and still get the job done.

In Photo 3–2, though, note that the 7 and 8-balls form an off-angle yet pocketable combination shot. The reason we don't play it that way goes back to straight pool: It involves an uncertainty. A good player could probably make the 8 and still control the 7 so it would be pocketable next, but he

Photograph 3-2

can't be certain where it will be. Further, notice that the 5 and 6 balls lie in advantageous positions to put us on the 7-ball; if those balls were up at the head end of the table instead, we well might have to play the combination.

Even though that 7-ball could be made in the side pocket, we play position to shoot it in the corner. A good player will seldom play position for a side-pocket shot when the opportunity exists to play position for the same ball in a corner, because the angles are far wider and his cue ball control will be far less inhibited.

Those same principles of position options carry over to Photo 3–3. We play for the 2 in the corner, not the side, and we hit that thin cut shot on the 1 just as we would in straight pool: soft, maybe even with a little reverse English to help hold the cue ball. Notice that on the 3, and especially on the 8, we can choose either no-rail routes or routes that involve a rail to help us get where we're going next. I chose a one-rail route between the 3 and 4, despite what w. p. 5 says, because that makes moving the cue ball easier. Ditto the 8-ball. If I had left the 8-ball straight with the cue ball, I'd have to draw the cue ball the length of the table; I'm capable of that, and so are you, but it's actually much simpler to stroke the cue ball at seven o'clock with a firm draw stroke and come off that side rail. Other players might opt to leave their cue ball close to the side rail following the 7-ball and play the 8-ball so as to use *two* rails to get back down the table. I

Photograph 3–3

wouldn't choose to do that, because that's not the way. I like to hit the cue ball, but that doesn't necessarily make it wrong. Nobody knows your stroke, and how you feel comfortable moving the cue ball, better than you.

Naturally, you should always try to run out the game when the layout of the balls dictates that that's possible. But they will frequently not do that, and what nine-ball does have in common with straight pool is that you generally strive to do whatever's easiest. Let's look at some examples.

Consider Diagram 90, with the 4-ball behind the 7-ball on the same rail. The position of the 1, 2, and 3-balls dictates against your being able to move the 7 before you get to the 4. So what do you do?

Well, what you *don't* do is go wailing in there between the two balls with all your might and main to see what you might luck in. You don't know exactly where your cue ball or either of those balls are going; for that matter, you don't know what the effect will be on any of the remaining balls. That's way too many uncertainties to make any pool sense.

The solution is really quite simple, as you can see in Diagram 91: Get your cue ball someplace where you can merely *hit* the 4, drive it out of there, and stop your cue ball dead next to the 7. You need only enough speed to be sure of moving the 4 where your opponent can't get to it; you need only enough accuracy to be sure that you don't *make* the 4 someplace, thus becoming a victim of your own snooker (unless, of course, the 5-ball or whatever's next is close at hand to where you leave the cue ball).

Remember, no rule says that you must

Diagram 90: Stuck with this?

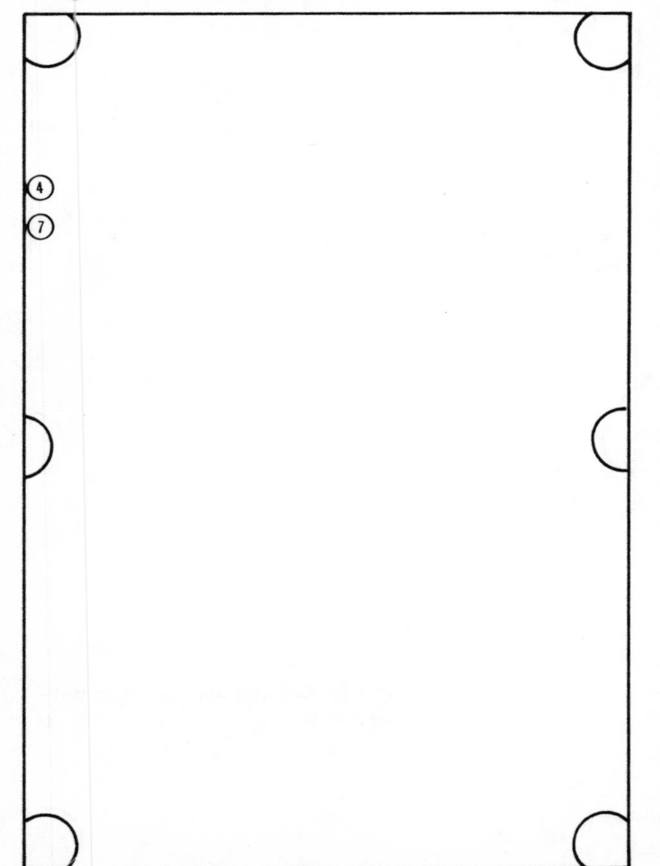

Diagram 91: Stick him with this.

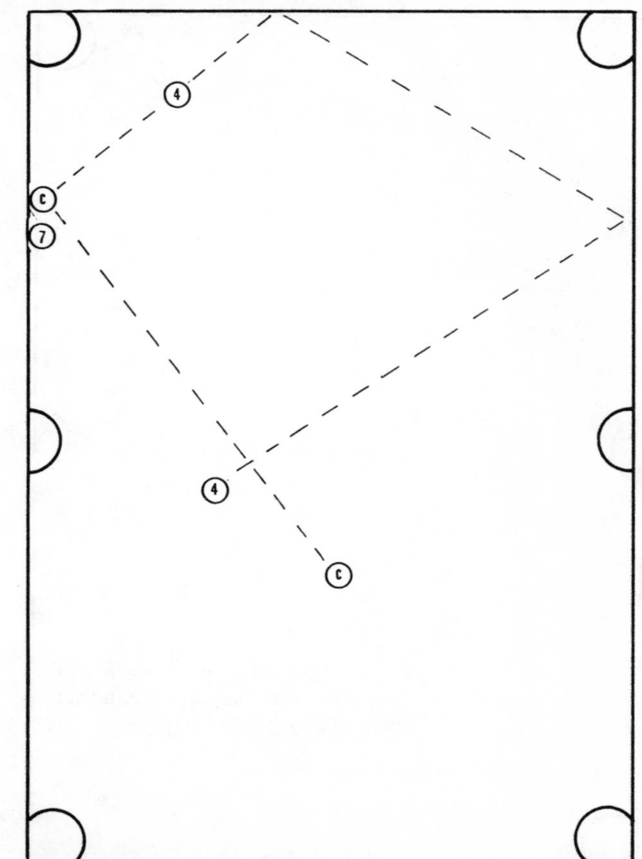

run out a rack of nine-ball in your only turn at the table. You don't get paid anything extra for doing so. And when you play good defense like this, you're doing everything you can to ensure that you'll be back at the table shortly if not directly. Be patient. You can certainly afford to wait for your next turn as long as one inning.

Diagram 92 shows you the same principle in the form of another layout. The 2-ball is pocketable as you see it, but consider (a) you've got a hideous angle to negotiate; (b) you can't be sure where the 1-ball will go for your next shot even if you do make the 2; (c) you'll have to drive your cue ball off two rails for position. Put them all together and they spell high-risk, low probability.

So play the good D instead, as in Diagram 93. Just roll off the side of the 1 and leave your opponent that sorry mess. You may even be able to put icing on the cake and hide the cue ball behind another ball, but even if you don't do that, your opponent is going nowhere fast with the 1 and 2-balls as you see them. If he's smart, he'll try and play *you* safe from there, and any time you can keep a nine-ball opponent playing safeties, you're playing the game right. Never lose sight of this, in nine-ball or any form of pool: *Denying your opponent an open shot is at least as important as making one yourself.*

The stymie of Diagram 94 comes up all the time in nine-ball: One ball blocks the path of another to a logical pocket, and you don't have a chance to play position for the latter ball somewhere else. It's similar to Diagram 92, except that here the balls are farther apart and farther off the rail, resulting in a high-risk combination shot that you

Diagram 92

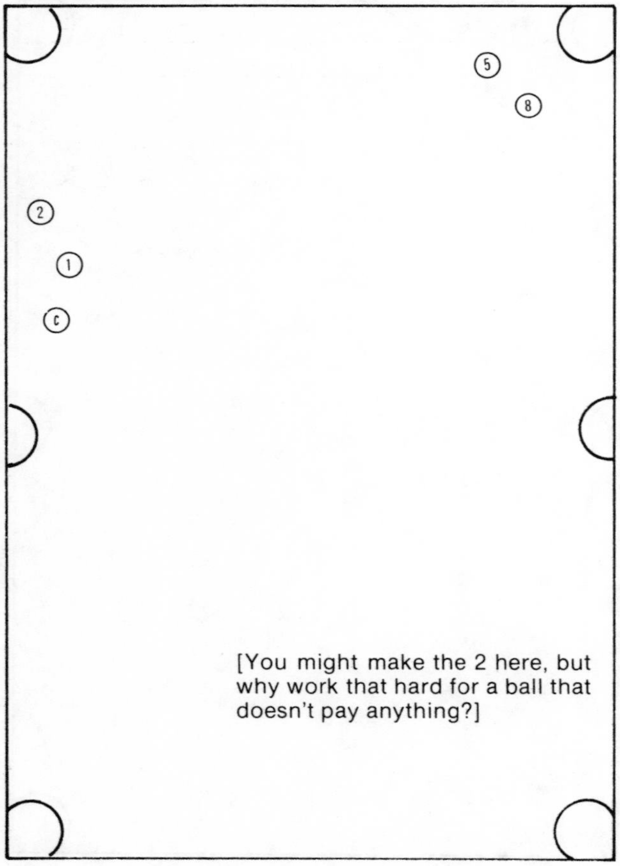

[You might make the 2 here, but why work that hard for a ball that doesn't pay anything?]

Diagram 93

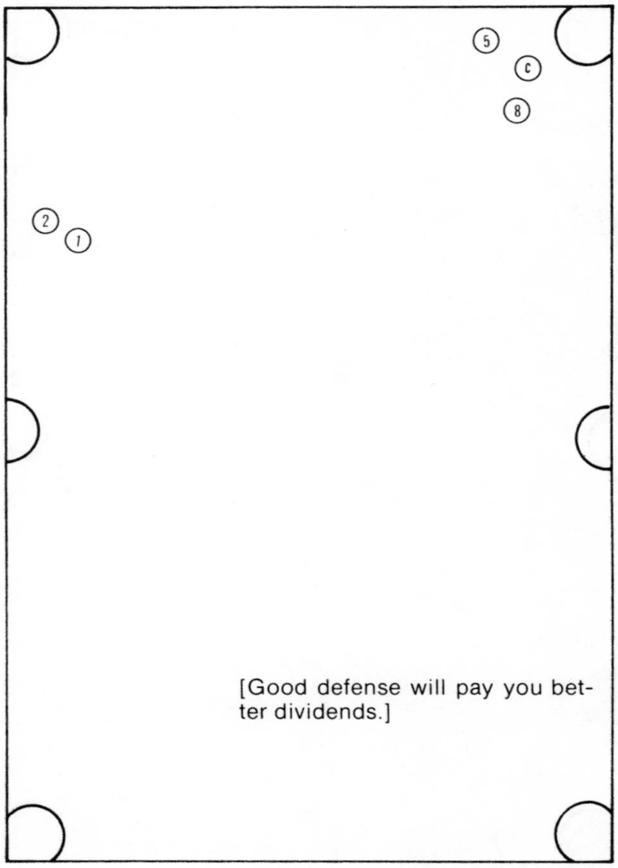

[Good defense will pay you better dividends.]

don't want anything to do with at all.

What you want to do is convert the ball that's working against you into one that works for you instead. Hide the 2-ball behind the 5, as in Diagram 95. All it takes to accomplish this is a soft roll of the cue ball. Even if you don't hide the 2-ball completely, you're just about sure of leaving your opponent safe. And it's light-years ahead of trying that nightmarish combination shot you were left.

Diagram 96 presents you with the same object-ball problem as Diagram 94, but this time the cue ball doesn't even line up for that miserable combination shot. Well, it so happens that this is an even better defensive opportunity for you. The principle is the same—use the second ball for a snooker—but this shot is a little harder to control. Your objective is as you see in Diagram 97:

Diagram 94

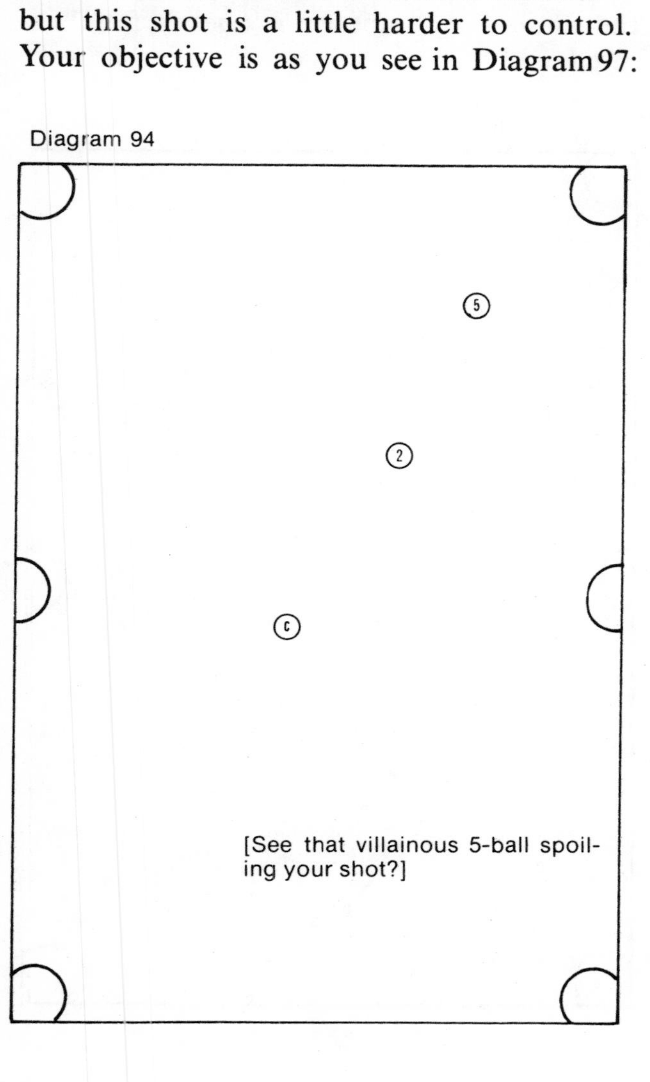

[See that villainous 5-ball spoiling your shot?]

Diagram 95

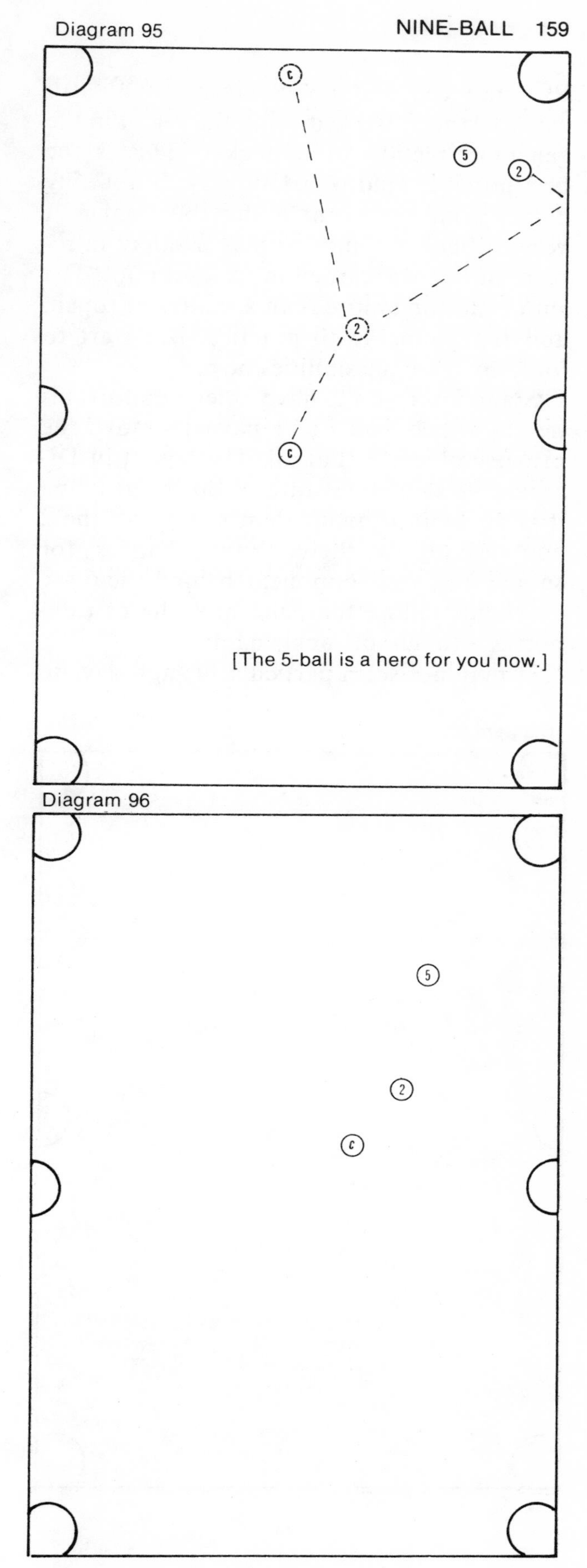

[The 5-ball is a hero for you now.]

Diagram 96

Roll the cue ball up as close as you can get it to the 5, while driving the 2-ball in the general direction of a pocket. This is the best possible kind of safety play: It not only denies your opponent a shot but makes it very difficult for him to play a safety in return, just as we learned in straight pool. The shot is nothing more than a matter of touch, and that comes with practice. But start to look for these possibilities now.

Sometimes you'll have safety opportunities in which you don't have to move the primary object ball at all. The layout in Diagram 98 is without future. But negotiating it is no more difficult than rolling off the 2 and leaving it there. Your chances for snookering your opponent behind the 6 are excellent; failing that, the most he can expect is a tough, off-angle bank.

It may not seem particularly aggressive to you, the notion of playing nine-ball defensively like this; but that's what I mean when I stress how mental a game pool really is. Good defensive play, in nine-ball or anywhere else, is simply another, much more effective way of playing to win. Get over that temptation to blast balls witlessly all over the table to see what might fall. I know it looks like fun to do that, but I think you'll find winning to be just as satisfying.

Caroms

The object of nine-ball is to sink the 9-ball. That's a concept that even the Jukes family could grasp. But since there are no guarantees that I know of that the 9-ball will fall every single time you try to move it, you will find it beneficial to move the 9-ball with the notion of "Suppose it doesn't fall?" in mind.

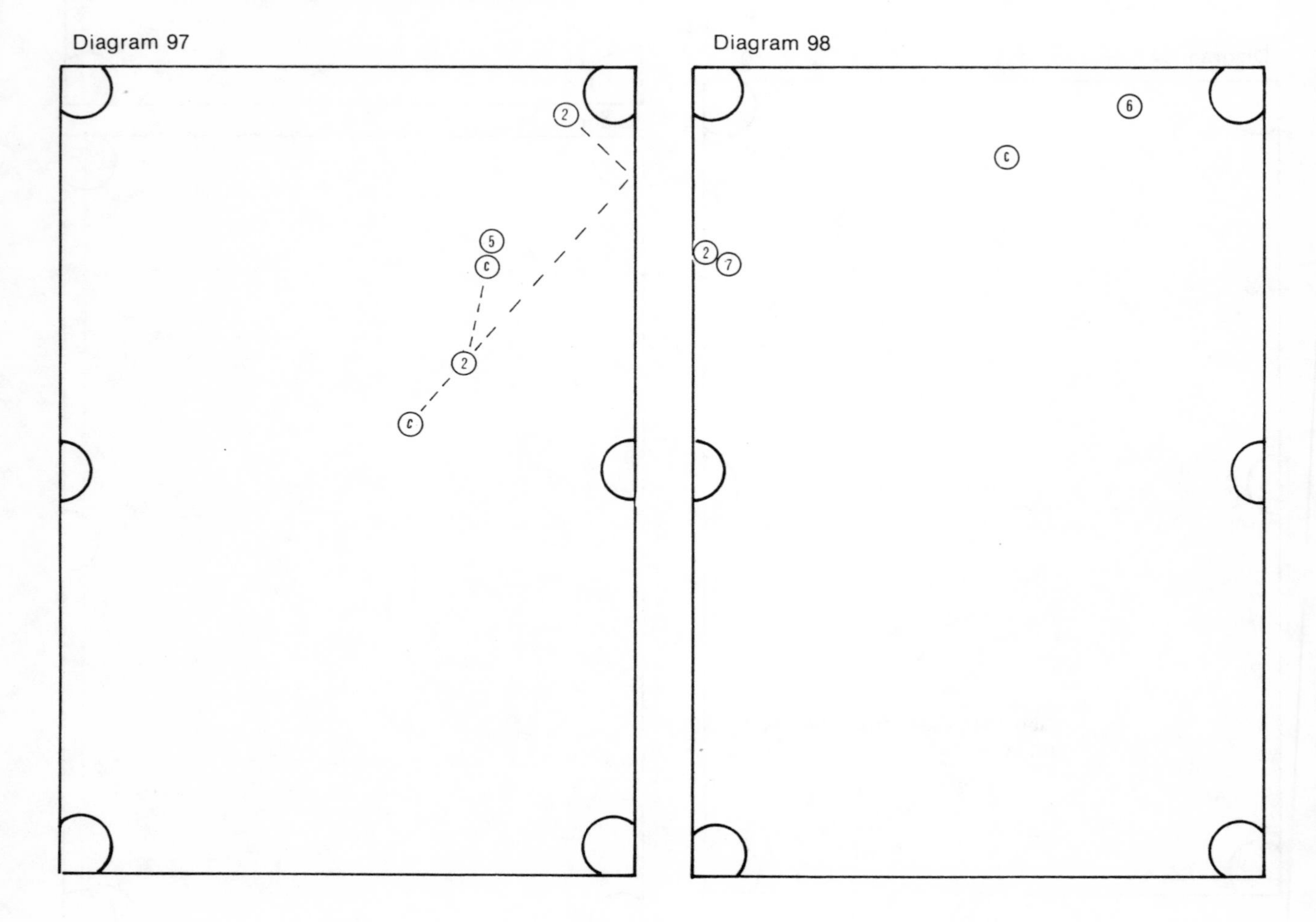

Enter the noble carom, an intimidating offensive maneuver that offers you (a) a reasonable, sensible chance of sinking the 9-ball and (b) a fail-safe chance to destroy the relationship between the 9-ball and the object ball you began with.

That last point is quite important, and Diagram 100 shows you what I have in mind. You *could* make the 9 by shooting the 1 into it; but it's a thin cut, made considerably tougher by the fact that you're dealing with two object balls instead of one. And if you *don't* sink the 9, you'll leave it in the vicinity of that corner pocket (unless you clobber the shot, which further reduces your chances of making it), with the 1 still between the cue ball and the 9. It's a completely poisonous set of circumstances.

The way you detoxify it is to pass up the combination shot and play a carom instead.

Diagram 99

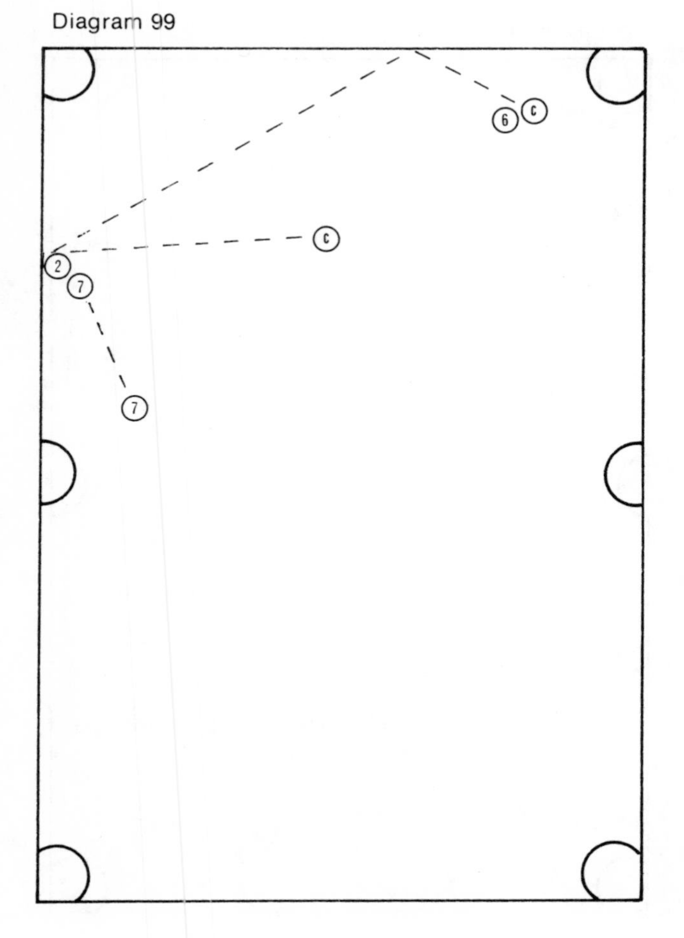

Diagram 100

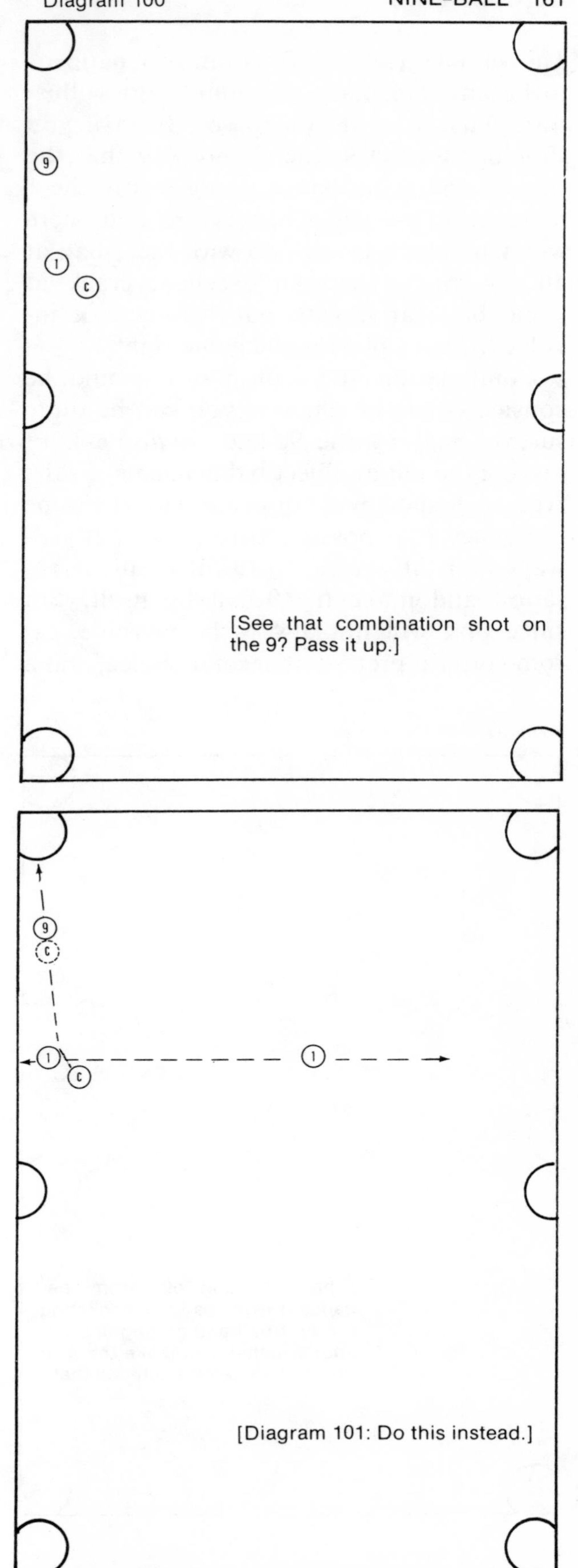

[See that combination shot on the 9? Pass it up.]

[Diagram 101: Do this instead.]

The shot you see in Diagram 101 happens to be an elementary one, but it does illustrate what I want you to see. Even if you should miss the 9, there's no way that the shooter following you is going to use the 1 to make it himself. Chances are that there won't be much he can do with the 1-ball at all. So you've had an excellent crack at game ball early, with hardly any risk involved. That's playing the game right.

Combination shots on the 9 should be considered no-no's unless you can be quite sure of making the 9, and *totally* sure of driving the initial object ball someplace safe. And such shots will not occur with the same frequency that possible caroms will. It's always best, of course, to run the balls in rotation and make the 9-ball by itself. But since that will not always be possible, caroms offer a pretty fair second choice, and a much better one than prayerful combination shots.

Diagrams 102, 103, and 104 show you some other typical carom shots. And good nine-ball players will find some exotic caroms that would never occur to the average player. You'll learn some, too, with experience. For now, it's important that you learn that caroms are generally quite superior to combination shots, and when you should opt for a carom in preference to trying to run the game out. There's a twofold answer to the latter question: You choose a carom either because you're quite sure it can be made; or the layout of the remaining balls indicates that you might as well go for the carom, because there are problems ahead anyway; or both. When the balls are pocketable as they lie, I'd say shoot them that way. But you know your shotmaking

Diagram 102

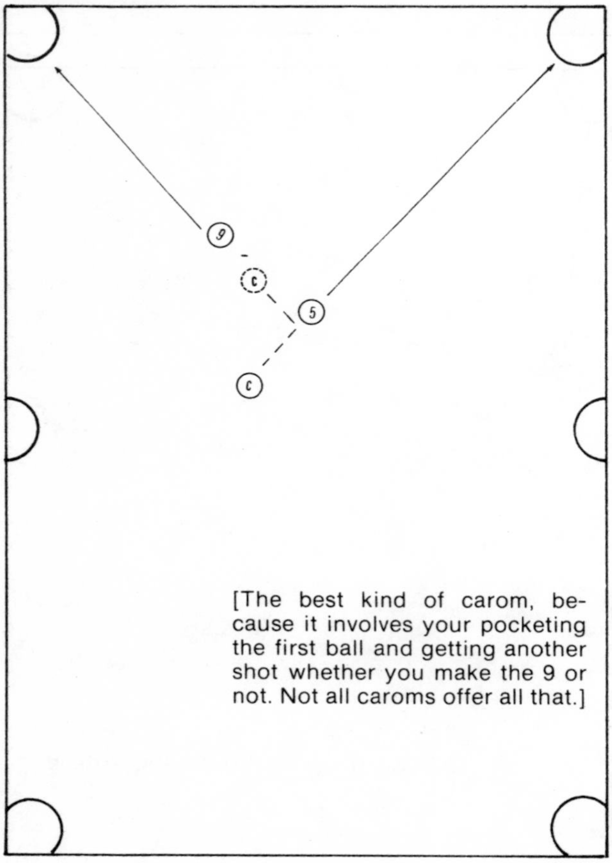

[The best kind of carom, because it involves your pocketing the first ball and getting another shot whether you make the 9 or not. Not all caroms offer all that.]

Diagram 103

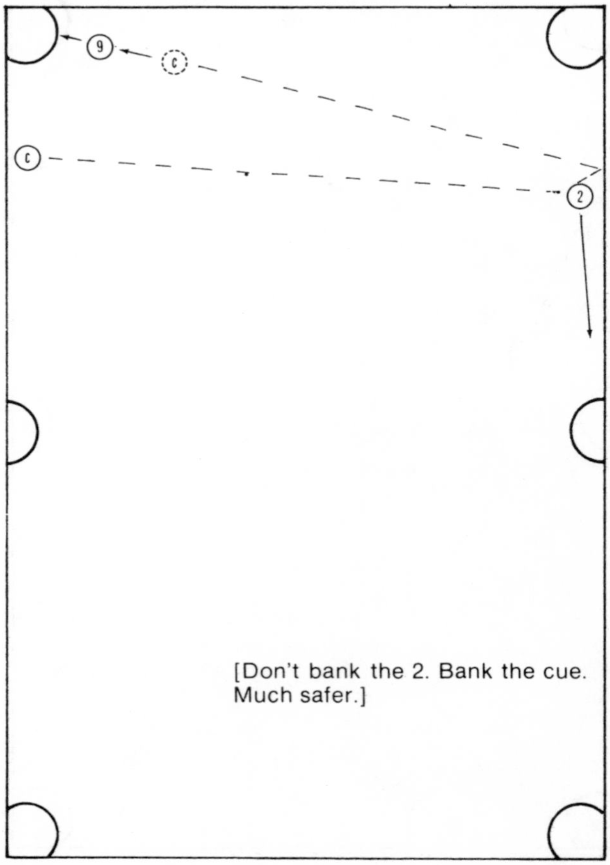

[Don't bank the 2. Bank the cue. Much safer.]

and position-playing abilities better than I do.

Rollouts

With the exception of tournament play, in which you must hit the correct object ball with each shot or else surrender cue-ball-in-hand to your opponent, nine-ball is almost always played with the rollouts rule. That means that if you simply cannot get the cue ball directly to the required object ball, you may roll the cue ball someplace where you can; your opponent then has the option of shooting what you left himself if he likes it, or making you shoot it if he doesn't. He gets cue ball in hand if you miss the right ball twice in a row.

The purpose of the rule is to ensure fair play. If there were no such rule, a player would, in effect, be penalized for his opponent's failure to hit the object ball as required if there were no resulting clear shot. But when good nine-ball players get it on, rollouts are an instrument of strategy as well as justice.

Obviously, the purpose in rolling out is to leave a shot that the shooter thinks he can make and his opponent can't. That is apt to be a pretty thin line, unless the players are far apart in ability. So playing rollouts the right way has a lot to do with what you know about what your opponent can do. If you don't know what he can do, rollouts are as good a way as any to find out.

A good rollout should result in one of two shots: a very long, very thin cut; or a tough, off-angle bank. There is no point in rolling out where your opponent can easily see the same defensive play you do; he'll just take it, and leave you on the defensive. So

Diagram 104

[Here the shooter abandons a chance to sink the 3. If he made the 3, he couldn't make the 9.]

Diagram 105

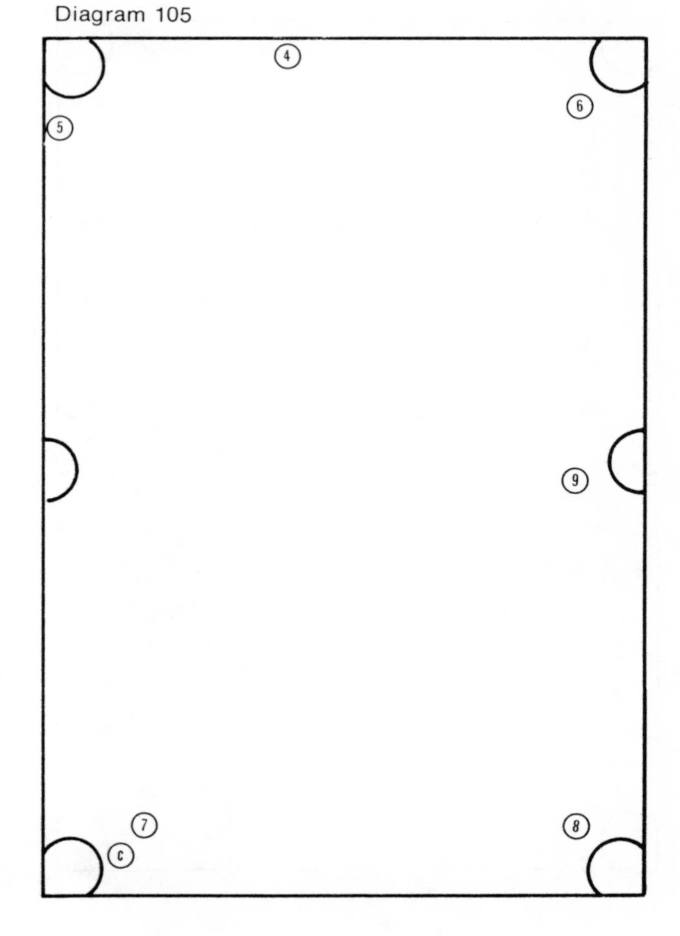

rollouts have an outguessing aspect to them.

Diagram 105 shows you as typical a rollout situation as exists. The 4-ball is clearly the last obstacle to running out the rack, as the rest of the balls are in the clear, but the shooter—let's say he's your opponent—can't get to the 4. So he rolls the cue ball over a few inches, as you see in Diagram 106. The 4-ball is available now, but it's no picnic; it's your choice to let him shoot this or shoot it yourself. What do you choose?

You'd correctly start out by estimating what *he'd* do with it if you elected to let him shoot it. Unless you know for certain that he's left a shot that's way over his head, and is bound to turn the game over to you by even trying that shot, letting him shoot is your weakest alternative. It takes all the control away from you.

Your choices, then, assuming you want this shot, are the same as with any shot in any game: you can cut it in, bank it, or play safe. There are good reasons not to bank this, unless you happen to be very good at bank shots: The 8-ball guards a piece of the pocket you'd naturally bank toward, and besides you can't leave the cue ball on that end rail for a safety if you miss. (You wouldn't want to do that anyway; if the 4-ball did go in, you'd have no position for the 5 except another bank shot.)

Diagram 106

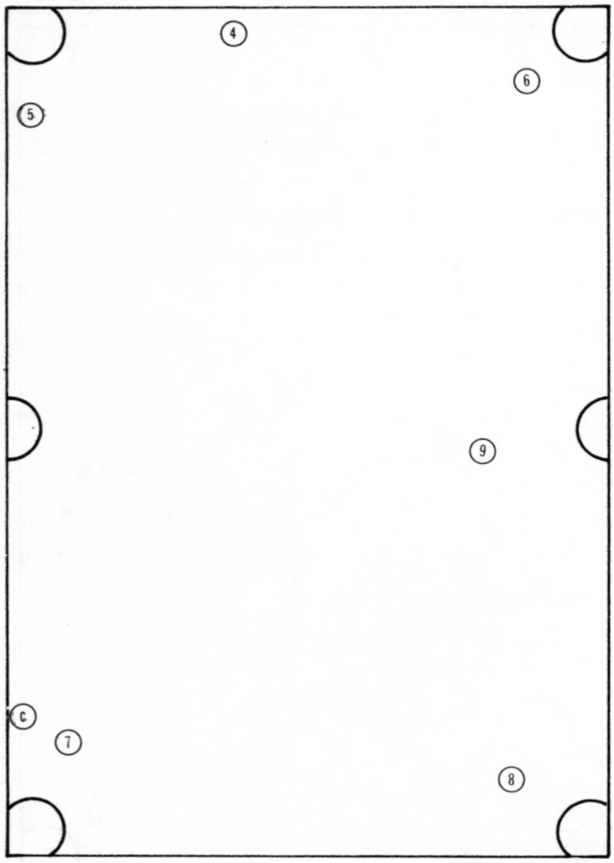

4
6
5
9
C
7
8

Want to cut it in? You know more about whether you're capable of that than I, but let me give you an important tip. On this and all ultrathin cut shots, you should address the cue ball with inside (in this case, right-hand) English. You then deliver a stroke with as little wrist action in it as you can provide. This will cause the cue ball to break the *other* way (left in this case), and make it far easier for you to achieve that thin hit than if you stayed with center-hit on the cue ball. Just be certain you don't stroke such a shot too purely, with wrist snap, because all you'll have then is a ball with a lot of right-hand English on it, and which in fact will curve slightly to the right, or counter to what you want. The shot, correctly struck, is more of a chop than a stroke. And the softer you hit it, the more break in the opposite direction you'll achieve. The technique does take considerable practice, no doubt about it, but it's well worth including in your game.

Another way to accomplish the same thing is to hit your cue ball low, with as exaggerated a follow-through as you can produce. That will keep the cue ball backspinning all the way to the rail, and backspin always enhances the effect of a thin hit.

Or you could elect to play safe off the *right*-hand side of the 4-ball, just feathering it and rolling it a few inches to the left. Again, you should consider your own abilities to cut a ball thin; the play you see in Diagram 107 takes a thin hit, but not as

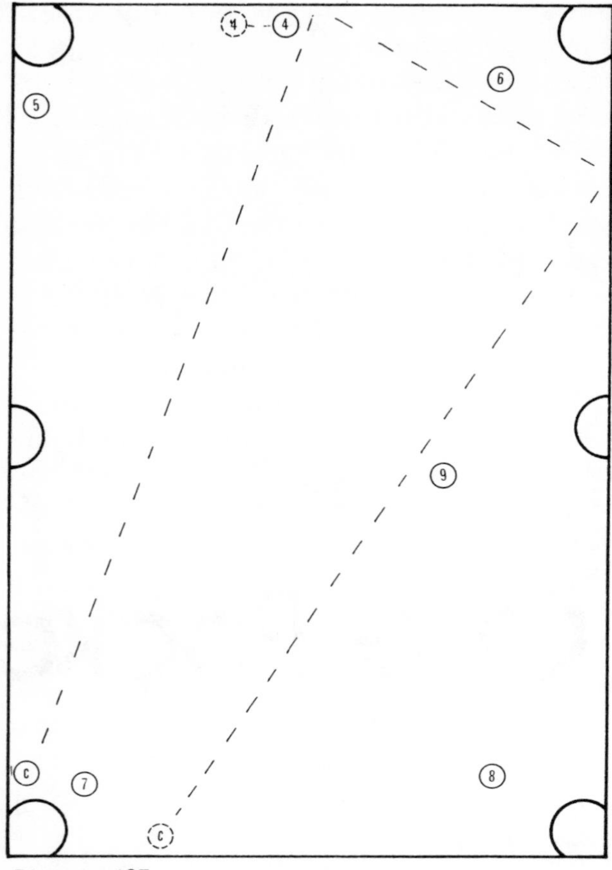

Diagram 107

thin as you'd need to pocket the ball. And your cue ball will travel as you see, back down in the direction of where you were. You need only hit your cue ball smoothly, without excessive speed. The position of the 7-ball ensures that you won't scratch, and even offers a possibility for hiding the cue ball again, just like you started him off with.

In choosing to roll out yourself, as we've already noted, you simply plan a leave that you think you can handle, one way or another, and your opponent can't. In answering your *opponent's* rollout, play to the strengths of your game, and select a shot, either aggressive or defensive, in which you have confidence. Nine-ball is most commonly played for cash, remember, and that's no time for experimenting. Confidence and sound planning are your best safeguards against the rollout situation where you're up the creek if you try shooting it and up the creek if you pass on the shot. Which, of course, is just what a good nine-ball player will try to leave you, insufferable bully that he is.

We'll skip the problem-solving photos this time; we've already had some of that in Photos 3-1, 3-2, and 3-3, and since the game offers you no choice of object balls, sequences tend to dictate themselves. Nine-ball is more a matter of *execution,* plain and simple, than other games. But don't forget to bring your pool brain along. It's a good friend.

4 Advanced One-Pocket

One-pocket, in more ways than one, is something else.

Jack Breit, a Texan by way of New Jersey who has been at the top of the game for a good 15 years, calls it a combination of chess and World War II. The second ingredient he names in his assessment is probably more accurate than the first. In chess, you have only one king, and it stays king the whole game. In one-pocket, any given ball can metamorphose from pawn to king in seconds.

As for the war, your most potent winning weapon is cue ball control. In a typical one-pocket game, you will have an open shot at your pocket perhaps one inning out of three. You'll spend most of the rest of your time driving balls *away* from a pocket—your opponent's pocket, of course—and any time you're not actually trying to sink a shot, what happens to the object ball you do hit is sheer trivia compared to what happens to the white rock.

If you watch good one-pocket at all, be a little analytical about it and you'll see that the game is lost far more often than it's won. Sure, the winning player has to get game ball into his pocket somehow, but he'll be able to do that as a result of the loser's mistakes much more often than he'll be able to create his winning opportunities on his own.

Watching one-pocket, in fact, is probably a better teaching tool than in any other kind of pool game. But you have to combine playing with your watching. There's a world of difference between watching the game when you play it yourself and watching the game when you don't know it. To an uninitiated spectator, the moves of one-pocket are about as clear as Sanskrit.

One of the first aspects of the game that

sets it apart from others (besides the fact that only two out of the six pockets count) is that it almost never attracts beginners. Total nonplayers play the first three games we've discussed (or, more accurately, play *at* them). But rare indeed is the player who comes to one-pocket without some skill in at least one other type of pool game. For that reason, we'll be able to take a look at the game on a reasonably sophisticated plane.

Remember the concentration technique I suggested in the straight pool chapter, about following the cue ball rather than the object ball after contact? I recommend that even more strongly for one-pocket, where it becomes even less mental and more functional. If you can get the cue ball where you want it, the object balls will take care of themselves in a sort of "Will Call" proposition; they'll be somewhere you can go back to and collect them from later. There's nothing radically new about watch-the-cue-ball's-flight; it's nothing more than what balkline billiard players were doing decades ago. But put it to work consistently for you in one-pocket and I think you'll be pleasantly surprised.

HOW TO BREAK

The break is a powerhouse advantage in one-pocket, at least as formidable as the serve in tennis. Obviously, if you never lost on your break, you could never lose a session, assuming you and your opponent were dividing the breaks evenly. But it goes further than that: You'll note a meaningful percentage of one-pocket games in which the incoming shooter never does recover from a really good break. He will be forced into purely defensive moves for the duration of the game, which is apt to be something less than long.

So let's learn how to break the right way. A good break will accelerate your progress in the game even while you're still learning good follow-up moves.

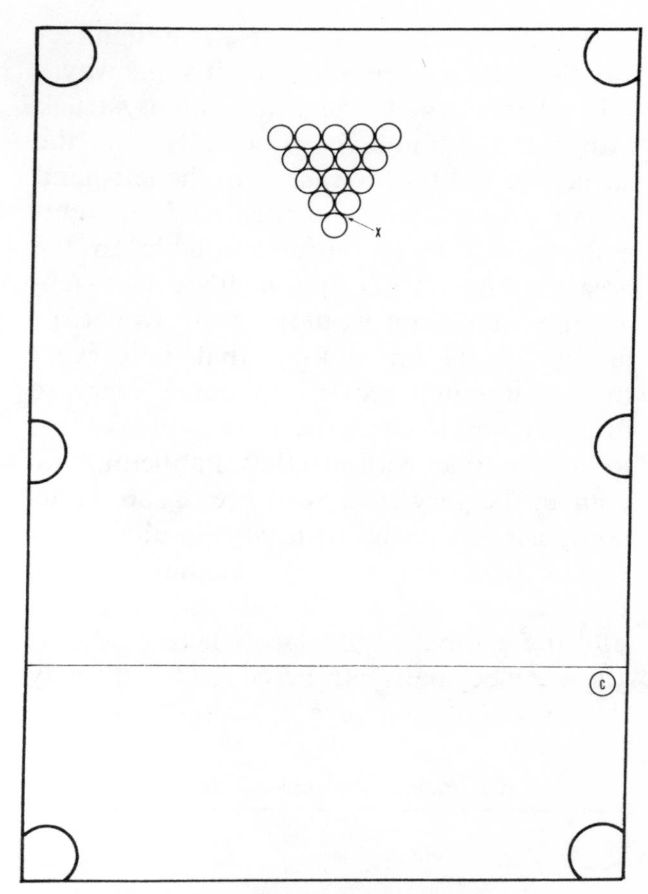

Diagram 108: One-pocket break position.

You start as in Diagram 108. (If you favor the right-hand corner pocket over the left-hand, just reverse everything you see and read.) The cue ball should be as close to the rail as you can place it and still address it with a full, comfortable bridge. Naturally, you check the rack for straightness and tightness first; then, you stroke the ball smoothly, not too hard, and very definitely with inside (left-hand in the diagram) English; you'll see the reason for that English in just a second. Your point of aim is the X you see, between the head ball and the ball just behind it; the catch is to hit the head ball as thin as you can—but you *must* hit it. When you miss the head ball completely, and that does happen, the cue ball goes *through* the side of the stack, rather than *off* it, and turns the break against the breaker. So even though you're aiming for a thin hit on that head ball, allow yourself enough leeway that you're sure of hitting it some way.

Breaks in which the head ball is struck with correct thinness will actually send the far corner ball in the rack *into* the left-hand corner pocket, now and then, and an eight-ball run-out is therefore available to the breaker without his opponent's ever reaching the table. You wouldn't want to bet the family jewels on sinking that ball every time, but you'll see it happening every so often. Completely satisfactory breaks are quite possible without that happening, of course; the very least your break should accomplish is to send at least one object ball to the bottom rail in the vicinity of your pocket, one ball to the side rail similarly, and the cue ball someplace where neither of those object balls can be contacted directly. That's where your reverse English comes in. It helps keep the cue ball close to the side rail, and not too far back up the table.

Occasionally you see more bizarre methods of breaking for one-pocket. Some players like to break as you see in Diagram 109, off that next-to-the-last ball, starting with their cue ball farther off the rail than before. This break moves more object balls than the break of Diagram 108, but it also sends the cue ball farther back up the table, and the object balls moved are usually available in some way to the cue ball for defensive plays. So overall, you'd have to say that this break is less efficient.

Diagram 110 shows you an even more rare break, popular for no apparent reason with black players. You start with the cue ball over on the *other* side of the table, go off the side rail, and into the middle of the right-hand side of the stack. As we noted in

Diagram 109: Another one-pocket break.

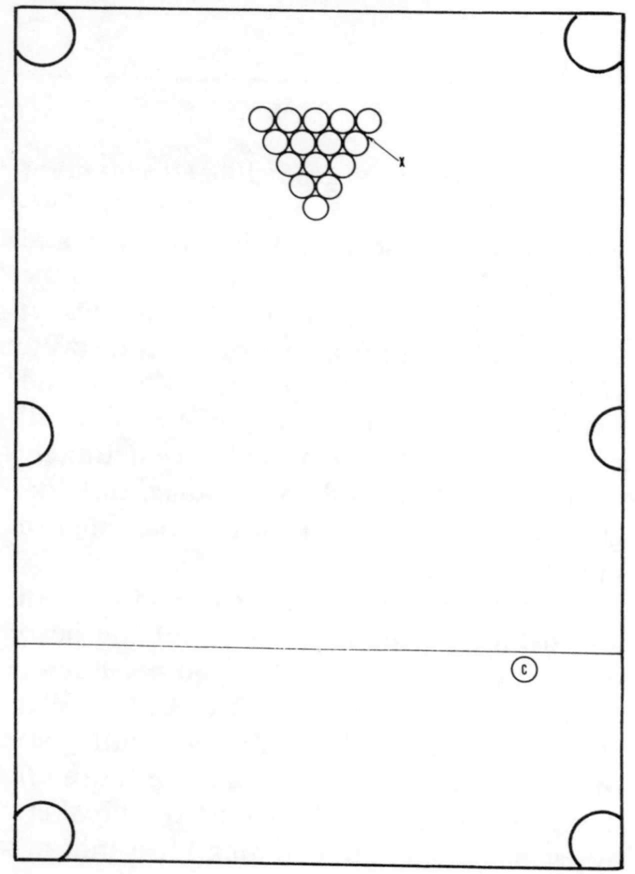

Diagram 110: And one more.

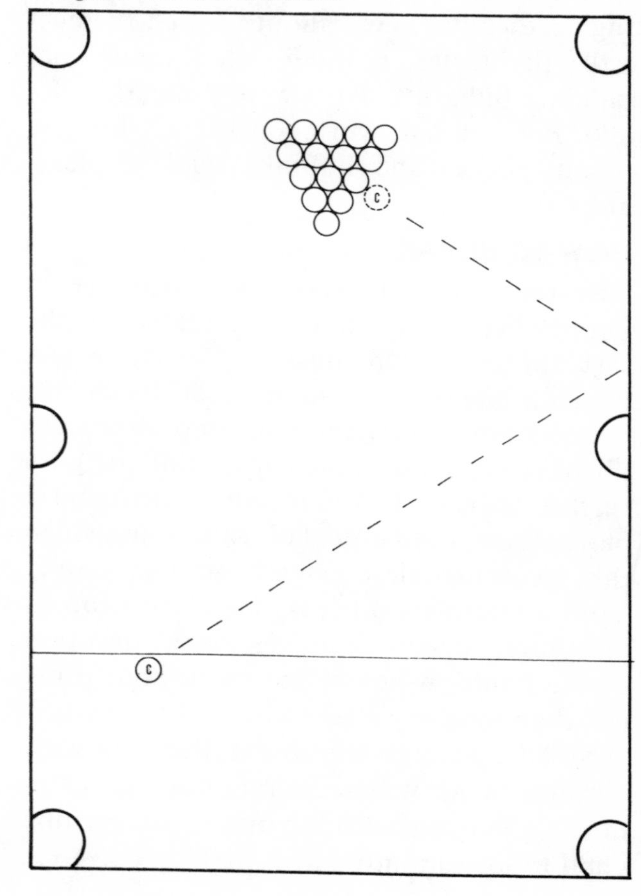

Photograph 4-1

straight pool, the cue ball will go absolutely nowhere from there, so you do have your opponent stuck; what you give up in return is that this break does not move a great many object balls. The break is almost completely safe, but not particularly aggressive.

My advice would be to stick with the break shot of Diagram 108, with this one cautionary note: On tables that run fast, settle for a little less English on the cue ball, and a slightly less thin hit on the head object ball.

In Photo 4-1, you see the typical results of a good one-pocket break. The 10 and 15 are close enough to the breaker's pocket to be legitimate threats if they become available to the cue ball; other balls are open to that pocket as well, and the cue ball occupies a position where the incoming shooter cannot do a great deal with the open object balls. (He'll have to do *something,* of course, and there's a move available to him; we're coming to that right now.)

ANSWERING THE BREAK

If the break in one-pocket is analogous to the serve in tennis, and I think it is, then the ability to answer the break corresponds to return of serve. A number of topflight tennis players stand out at that, even more than their peers; Jimmy Connors is about the best at it, and it's helped him enormously to become one of the world's best. And some pool players are awesome, in the corresponding way, when it comes to answering an opponent's break. They not only get out of immediate trouble, but frequently they are also able to turn the game in their favor, right from the beginning.

If the tennis analogy doesn't appeal to you, consider the notion of counterpunching in boxing; that is precisely the principle of answering a one-pocket break correctly, as well of the subsequent moves in a well-played game. If Jack Breit has analyzed the game accurately, perhaps "counteroffensive" is the best word of all to describe the nature of the strategy. What I want you to come away with here is not semantics, but the notion that the best defensive moves of one-pocket have an offensive aspect to them too.

All right. Answering the break is obviously your first defensive opportunity. If you accomplish nothing else with your response, you certainly want to deny the breaker any open shots at his pocket. That means you must get the cue ball between his pocket and any object balls; what you must also do, for a successful response, is put the cue ball someplace where *he* must defend, rather than simply put you right back in trouble again.

Diagram 111 shows you the identical layout to Photo 4–1. In one-pocket, there are two principal areas of defense that you must never lose sight of: the remaining stacked balls, and, more dangerous but more effective, the area closest to the breaker's pocket.

I see no ready sanctuary in the stack in Diagram 111. We could drive the 7-ball to a rail and stop the cue ball dead at the head of the stack; but if we did that, the breaker would simply roll the cue ball back in the direction we came from, or maybe even up to the head rail, and we'd be back in trouble

Diagram 111

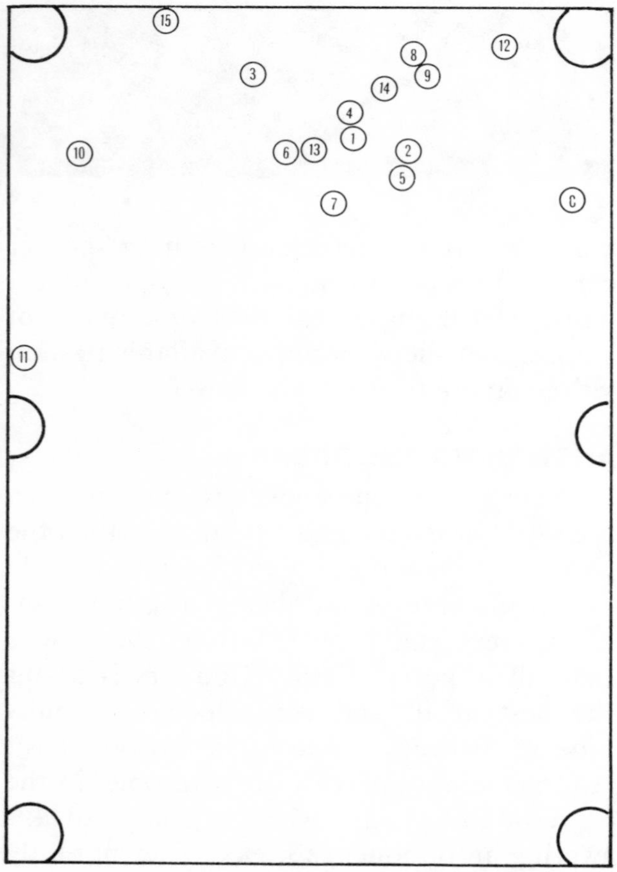

Diagram 112

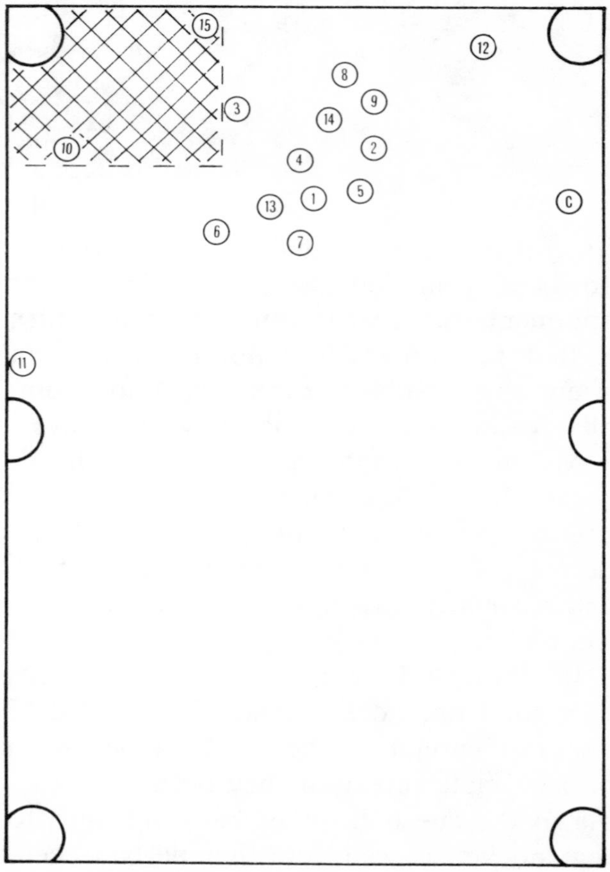

again. As of now, we have nothing near our pocket to threaten him with.

So let's deal with *his* threats. In Diagram 112, the shaded area represents the only available table area from which neither the 10 nor 15 ball can be made. Naturally, the closer those object balls are to the pocket, the smaller the safe area becomes. But it's ample in this case; our problem now comes how to get the cue ball there, since most of the rest of the stack is in our way.

Diagram 113 shows you how to get there: off the one ball that isn't part of the stack any more, the 12. At the same time, you move the 12 to a much more menacing position in front of your own pocket, and the cue ball is where your opponent can't move that 12. The game isn't completely turned around in your favor yet, but you've got a good start, because you've forced the breaker into doing something defensive, just one inning after he broke the balls well. The 12-ball is now more or less "king," in chess terms. Every move he makes must be made in consideration of the 12, which is pocketable by you from just about any point at which you can "see" the ball with the cue ball.

You accomplish this move with the very bare minimum of speed, and by hitting the cue ball southwest of its center. It's important that you note that the move (and just about *all* of one-pocket's defensive plays) has varying stages of success to it. Just getting your cue ball into that shaded Twilight Zone is worth something. But the play is worth vastly more if you can achieve the *optimum* with it, which in this case would be to get between the 10-ball and the side rail. You'd really have your opponent's

Diagram 113

Diagram 114

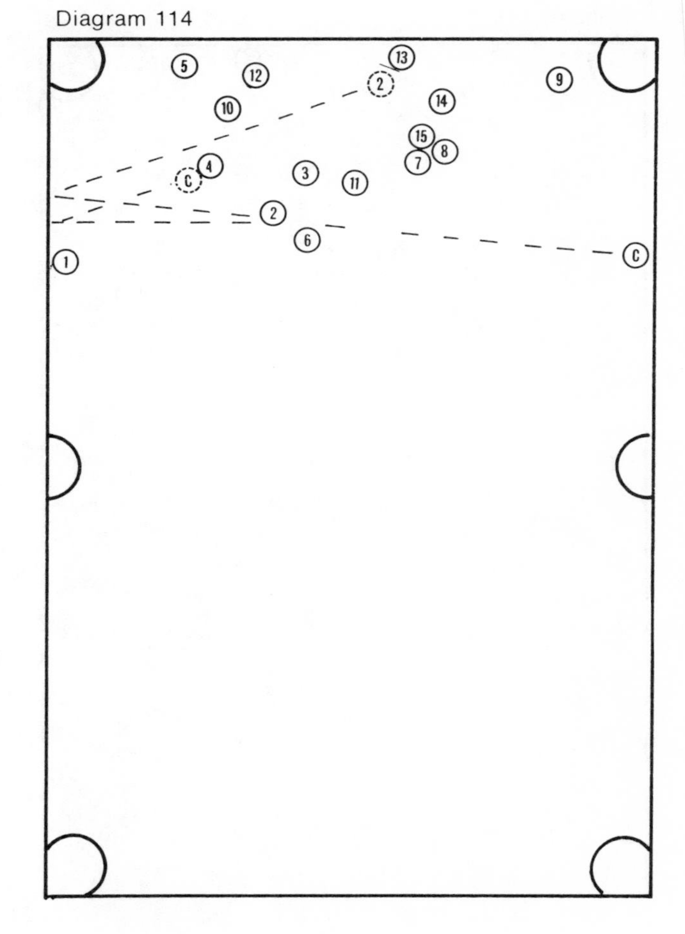

toilet flushed from there. If you merely get to the Twilight Zone but leave him breathing room to retaliate, your position is not nearly as strong. One of New York's legendary one-pocket players was reputedly able to achieve the absolute maximum with just about all his defensive moves; and he wasn't nicknamed "Bob the Destroyer" for nothing.

Let's get you involved with this phase of the game right away. The next four pages will present photos of good but answerable one-pocket breaks. In each case, the breaker has chosen the left-hand corner pocket, and you've got the pocket on the right. What do you do? You've already been given enough information to help you formulate responsible solutions.

Diagram 114 shows you the layout of Photo 4–2. You can't get to the Twilight Zone here, but you can bank the 2-ball without much risk. The 6-ball will help keep the cue ball from going up the table, which would expose the 1. You can't pocket the 2, of course, but as long as you can get it cleanly between the 10 and 4, you'll still do some damage. Your opponent will now have to guard against the 9-ball near your hole, as well as whatever else you might knock over that way with the 2. The defensive optimum is as you see it diagrammed, up against the 4 and 3-balls; the next-best position would be on or near the side rail.

Diagram 115 corresponds to Photo 4–3. This is as good an example as any of the concept of "Play the cue ball, not the object ball." As you see, you drive the 12-ball to the rail behind the 5 and 14-balls and out again; if it goes in and out cleanly, it will contact the 13, and possibly the 9, and move

Diagram 115

Diagram 116

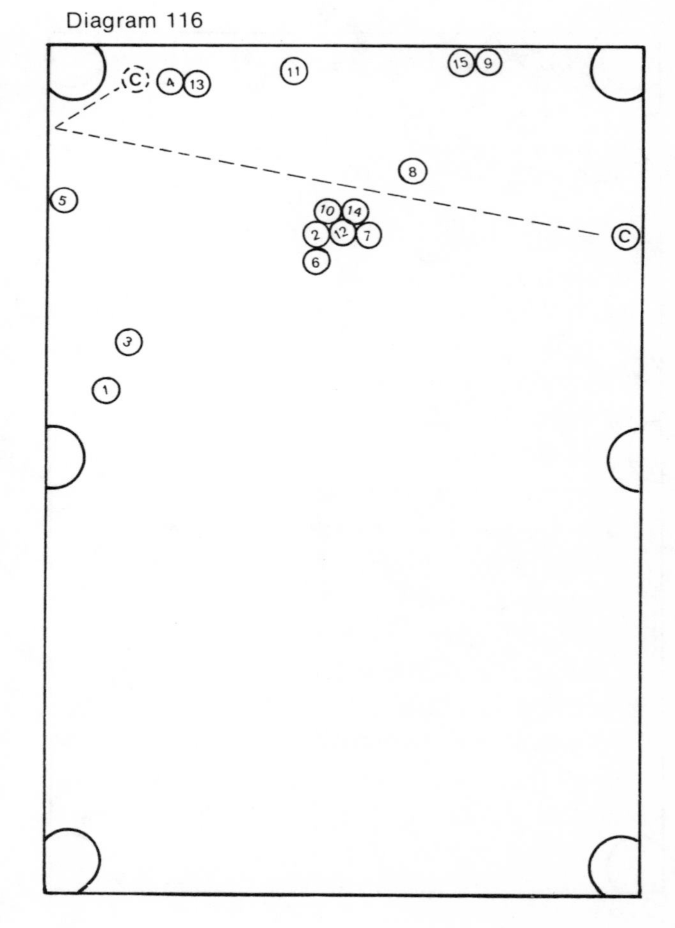

Diagram 117

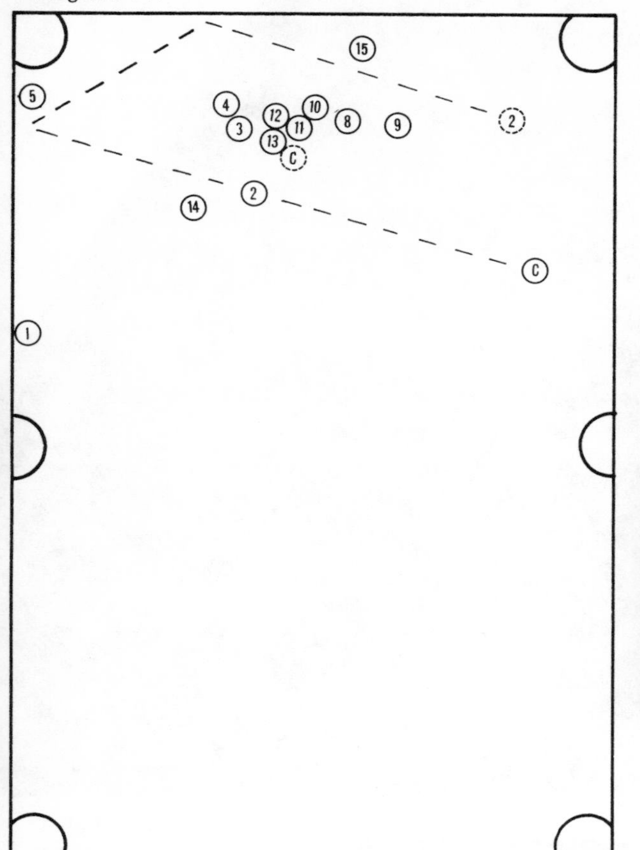

Photograph 4-2

either or both toward your pocket. But much more importantly, you roll this shot with follow English so as to leave your cue ball behind the 5. The optimum here would be to freeze your cue ball on the 5; but failing that, you can see that the least you should do is get the cue ball past the 5.

Diagram 116 represents the layout of Photo 4–4, and shows you perhaps the most valuable single defensive move that one-pocket has to offer. Its principle is similar to the last move we discussed, in that we're going for the "coffin corner," but this time the movement is confined to the cue ball. You simply roll the cue ball so as to graze the rear of the stack and fit in there snugly behind the 4. You'll have to overcome your fear about scratching in his pocket; that possibility does indeed exist, but practice and confidence will give you the cue ball control you need to avoid it. The reason this move is so important is that it recurs frequently, in modified forms, throughout the game. In this case, your opponent is shut off from guarding against your potent 15-9 combination near your pocket; and if you play this shot right down to the gnat's tailbone, the possible bonus is that you'll ruin his 13-4 combination so that neither ball can be made. In any case, the art of rolling the cue ball into the coffin corner is well worth your recognizing and practicing. A good one-pocket player wants to see his opponent spending part of his life down there.

And if he can't get his opponent there, he'd love to stick him in the remaining stacked balls. Diagram 117 shows you just such a solution to Photo 4–5. Simply bank

Photograph 4-3

Photograph 4-4

Photograph 4-5

the 2-ball and sit your cue ball right down on top of the 13, or close to it. You'll have the 2 near your pocket to threaten him, and he'll have a headache. But wherever the 2-ball does go, you can see how important it is to plop that cue ball down accurately and shut off his field of vision with it.

The reason that responses to the break are so important in one-pocket is not simply that they can inhibit or take away the breaker's advantage. It's that the principles of those shots comprise the lion's share of *all* one-pocket defensive play. As you learn the game, you'll see these strategies cropping up all through the game, even with increasingly fewer object balls on the table. We haven't covered them all, of course, and we never could, but this is a pretty fair start. And these shots are not much more than your getting to know the cue ball, and what you're able to do with it.

OPENING OFFENSIVE AND DEFENSIVE STRATEGIES

Needless to say, the best-played one-pocket games involve the most innings between the break and the point at which a clear, open shot at a pocket occurs. When a player in such a game does score successfully, he's apt to do it with a run of some balls, rather than a single shot or two. The best players, of course, are the players we want to emulate. So in learning one-pocket, you would benefit if you could bring along the added tool of patience.

Suppose you had the left-hand corner pocket in Diagram 118, and it's your shot. That 2-ball looks like it can be banked. But

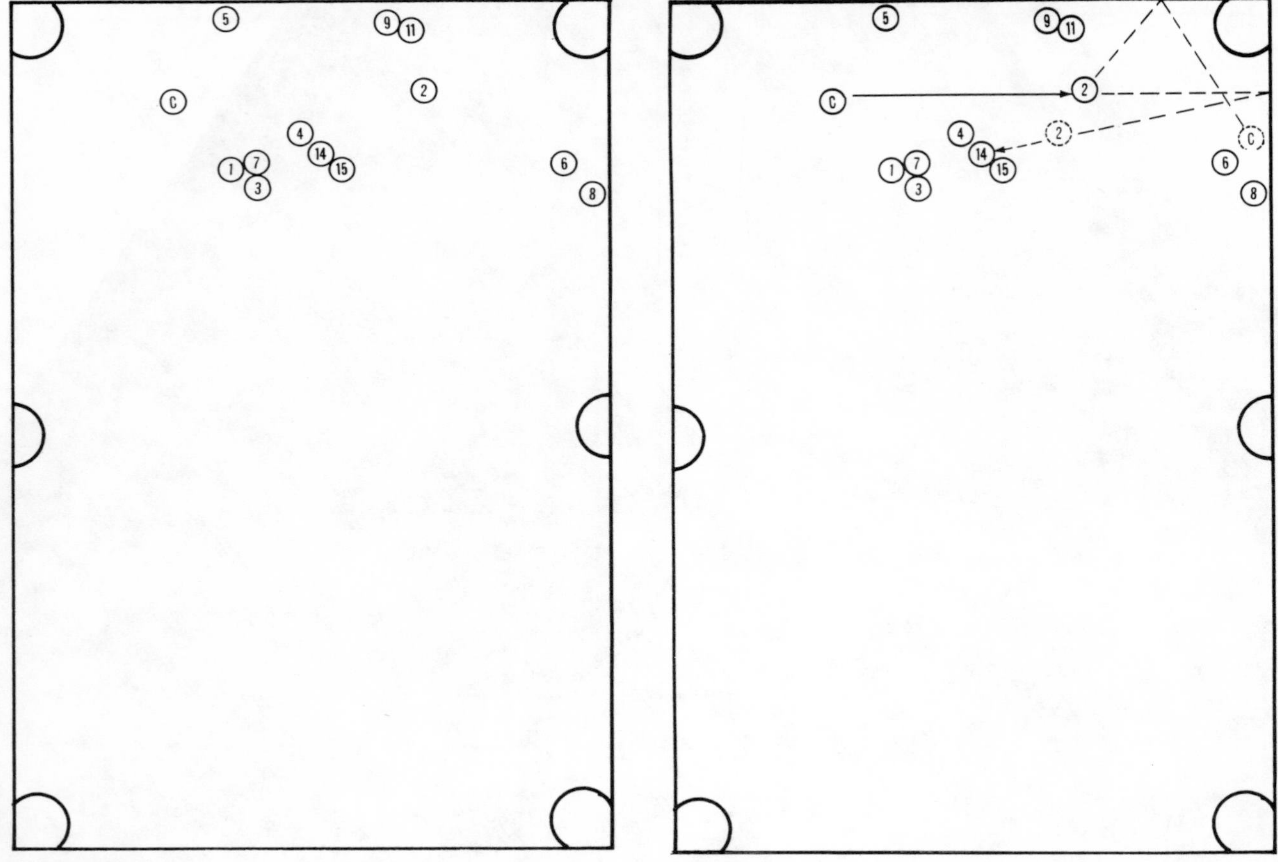

Diagram 118

Diagram 119

consider these factors in the shot: The 5-ball on the rail actually guards part of your pocket on a short-angle bank like that. You can't help but go past the 6 and 8 balls, leaving two clear, easy shots if your bank doesn't score. And even if you make the 2, you don't have a second shot.

It's a matter of "Penny-wise, pound-foolish" to try and score that lone 2-ball. What you should do is shown in Diagram 119: Slap the 2 off the side rail and back into the stack. It will tear a whole gang of balls loose and in the direction of your pocket, for him to solve. There's an excellent chance he won't be able to get directly to the balls nearest your pocket. The optimum on this shot would be to drop the cue ball in that little inlet under the 6 and 8-balls. You passed up a chance to score one, but you've given yourself a chance at scoring four or five an inning or two from now, and that's certainly a worthwhile consolation.

This is a very important move that you should learn; the opportunity to play it comes up frequently. As you can see, it's nothing more than cue ball control; as long as you leave the cue ball safe, the move must work to your advantage. The shot comes up most often within two or three innings of the opening break. If the ball to be banked is closer to the side rail than the 2-ball in the diagram, see if you can combine the shot with the "coffin corner" principle we discussed in the last section, leaving the cue ball on the bottom rail behind the nearest ball to the corner. Learning the move will cost you a few scratches and exposed shots at first, but it will more than repay you once you get it down.

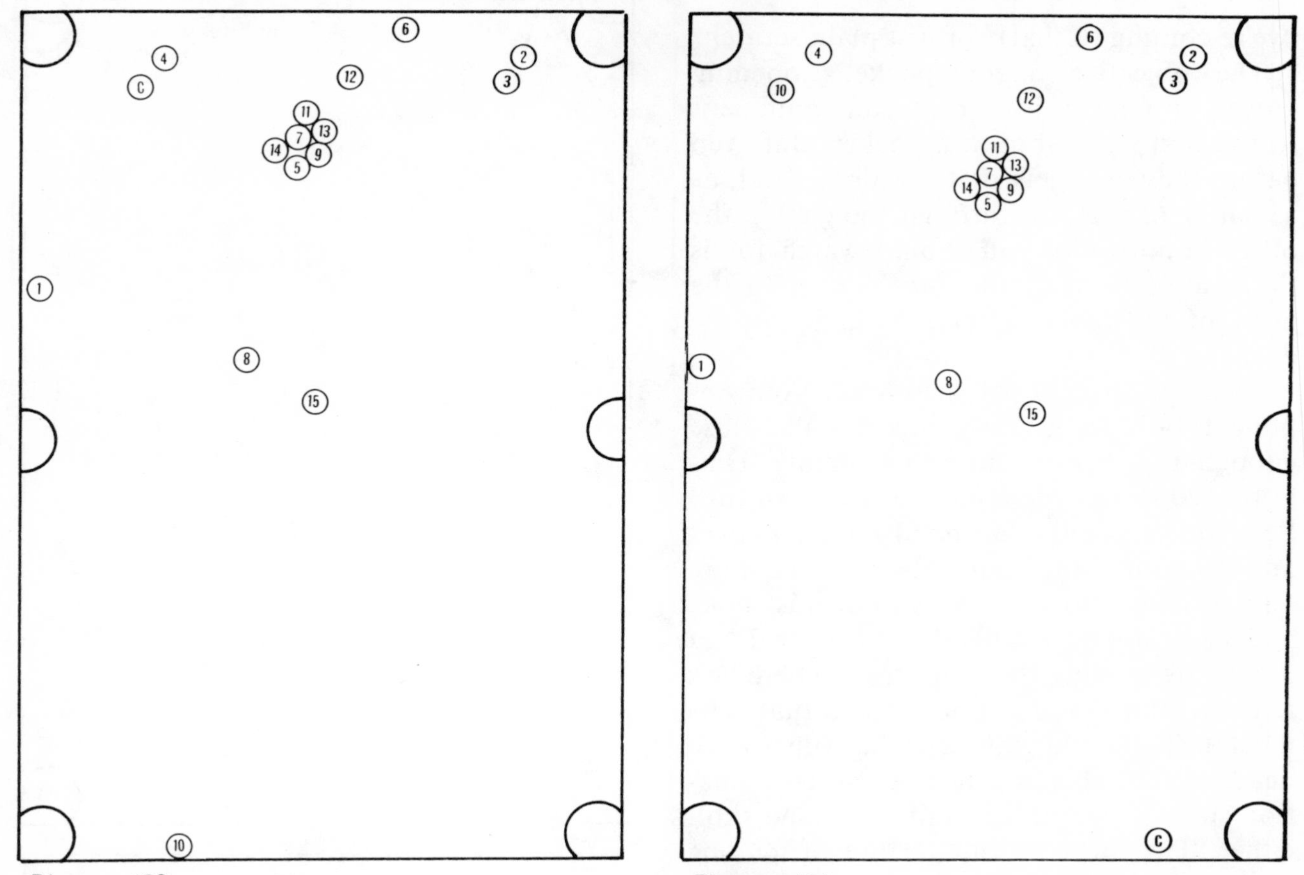

Diagram 120

Diagram 121

An aggressive one-pocket player will move balls away from his opponent's pocket and toward his own; a more defensive player will settle for simply moving them away, usually up the table. There is nothing right or wrong with either style; what counts is that you pick the style you're comfortable with. Safe defensive play will probably serve you best as you learn the game; with experience at the game and added confidence in your cue ball control, you can always add offensive moves to your defensive game. But many one-pocket players of years' standing, as well as beginners, prefer the defensive game.

The first objective of players like that will be to send the maximum number of object balls up to the head of the table, to be bunted about and banked the length of the table endlessly. I call this strategy, somewhat uncharitably, "*Alter Kocker's* Revenge." You see it a lot between players who do not consider themselves shotmakers, or who fear their opponent's shotmaking ability. The resulting game is about as scintillating to watch as a mutual fund, and it's not too much more fun playing such a game than watching one; but A. K.'s Revenge is efficient, in that it just about destroys anybody's chance at a meaningful run. The scoring in such games is invariably one ball at a time, or something close to that.

Driving object balls up to the nonbusiness end of the table doesn't make you a bad guy, but such balls should end up closer to your side of the table than to his no matter how far up the table you drive them. Also, always try to have at least one object ball clear of the head string, available to shoot should your opponent intentionally scratch

Diagram 122

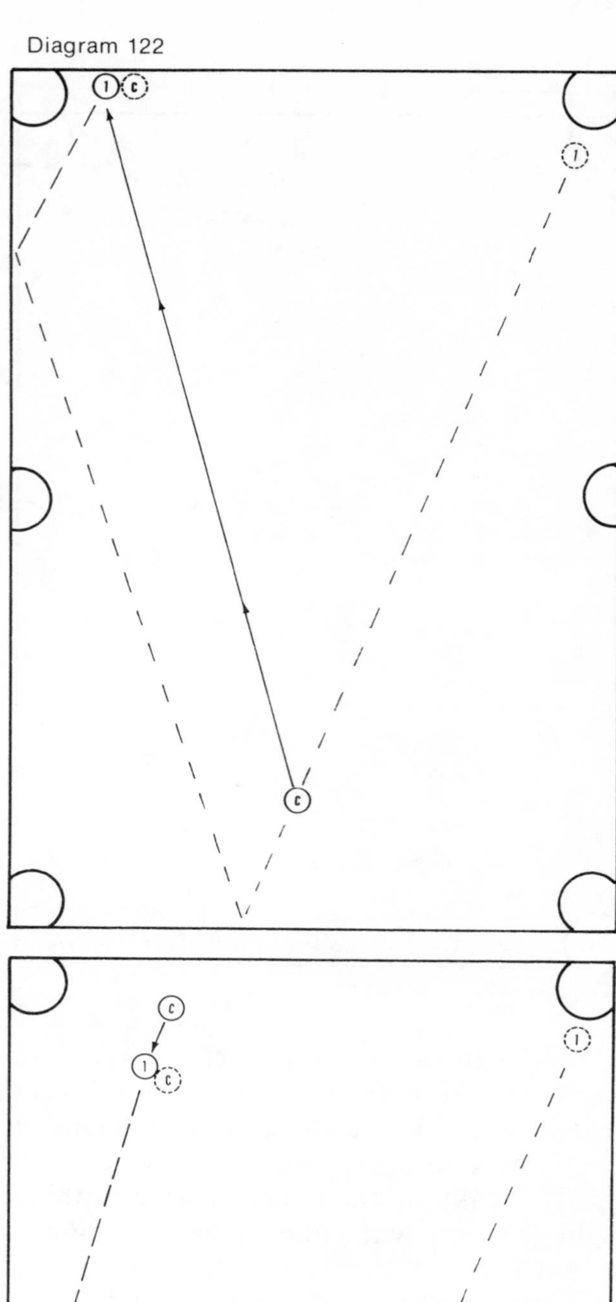

(we're coming to that) or just plain scratch.

The objective of one-pocket's opening moves, of course, is to beat your opponent to the first open shot at a pocket. But even before the game gets that far along (and, as a matter of fact, all through the game), the other opportunity you should watch for is the chance to send the *cue* ball up to the head of the table, without risk, before he does.

This opportunity will arise when your opponent fails to get any object balls close enough to the side rail to be threats. Diagram 120 shows you a good example of this. Say you've got the left-hand corner pocket and it's your shot. Your opponent has more balls near his pocket than you at this stage, and you can't even defend against the 2 and 3 balls by moving them out from where he's left you. But you don't have to do that. The most he'll have if you send him up to the head of the table is a heathenish combination shot. It guarantees him no second shot, either. The most he can get out of making the shot is a single ball, with secondary balls moved in the direction of your pocket and his cue ball on the wrong side of the table. The correct response here is to try banking the 10, stroking your cue ball low enough to keep it near the head rail after contact. If you make the bank, a run becomes available at once. But even if you don't make it, you can see from Diagram 121 that the game clearly favors you now; you have the threatening balls nearest the pocket, sinkable from most positions on the table, and the 8 and 15 guard against his defensive plays.

You don't always win in one-pocket just by doing a better job of shooting (although good shotmaking can't possibly hurt you). Sometimes you can win by doing a more efficient job of waiting.

Look for the defensive move first. If your opponent does maneuver you into a trap where you simply can't find a defensive play, then take the offense and do your best

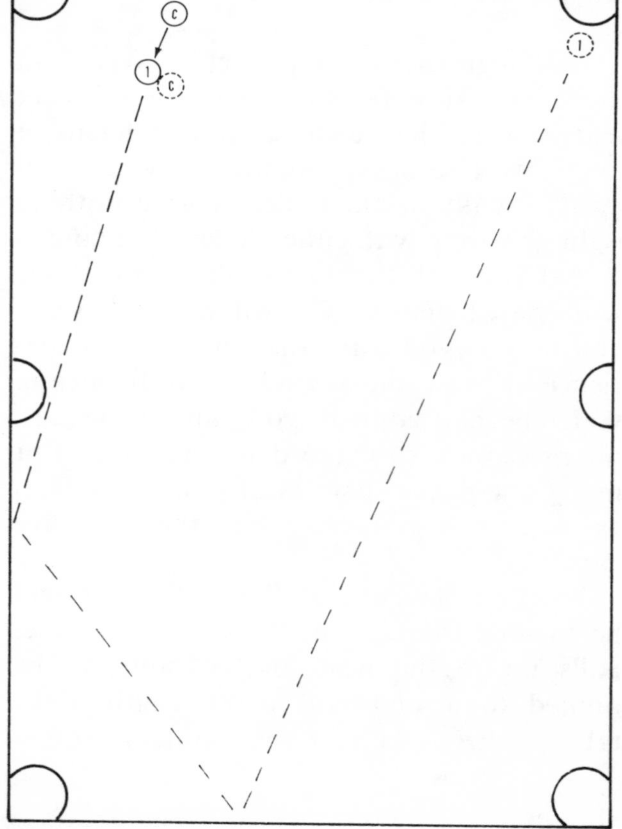

Diagram 123

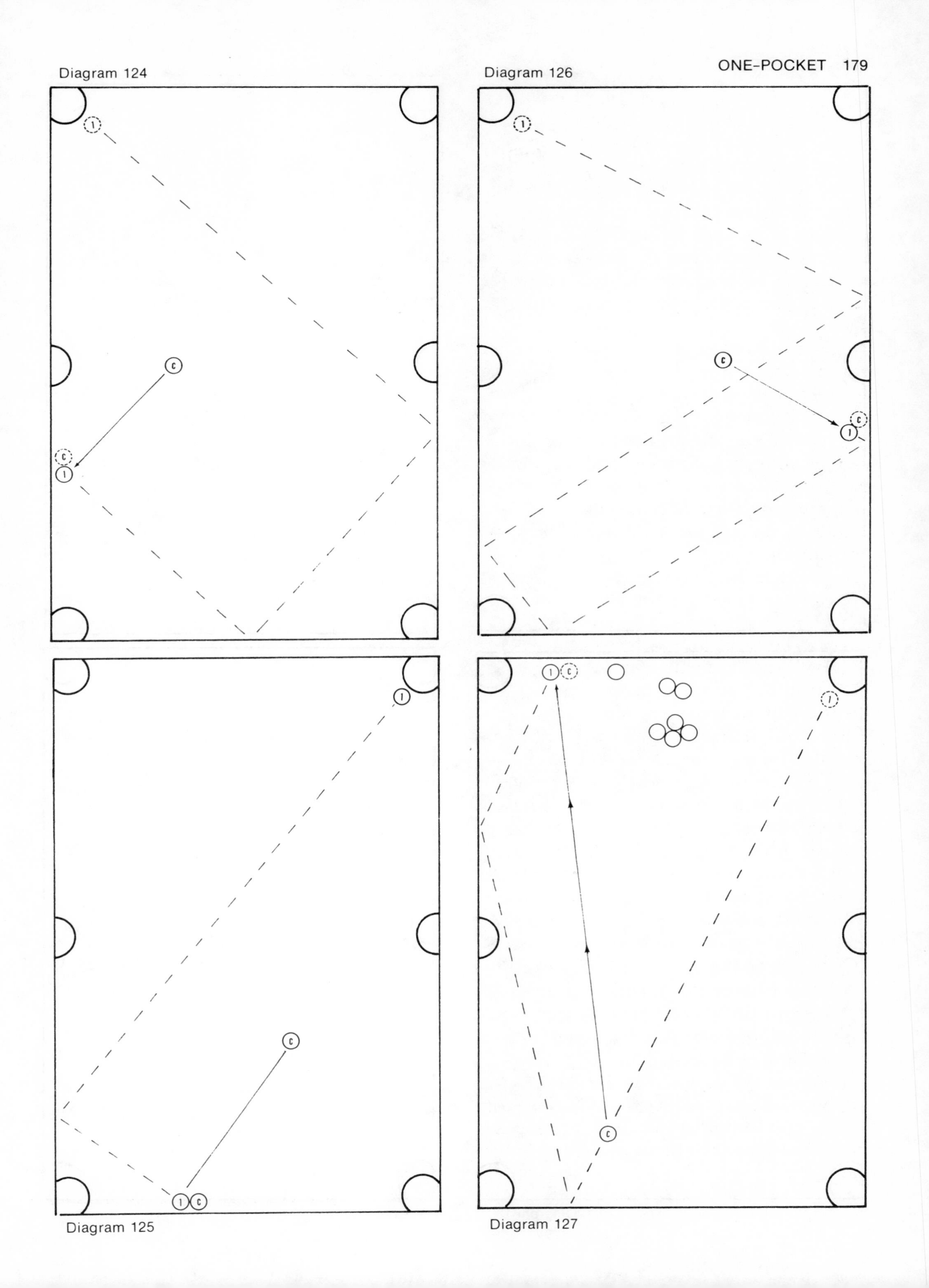

Diagram 124

Diagram 126

Diagram 125

Diagram 127

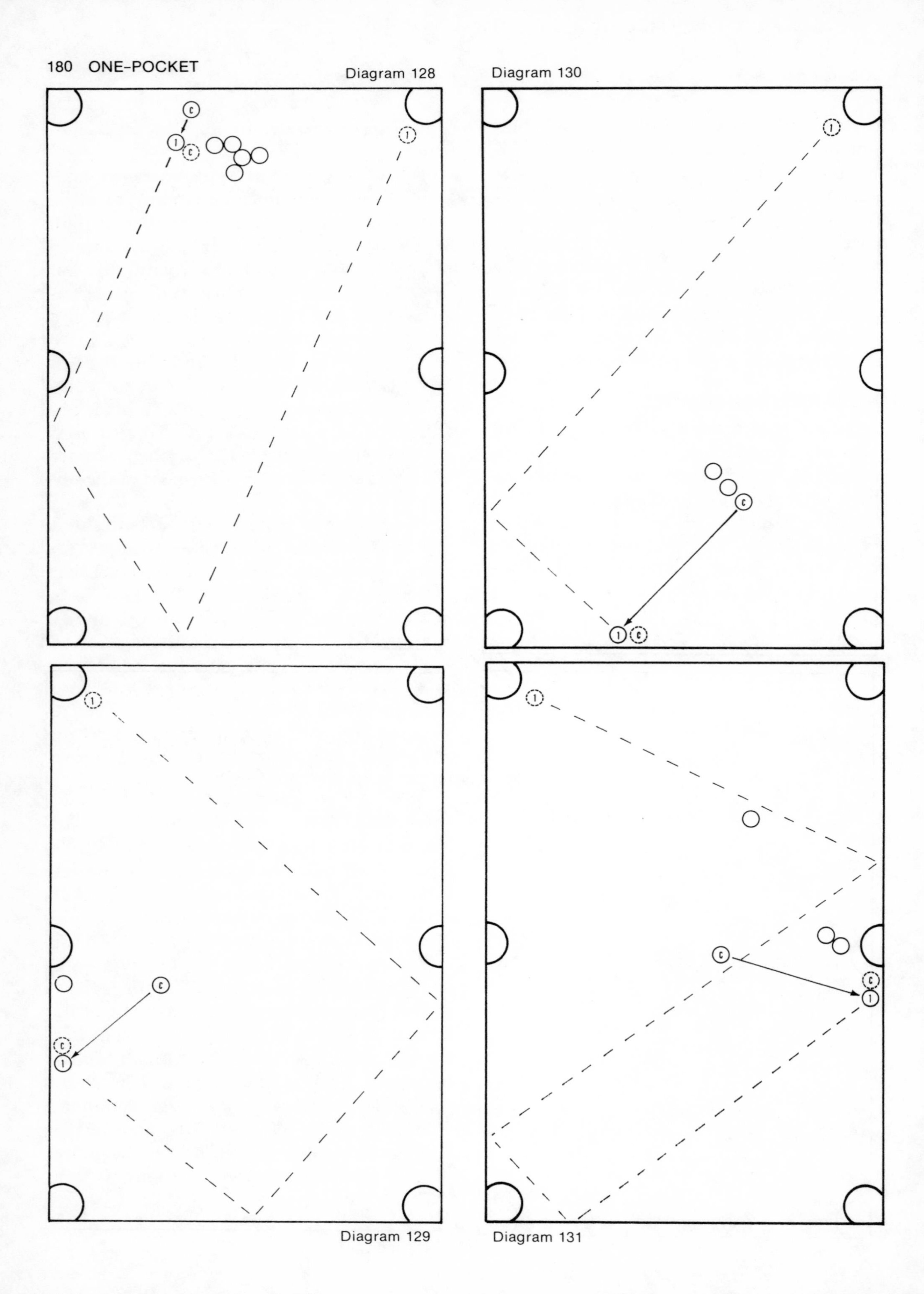

Diagram 128

Diagram 130

Diagram 129

Diagram 131

to get a ball near your pocket so you'll have something to work with when he's done shooting, or in case he misses. For instance, a good player who comes up against a leave like that of Diagram 121, and finds no defensive plays with which he feels comfortable, might try cutting the 15 in the right-hand corner. Tough shot, but it's a chance to take away your edge, and he's got to do *something*. This sort of desperation shot has bailed out many a one-pocket game.

MULTI-RAIL BANK SHOTS

Diagrams 122 through 126 show you bank shots off two or more rails that occur frequently in one-pocket. We won't get into exactly what you do to make these shots; they're far too difficult to be learned out of a book anyway. The purpose in including them here is to get you to be aware of the opportunity for them. Shots like these also figure prominently in one-pocket's end-games.

When this sort of shot arises in mid-game, though, its purpose is more to move balls and thereby create traps than it is to pocket the banked ball. It's always nice to pocket a bank shot like this, naturally, but you can enhance your cause in the game tremendously just by hitting the shot well and getting the ball reasonably close.

The next five diagrams re-create the last five, and show you how they might commonly be used in conjunction with other object balls to your advantage. Note in each case that placement of the cue ball is more critical than the precise placement of the object ball.

Also, stay on the lookout for situations where two object balls come together on your opponent's side of the table so that neither ball is pocketable. The two balls nearest the cue ball in Diagram 131 are an example of this; not only can they not be made, but they dictate against a lot of long bank shots your opponent might otherwise try. *Leave balls like that alone.* They're working for you. Until he breaks them up somehow, they'll help you stay a move ahead of him.

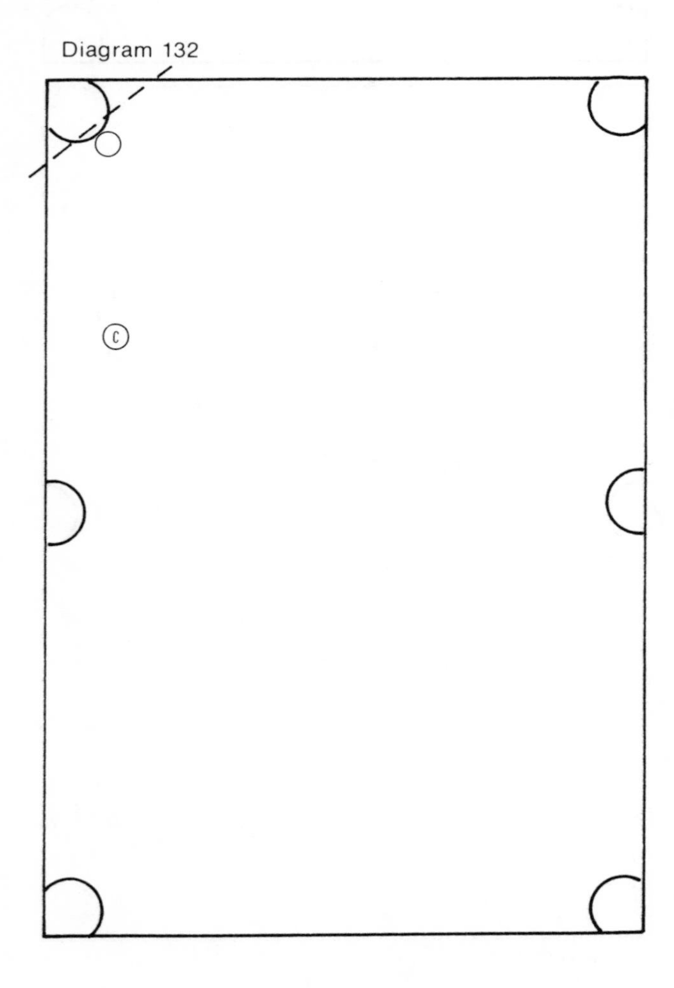

UNPOCKETING

No, it doesn't have anything to do with 7-Up. What it refers to is the taking of object balls away from your opponent's pocket when they're all but in there already.

See the dotted line in Diagram 132? That line connects the edges of the two rails where they cut back to form the corner pocket, and it's something of a point of no return. If the base of any object ball has crossed that line, you can forget about knocking it away. But there will be shots that require some very careful inspection on your part to see just where the base of the ball does lie. The object ball in Diagram 132, of course, is playable, as long as you can get between it and the side rail and kill your cue ball upon contact.

The technology of pool will help you with this phase of the game. The same factors that make pockets "tough" and unreceptive to object balls not coming right down the center of the pike actually increase your chances of driving object balls away from your opponent's pocket.

Pay close attention to the areas you have available to work with in shots like this. If the object ball in Diagram 132 were slightly closer to the cue ball, for instance, you'd want to spin the cue ball in *behind* it and take it out that way, killing the cue ball so there's no chance of scratching. From-behind is the best unpocketing route, but it won't always be available.

When your opponent does get an object ball in there deep where you can't go get it out again, the right move is to make it for him and leave the cue ball right in the jaws where it's hard to shoot. It's quite possible that you'll have open shots first, since the ball hanging in his pocket is the product of a close miss. Just make sure that you can get to his ball when you're done cleaning yours off; you certainly don't want to leave it there for him.

You also don't want to concede a ball to him that way when he is within one or two balls of game. By that time, of course, a good many object balls will have been cleared off, and now you can see why it's so important whether any object balls lie outside the head string or not. *If your opponent needs a ball or two, and has a hanger, your correct move is to make the ball for him and follow it in with the cue ball.* It costs you one of the balls you've already pocketed, but he doesn't get credit for the one you've made for him. Both your ball and his get respotted in tandem; he gets cue ball in hand behind the string, with no open shots—*unless* object balls lie in front of the string where he can get at them. If such

Diagram 133

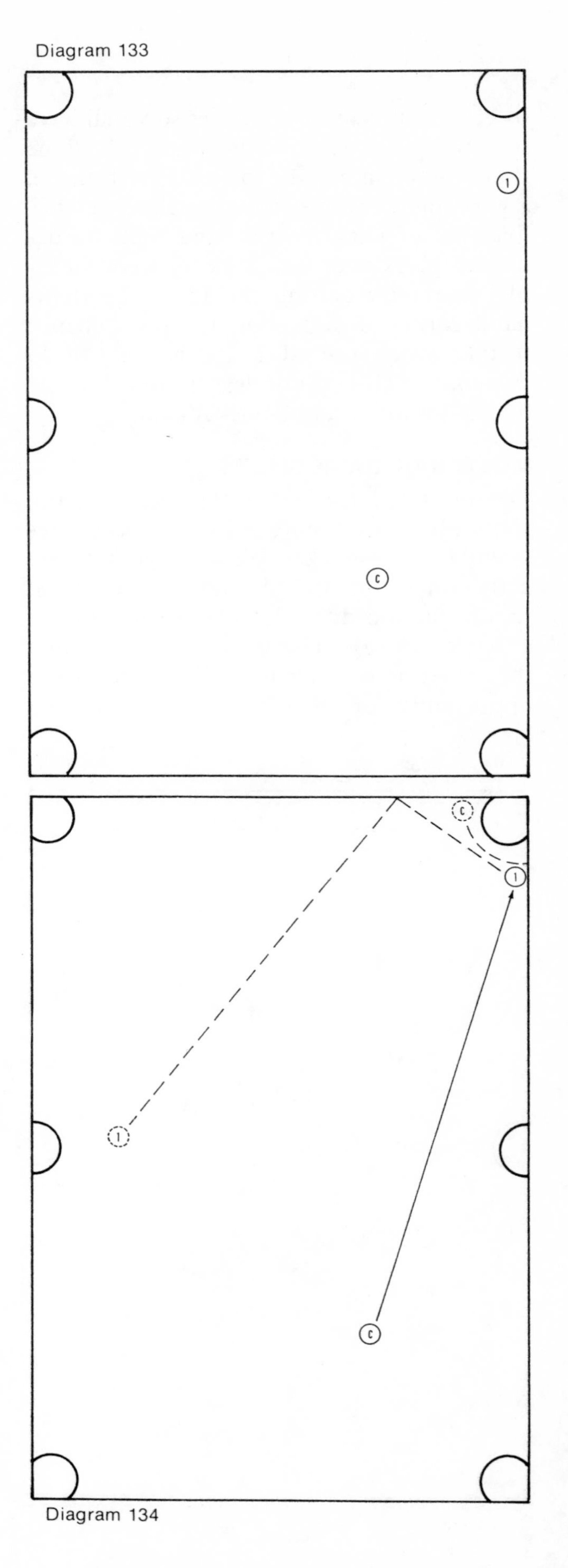

Diagram 134

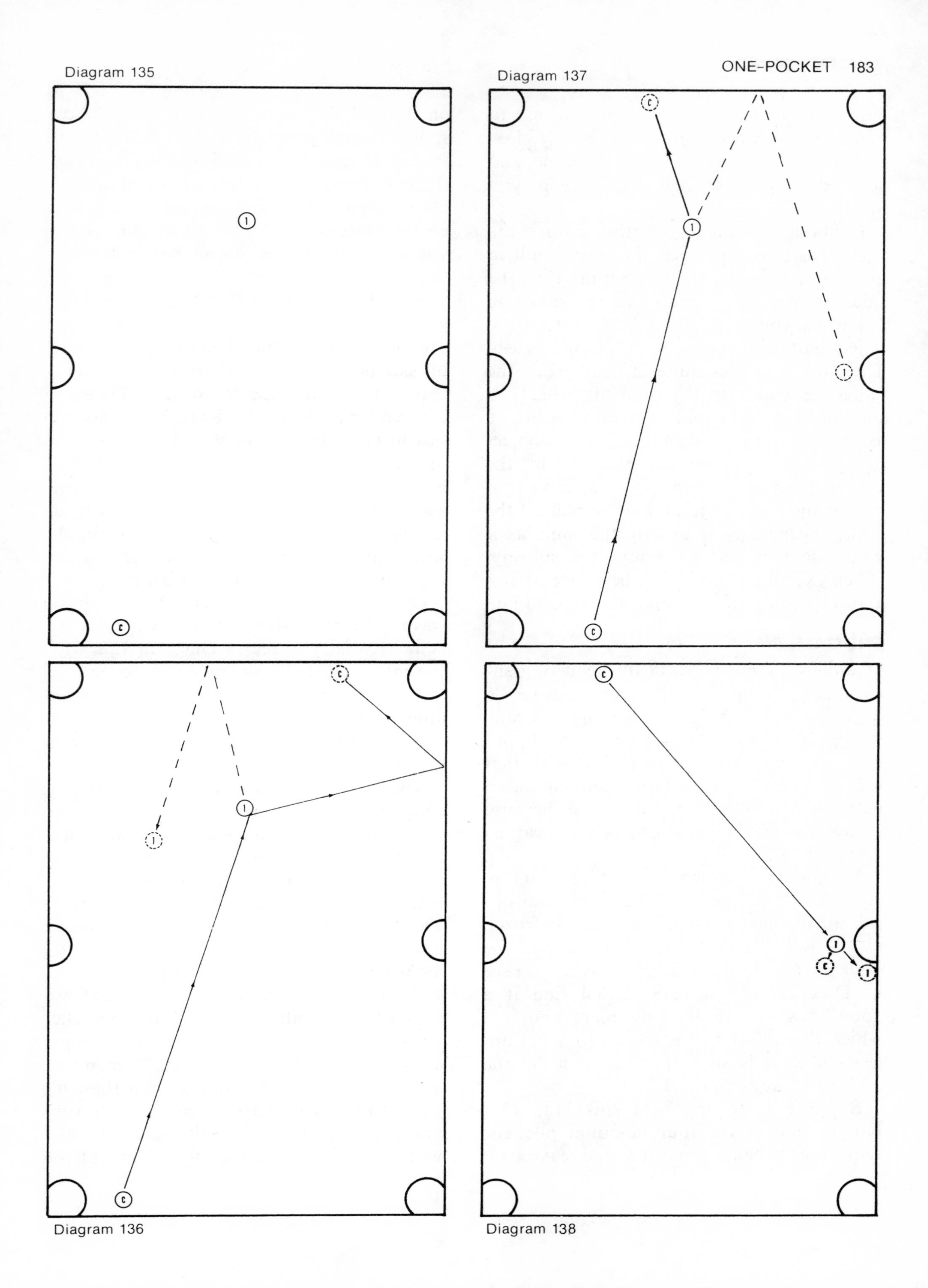

Diagram 135
Diagram 137
Diagram 136
Diagram 138
1
C

balls are out there, he's almost a cinch to make one or more unless they're very close to the side rail on your half of the table, and your deliberate scratch won't help you much.

Deliberate scratches of this nature are vastly easier to do when the object ball in question lies nearer the bottom rail than the side. All you have to do then is what you did when you were still a beginner: hit the object ball dead center, with follow English. The shot is in fact quite difficult when the hanger is closer to the side rail; what you should do in that case is jack up your bridge as though you were shooting over an object ball, aim high on the cue ball, and hit the shot as hard as you can. Your objective is to pocket the ball and jump the cue ball off the table; the penalty is exactly the same as if your cue ball had gone into the subway. When executing this move, be a nice person and warn spectators behind the pocket first.

ENDGAMES

One-pocket's most identically recurring situations come up once the score goes to 7-6 or 7-7. Unless you do something radically wrong, it's fairly simple to deny your opponent an open shot for his pocket with that few object balls on the table; denying him a bank shot is something else again, because as we've seen, the game's bank shots can be quite versatile.

Diagram 133 shows you a typical setup; yours is the left-hand pocket, and your opponent has just missed. The 1-ball is frozen to the rail. *Don't try to bank the ball for your pocket.* Drive it safely away as you see in Diagram 134 instead. You'll find it a good idea not to try any bank shots in which the object ball is frozen to a rail unless the shot is such that you can cut the object ball quite thin.

Suppose your opponent sinks the 15th ball in one of the four no-count pockets, requiring its being respotted, and leaves you on the end rail, as in Diagram 135. The response you'll generally see to this shot is that of Diagram 136: Roll off the far side of the ball, bringing it halfway back up the table or slightly less, and leaving the cue ball on the bottom rail. You can't scratch, unless you err and hit the object ball extremely thin.

Still, I think you'll find the play of Diagram 137 to be even tougher for him to figure out: Give him the object ball as close to his side pocket as you can without making it there. If you play the response of Diagram 136, you may leave the 2-rail bank shot we saw in Diagram 123, or you may leave your opponent the chance to merely bunt the ball back to his side without risk. But if you leave him the shot of Diagram 137 instead, the *most* he'll have is a tough 3-rail bank, with imminent danger of scratching or leaving you something quite negotiable.

(If the no-account is smart enough to leave *you* that shot, by the way, try to achieve what you see in Diagram 138, with the softest cue ball roll you can manage.)

The shot you see in Diagram 136 is more appropriate when there are two or three balls spotted in tandem than when there is only one.

The least you should accomplish with any endgame ploy is leave the cue ball on or very near a rail someplace. Assuming you haven't left an open shot, leaving the cue ball close to a rail minimizes your opponent's chances for a bank shot; 99 out of 100 players prefer to hit their bank shots with draw on the cue ball, and that's no picnic when you're shooting off a rail.

As with the rest of one-pocket, defense comes first in endgames. Don't try to pocket any ball you're not sure of; there will almost always be a defensive option. Remember, one-pocket is lost far more often than it's won. Unless you get very careless (or very unlucky), the game is quite likely to end with a bank shot, either the length of the table or similarly to the shot you see in Diagram 133. Before you try winning the game with a bank shot, I'd recommend that you wait for a shot in which the object ball is at least an inch off the rail. If that 1-ball in Diagram 133 were comfortably off the rail, your shot would obviously be one in which the cue ball *passes* the object ball; the inch would be enough to allow the object ball to go to the near rail and come out again while the cue ball is on its way out of there. A double-kiss, which is what you'll get if you don't get the cue ball out of the way, will be at least mortal and quite likely fatal to your cause.

As a last word of encouragement, let me advise you that in order to have any success with these pass-over bank shots, you need not be Jewish.

EPILOGUE: ONE LAST RACK

As they used to tell me in the Army, back when the earth's crust was still cooling: There's a reason for everything. And I suspect that a partial reason for the lack of books on advanced pool today is that the game is too complex to be learned that way.

Obviously, I can agree only partially with that. True enough, it will take more than your agreeing with the concepts I propose in this book to make you a player of consequence. You won't be able to play at all without your fair share of that 20 percent physical aspect of the game that we've discussed before, and the only marketplace in which that is available is the pool table itself. Whatever your natural aptitudes for the game, you should be playing as often as you can. The game of pool is more delicate than you'd believe.

On the other hand, the best players are the *thinking* players. I can't show you how to play in the absence of actual equipment, but I can give you an idea of how to think. That's what this book is all about, and my fondest hope is that, in that sense, you've found it a departure from whatever else you might have read. (I'm not saying the others are bad books; they surely are not. You've got to start someplace. My opinion is that they just don't go far enough.)

Make the most of your time at the table. When you practice, for instance, there should be more to it than simply driving balls into holes (unless you're getting ready to compete, in which case slapping a few balls home can help loosen you up, but I'm talking about more concentrated practice than that). Practice is the best arena in which to test the principles I've shown you here; as an exercise in creative problem-solving, which is how I see the game, it's also extremely therapeutic. A nicely executed sequence is good for a nice little glow. Even if nobody is watching you.

Along similar lines, make the most of the opportunities you have to watch good players. Who beats who, by how many balls, and for how much, are not nearly as significant as *how* the game was played, and I mean that literally, not in the metaphysical sense. You can learn from other players' mistakes just as you can learn from your own, and every player alive makes them. Theoretically, it's at least as possible to run balls infinitely as it is for the proverbial infinite apes to re-create the works of Shakespeare on their infinite typewriters over an infinite period of time. But, more practically, apes will generally type gibberish; and the longest pool run of all time is only a matter of hundreds of balls. It's one tough game.

You'll be light-years ahead of other students of the game if, when watching good players, you recognize how *pretty* the game really is when it's really, really played right. When two spheres touch each other, the actual point of contact is merely a pinpoint, and the margin for error not much greater than that. So the game offers marvelous subtleties, and reducing these subtleties to the certainties we've discussed throughout is a lovely thing to see.

And you'll also do well to try playing the game prettily. The game will return the favor to you almost at once. You can't look good while you're playing badly, naturally, but somehow looking good seems to make you play well too. It's very much like life, a point we've already considered.

I hope you'll come to shoot a great game of pool, Fast Eddie. Even better than that, I hope you'll come to enjoy the game as much as I do. When you get right down to it, I could hardly wish you more.

Index